Introduction to the Music Industry

D1236173

Introduction to the Music Industry: An Entrepreneurial Approach is a textbook that offers a fresh look at one of the fastest-changing businesses in the world today. Emphasizing the importance of entrepreneurial thinking for the music industry, this textbook engages college-level students in learning the fundamentals while discovering ways to shape the industry's future. Every chapter explores the inner workings of the music industry using creative problem-solving exercises, discussion questions, collaborative projects, case studies, hands-on activities, and inspiring stories of actual music entrepreneurs. The textbook's companion website provides multi-media content, study guides, and an instructor's manual with lesson plans and suggestions for assessing students' work.

This book will be beneficial to students who want to be involved in the music industry in some way: as a professional working in support of artists, as an artist trying to launch his or her performing career, or as an active fan.

Catherine Fitterman Radbill is the Director of the New York University Steinhardt School's Undergraduate Music Business Program.

Introduction to the Music Industry

An Entrepreneurial Approach

Catherine Fitterman Radbill

Routledge
Taylor & Francis Group

NEW YORK AND LONDON

Please visit the Companion Website at
www.routledge.com/cw/radbill

First published 2013
by Routledge
711 Third Avenue, New York, NY 10017

Simultaneously published in the UK
by Routledge
2 Park Square, Milton Park, Abingdon, Oxon OX14 4RN

Routledge is an imprint of the Taylor & Francis Group, an informa business

© 2013 Taylor & Francis

Library of Congress Cataloging in Publication Data
Fitterman Radbill, Catherine, author.
   Introduction to the music industry : an entrepreneurial approach /
   Catherine Fitterman Radbill.
   pages cm
   1. Music trade. 2. Music entrepreneurship. I. Title.
   ML3790.F596 2013
   780.68—dc23
   2012009974

ISBN: 978–0–415–89638–2 (pbk)
ISBN: 978–0–203–09669–7 (ebk)

Typeset in Stone Serif
by Swales & Willis Ltd, Exeter, Devon

Senior Editor: Constance Ditzel
Editorial Assistant: Elysse Preposi
Production Manager: Sarah Hudson
Marketing Manager: Joon Won Moon
Project Manager: Swales & Willis Ltd, Exeter, Devon, UK
Copy Editor: Janice Baiton
Proofreader: Swales & Willis Ltd, Exeter, Devon, UK
Cover Design: Salamander Hill

Printed and bound in the United States of America by Sheridan Books, Inc. (a Sheridan Group company)

BRIEF CONTENTS

DETAILED CONTENTS

PREFACE

I'd like to tell you a story. It's a tale based on the hopes, fears, successes, failures, and collective wisdom of the thousands of students and music professionals with whom I've had the distinct honor of working for more than 14 years as a music entrepreneurship evangelist.

I've met you in classrooms, meeting rooms, coffee shops, railroad stations, airports, and on line. You are 17, or 30, or 55. You are performers, educators, composers, technicians, administrators, inventors, venue managers, DJs, recording artists, bloggers, music retail store workers, record label owners, publicists, or a hundred other things—all working in the service of this thing we can't live without called music.

When I founded the Entrepreneurship Center for Music at the University of Colorado in 1998, I spoke the musical language of the faculty and students: nonprofit classical music, jazz, and composition. Since moving to New York University in 2002, my vocabulary has expanded to include commercial music—pop, rock, hiphop, country, electronic—and the variety of ways music is used to make money.

No matter where I've met you or what you're doing for a job, your stories all revolve around a common underlying question: How can I make a living doing what I love? Or specifically: How can I work in the music industry in whatever area I'm passionate about right now, and sustain myself economically?

The answer is straightforward: You will need to learn how to think and act like an entrepreneur. Music is a business with its own distinct culture. If you want to find your place in it, you'll need to look under the hood to see how all the moving parts fit together. Learning to think like an entrepreneur as you explore the inner workings of the music industry will catapult you into a mindset that allows you to see opportunities where others see only problems. The world around you will look like one gigantic suggestion box, full of great ideas for you and other entrepreneurial thinkers to play with. You will be able to control your own destiny, whether you decide to work for yourself and create a new product or service, or choose to make meaning in the world by being an entrepreneurial thinker as an employee.

The market conditions are perfect for entrepreneurial activity in the music industry. Everything is in flux as it adapts to changing consumer habits and new technologies. There is no longer a fixed shape or direction to the landscape. How did we get here? Where are we going? It's messy and chaotic. It's a perfect *entrepreneurial opportunity*.

Creativity, innovation, opportunity, and a "why not...?" attitude are the hallmarks of entrepreneurship. These are the skills and tools you will acquire in the chapters ahead. We'll apply some myth busting to conventional wisdom and reject a "that's just the way things are done" mentality so you can find your place in the music industry. In each chapter, I will urge you to ask questions, challenge my answers, look under every rock for opportunities, and make meaning in all that you do. I invite both teachers and students to add their own imagination, creativity, wisdom, and energy to this story.

As an entrepreneurial thinker, how will your passion and enthusiasm guide the music industry? What areas of the business will intrigue you? What creative ideas and insight will you bring to solving some of our industry's challenges? The opportunities for you to have a satisfying and sustainable career in the music industry are abundant if you learn how to develop an entrepreneurial mindset.

I want to hear *your* story. Please contact me through the book's website as you journey through the textbook with your class. I look forward to hearing from you.

GOALS OF THIS BOOK

Introduction to the Music Industry: An Entrepreneurial Approach is a textbook that offers a fresh look at one of the fastest-changing businesses in the world today. It is written for the first course—and in some schools the only course—in the fundamentals of the music industry, in the course called *Introduction to the Music Business* (or by a similar name). Emphasizing the importance of entrepreneurial thinking for the music industry, this textbook engages college-level students in learning the fundamentals while discovering ways to shape the industry's future. As entrepreneurial thinkers, students develop a creative mindset that allows them to recognize opportunities where others see only problems.

Introduction to the Music Industry: An Entrepreneurial Approach does not engage in the history of the music business as much as its present-day workings. It doesn't predict the future, but acknowledges a future that is likely to be more technologically driven than it is today. It acknowledges a future that requires entrepreneurial thinking from day one. For a history of the music business, there are other fine books. This book is more applied in its approach and is intended to help students "hit the ground running."

It will be beneficial to students who want to be involved in the music industry in some way: as a professional working in support of artists, as an artist trying to launch his or her performing career, or as an active fan.

In coursework, this textbook is designed to help create lively classrooms that enhance learning. Every chapter includes hands-on activities, discussion questions, collaborative projects, and inspiring stories of actual music entrepreneurs. The textbook's website provides multi-media content, study guides, and an instructor's manual.

HOW THIS BOOK IS ORGANIZED

Introduction to the Music Industry: An Entrepreneurial Approach is structured chronologically in four parts:

1 Thinking Like an Entrepreneur

2 Contacts and Contracts

3 Performing and Recording

4 You as Entrepreneur

In Part 1 we'll focus on the fundamentals of entrepreneurship and entrepreneurial thinking, tackle creative problem solving, and explore the concept of music and branding.

Part 2 will help students understand and master the basic building blocks of the music industry: copyright, publishing, licensing, and performing rights societies.

Part 3 allows students to see the music industry in action through live concerts and touring, recorded music, and a look at the newest and fastest-growing frontier, digital music services.

Part 4 consists of two long-form music industry case studies that put students in the driver's seat as entrepreneurs. In both of the cases, students will step into the role of a company's founder, using the skills they've acquired in this textbook to engage in thoughtful reflection and tough decision-making.

An Appendix introduces students to the world's largest music products trade show, NAMM.

LEARNING TOOLS INSIDE THIS BOOK

The music industry seems to change shape almost daily, so I've designed this book to be used alongside an open internet connection. The book's companion website, with links to each chapter, will keep students posted on changes and developments in the many areas that impact the global music industry, such as digital technology, copyright law, consumer behavior, communications, and music trends. The links also will provide context and background for each chapter, and give a jumping-off point for class discussion.

I've designed each chapter so that students will have different ways to learn the material and prepare for class. Here are some of the tools:

- Chapter Overviews—each chapter begins with an overview of topics to be presented, and key terminology that will be discussed in the chapter

- Entrepreneur's Stories—candid snapshots of working music entrepreneurs

- Industry Essentials—a thorough overview of the inner workings of the chapter's topic

- Opportunities Ahead—highlights entrepreneurial possibilities for students to explore

- Self-reflection—questions and activities for students to reflect upon as they read each chapter

- Talking Back—activities, discussions topics, and projects that help students prepare for lively class discussions

- Internet Resources—suggested resources that encourage deeper study of the chapter's topic

- Links in each chapter on the book's companion website to articles and blogs, video material, study guides

- Case Studies in Part 4 will help students learn how to make convincing arguments based on solid evidence, astute analysis, and good communication skills.

We learn well through stories, and there are many storylines flowing through the book to help illustrate key points. Students will find plenty of insight and humor in the short Entrepreneur Sound Bytes and more detailed Entrepreneur Profiles. All of the characters in the stories are real people, but in some cases I've given them new names or a slightly altered circumstance to protect their privacy.

As students read through this book, they will become advisors to the Third Rail, a fictional indie band trying to launch its music career. They'll help Third Rail master the key elements of entrepreneurial thinking, and find opportunities to build its fan base, launch a tour, license its music, and start a record label.

Using case studies is a very effective pedagogical tool for creating interactive classrooms. In addition, the case study method helps students acquire analytical and diagnostic thinking skills, which they will put to use in a free-flowing environment where circumstances are always changing. The classroom becomes the laboratory for comparative reflection on and lively discussion of the students' findings and conclusions

ONLINE RESOURCES

www.routledge.com/cw/radbill

The companion website for *Introduction to the Music Industry: An Entrepreneurial Approach* features:

- Flash cards—to help students master the key concepts of each chapter

- Links to videos, interactive materials, and useful websites

- RSS Feeds for social media, blogs, and industry news updates

- PowerPoint presentations that reinforce chapter learning goals

- Instructor's Manual and test bank.

One of the challenges of teaching a course that tries to cover the sprawling music industry in one school term is that some students may want to delve more deeply into issues and topics than we have time to discuss in class. To help with that, the book's website includes suggested resources for deeper research and study.

INSTRUCTOR'S MATERIALS

The textbook's companion website includes an Instructor's Manual that is not accessible to students. In it, instructors will find a guide to creating a syllabus for the semester and weekly lesson plans. In addition, the manual will include helpful tips on how to:

- Incorporate interactive projects and media into traditional lectures
- Use a long-form case study
- Create homework assignments and projects for both small and large classes
- Assess students' work
- Help students enjoy the class and become life-long learners.

ACKNOWLEDGMENTS

There are many people to thank for their inspiration and encouragement in writing this book. First, I would like to acknowledge the hundreds of students with whom I have had the pleasure of learning and teaching. Their passion for music has inspired me to find new ways to think about the music industry, resulting in this textbook. Gregory Allis, Pedro Avillez Costa, Katonah Coster, Jillian Ennis, Shrayans Jha, Chris Lane, Christine Mayer, and Yifan Qin are former students who contributed to researching and writing several sections of the book.

My academic colleagues Jim Anderson, Cathy Benedict, Judith Coe, Lawrence Ferrara, Catherine Moore, Rich Nesin, Robert Rowe, Peter Spellman, E. Michael Harrington, and Shirley Washington spent many hours reading and editing my drafts and encouraged me during those dark moments when I was tempted to walk away from this enormous undertaking. Chief among these wonderful colleagues is Angela Myles Beeching, whose weekly phone calls guided me with a patient yet firm hand to my deadline.

Special thanks to Ray Sylvester, whose presentation at a MEIEA conference was so impressive that I invited him to contribute Chapter 3 of this book.

The entrepreneurs who generously shared their stories and inspiration are the bedrock of this book. With deep gratitude I thank Aaron Bisman, Andrew Cyr, Peter English, Tony Falco, John Janick, Kimberley Locke, Brian McTear, Chris Stanchak, Marni Wandner, and Alex White.

My music industry colleagues shared their wisdom and insight with me throughout the years that I researched and wrote this book. I would particularly like to thank Gary Bongiovanni, Keith Fitzgerald, Savannah Haspel, Neeta Ragoowansi, Craig Rosen, James Thompson, and Heather Trussell.

I owe a debt of gratitude to my editor, Constance Ditzel, who wisely rejected my first book proposal, and who performed wonders with the second. I am grateful to the anonymous reviewers who read my drafts and give me valuable insight into how to make this a better book.

Finally, to my family—whom I am amazed and delighted to say are still speaking to me after the burdens I placed on them while writing this book—I give my deepest thanks. My daughter, Ariel Fitterman, shared her artistic talents by giving life to the Third Rail. My son, Ben Fitterman, and my sisters, Caren Leach and Caral Markwood, reviewed many chapters and kept up my spirits with frequent text messages, cards, and phone calls of encouragement. My mother, Cass Maccubbin, served as head cheerleader, celebrating my successes and pulling me up from my failures. And lastly, to my patient and devoted husband, Michael Radbill: you may now read my book!

PART 1

Thinking Like an Entrepreneur

CHAPTER 1

Fundamentals of Entrepreneurial Thinking

CHAPTER OVERVIEW

This chapter introduces the concept of entrepreneurial thinking and discusses how it can benefit you in whatever career you choose. Entrepreneur Brian McTear will explain how his company, Weathervane Music, is helping to build a healthy musical ecosystem in Philadelphia and beyond. We'll explore music as a venerable industry in transition and reflect on the tension between music as art and commerce. You will be encouraged to consider why we as humans are addicted to music, and how we struggle to balance the artistic and the commercial aspects of art. You will meet Third Rail, the fictional indie do-it-yourself (DIY) band whose adventures will reappear throughout the book. Chapter 1 concludes with Talking Back, a section in every chapter that will help you review the key concepts and prepare for a lively class discussion.

KEY TERMS

- A&R
- Brand identity
- Cognitive science
- Curator
- DIY artists
- Exploit (as it is used in the music industry)
- Fixed mindset
- Growth mindset
- Left-brain, right-brain characteristics
- Low (or high) barrier to entry
- Millenial generation
- Music business ecosystem
- Shaking Through and Weathervane Music
- Status quo

An Entrepreneur's Story: Brian McTear and Weathervane Music

One young Philadelphia-based entrepreneur is working hard to support and advance the careers of indie artists. Brian McTear is a producer/engineer and musician/songwriter who tours and records with the band Bitter Bitter Weeks.

McTear has deep roots in the Philadelphia music scene and a laser focus on strengthening and securing the future of music in our society.

"We need to build a healthy music ecosystem," he explains. "The people who make the music we love need to be actively and consistently supported in their communities."[1]

McTear's definition of a music ecosystem encompasses all the necessary working parts to bring music to our culture. This includes the people making, recording, and promoting the music, and the audience that supports it.

States McTear: "In this day and age, the audience isn't even at the end of the process, really. We're seeing more and more people working in a fan-funding model, where fans get in before it even happens. We want to inspire more of that type of logic with our audience as well. In other words, we want the audience to potentially see themselves as ground floor 'owners' of all parts of the process."[2]

As a member of Philadelphia's thriving music community, McTear meets many talented and eager young bands trying to make careers in music. He is in a unique position to help, as he is the co-owner and co-founder of Miner Street Recordings, a state-of-the-art studio where many of Philadelphia's most beloved and influential musicians produce nationally acclaimed records.

"I always loved recording these young musicians. I would try to connect them with people I knew who might be able to help them," he said. "But there was one very bleak moment a few years ago when I realized there was no way for these guys to make it. Sure, critically acclaimed records were being made, but without an involved and nurturing community, their musical careers were not sustainable."

With the ongoing massive retrenchment in the recording industry, most record labels will not take on a band that hasn't already proven itself in the marketplace. The result of this, along with the fact that music audiences are unaware of their role in bringing music to the marketplace, is a music ecosystem that is out of balance. There are fewer opportunities for extraordinary young musicians to find the support they need to become professionals who can make a living through their music.

"The internet is a great resource for musicians, but it's a ridiculously crowded marketplace," states Peter English, assistant director of Weathervane Music, and producer of its music and video series, Shaking Through. "Everybody is chasing after eyeballs and ears. With so much distraction, listeners' attention spans get shorter and shorter. Songwriters feel pressured to accommodate, so their songs can sound really hollow. They're a lot less satisfying musically."[3]

McTear knew first-hand how hard it was for artists to keep their vision intact when they couldn't even pay their rent, let alone afford healthcare or save toward a retirement. He also felt there were many other people who shared his hunger for authentic, high-quality music. So he began searching for a way to create a vibrant community-funded non-profit that would build community around, identify and nurture promising new artists.

In 2009, McTear and high school friend and fellow musician Bill Robertson established Weathervane Music, a non-profit organization dedicated to supporting musicians and giving the community an active role in the artistic process.[4]

Shaking Through is one of the most intriguing projects undertaken by Weathervane. It is a music and video web series that allows fans to witness the first recording of a new song by some of the most exciting minds in indie music.[5] Shaking Through is produced through a partnership between Weathervane Music and WXPN, the non-commercial, member-supported radio service of the University of Pennsylvania. McTear is the creator of Shaking Through. The series episodes are recorded at McTear's Miner Street Recordings, which sponsors the series by donating studio time.

A revolving cast of music professionals function as guest curators of the Shaking Through series, selecting creative and self-motivated bands they feel are just short of achieving sustainable careers.[6] The curators are well known in the music industry, bringing heightened visibility to the Shaking Through project.

Says English, "The curators select young artists who are excellent songwriters, passionate about music, and hungry for knowledge. Curators play an active and crucial role in the success of artists who participate in Shaking Through. Sometimes the bands are very raw, with little or no professional experience. But they're real artists: authentic, and committed to their own vision. We're here to support and facilitate their learning."[7]

Here is a partial listing of some of Shaking Through's curators and the bands they've selected:

- Scott McMicken (singer, Dr. Dog)—Floating Action, Springs, The Man Suits
- Bruce Warren (radio programmer, WXPN)—Hezekiah Jones
- Mark Schoneveld (music blogger, YVYNYL)—Twin Sister, Party Photographers, Reading Rainbow
- Peter Silberman (singer, The Antlers)—The Antlers, Port St. Willow
- Elise O. (music blogger, Pixel Horse)—La Big Vic, A Classic Education
- Daniel Smith (singer, Danielson)—Ben + Vesper, Sonoi, The Strapping Fieldhands
- Daniel Rossen (singer, Grizzly Bear)—Family Band
- Sean Agnew (major indie promoter in Philadelphia)—Creepoid.

 Watch video: all the Shaking Through web episodes.

How It Works

Shaking Through has a selection committee comprising Weathervane board and staff that selects guest curators to aid in finding new artist participants. Guest curators are well known and respected voices from the music community, including musicians and music bloggers, as well as professionals in the music industry, such as label owners, radio programmers, and others (Note: label owners are prohibited from selecting artists on their label.) Guest curators are selected based on their taste in music and the potential reach that their network will bring to the project.

The guest curator suggests two or three prospective artists. Shaking Through's selection committee vets those artists' eligibility and availability, and discusses the merits of episodes for each of them along with the curator. When the final artist is chosen, the curator and selection committee work with the artist to select the song they will record from their catalog of new songs. The song is decided upon based on its quality as well as the potential narrative arcs it may inspire for the video episode.

From the moment a band is selected by a curator, they are enveloped in the Shaking Through family. As the artists prepare for their trip to Philadelphia to record, they discuss all the details with McTear and English on the phone and through email.

Once they arrive in Philadelphia, the musicians hunker down in the Miner Street Recordings studio for two to three days while 'giving birth' to a new, previously unrecorded song. A professional video crew captures the entire process. After the episode is completed, Weathervane initiates a PR process accessing their own, as well as the artists' and curators' networks. New web episodes air on ShakingThrough.com on the third Tuesday of each month.

"The bands come in as amateurs and leave as professionals," explains English. "For some of the artists, this is their first time recording in a high-end studio. They learn what the process is like, working with producers, engineers, and other musicians. It is pivotal for their fans to see the growth as it is happening."[8]

Miner Street Recordings donates studio time for the series free of charge to the artists. WXPN airs promotional segments for the episodes and backs it up with marketing outreach to traditional and new media outlets. WXPN may also add Shaking Through artists to their regular airplay rotation, or consider the artists for other WXPN programs such as their NPR distributed program "The World Café" if the music matches the station's aesthetic. The artists' work reaches a global audience via the high visibility of both websites and terrestrial and online radio.

"The artistic marriage of music and video, and the significant financial and resource commitment to the partnership by Weathervane and WXPN, is helping artists hone and develop their craft, while sharing their work with a growing community of listeners and supporters."[9] The worldwide creative community is invited to participate in Weathervane Music's 'Media-Share Project,' where raw multi-tracks and mix-stems from Shaking Through recording sessions are available for downloading, remixing, and sharing.

Pitchfork called Shaking Through "an inspired recording project"[10] when reviewing Shaking Through's first episode in January 2010, which featured Brooklyn-based Sharon Van Etten's "Love More" track.

Sharon Van Etten

"We had known Sharon Van Etten by name for a while," explains McTear.[11] "So we weren't surprised when her name was put forward by several friends, including Greg Weeks (of the band Espers), and well-known singer and musician Sufjan Stevens."

Van Etten's record label had just gone under, and she was in the process of figuring out what to do next when McTear approached her to be their first recording artist in the series. She eagerly embraced the innovative concept of Shaking Through. As with so many artists, there weren't any 'next moves' from the traditional music business that could support her.[12]

Van Etten had collaborated infrequently with other musicians, and had recorded her music in small-scale studios. For her Shaking Through session she brought two other artists from Brooklyn, Cat Martino and Jeffery Kisch. Her recording session at Miner Street was 'eye opening,' as Van Etten stretched her wings in new territory.[13]

Hundreds of people watched the Shaking Through video of the band making Van Etten's single "Love More." Thousands more downloaded the song. A YouTube video surfaced showing members of Bon Iver and The National covering "Love More." Three months later Van Etten was signed to a recording contract and created a new album entitled *Epic*, featuring her Miner Street-recorded track.[14] Since then, Van Etten's touring has grown to include shows at the Pitchfork Festival, Bonnaroo, SXSW, a world tour with The National, and the Bumbershoot Festival in Seattle.[15]

Watch video: the making of "Love More."

Dreamers of the Ghetto
Shaking Through asked curator Ben Swanson, co-founder of Secretly Canadian Records, to think of an artist to whom he personally wanted to give a huge career opportunity, but who wasn't on his label. Without hesitation, Swanson chose Bloomington, Indiana natives Dreamers of the Ghetto.[16]

Says McTear, "This band knows exactly who they are. There's no pretentious identity whatsoever. They are all family, all best friends, and that was really inspiring to us."[17]

This was Dreamers of the Ghetto's first time as a band to actually travel and do a legitimate recording project. Luke Jones, Dreamers' lead vocalist, says of his Shaking Through experience: "There's some intimidation that comes with the recording process but when you're working with good people you have nothing to be afraid of. It brought out the best in us."[18]

Dreamers of the Ghetto recorded the song "Heavy Love" over the course of their two-day session at Miner Street. McTear produced the track using boutique tube microphones provided for Shaking Through by frequent sponsors Studio Logic Sound and TELEFUNKEN Elektroakustik.[19]

 Watch video: the making of "Heavy Love."

Big Troubles
Curators Jenn and Liz Pelly, the twin sister co-authors of PellyTwins.blogspot.com, chose the band Big Troubles for a Shaking Through episode. The band brought their song "Phantom" to Miner Street Recordings, the first song Big Troubles had ever tracked in a real studio.[20]

"Having a team like this to help out bands who . . . don't have some label to throw money at them is awesome" says Alex Craig, the songwriter and frontman for the band.[21]

 Watch video: the making of "Phantom."

"I think what we really like the most about the Shaking Through series is the depth that it goes into, in terms of the process of creating one track," states Liz Pelly. "The music media/online media landscape . . . needs some longer form narrative content where people are . . . spending time to look at the actual process of making music."[22]

IFC.com reviewer Grayson Currin had this to say about Shaking Through: "Led by the remarkable producer and musician, Brian McTear, Shaking Through treats every band they feature and every song those bands make like a cross between sanctuaries and stories. For McTear and his crew, this music and the chance to make it seems sacred, each three or four minutes of audio a new chance to put something perfect and daring into the world. It makes sense, then, that Shaking Through releases some of the best takes ever by some of the bands it brings into the studio."[23]

"The Shaking Through venture with WXPN has been a phenomenal first project for Weathervane Music and the 20-plus indie musicians we've worked with so far," concludes McTear. "We've been lucky to collaborate with such extraordinary and talented people in helping these musicians. It's gratifying that we are actually making it possible for them to take their first steps toward sustainable careers in music. As time goes on, we hope the general public will gain a deeper understanding of their importance in being active players in all artists' success."

As you read the pages ahead, look for a connection between nurturing young artists, entrepreneurial thinking, and music as both art and commerce. What could you do in your community to support artists, fans, and a healthy music ecosystem?

INDUSTRY ESSENTIALS: THE FUNDAMENTALS OF ENTREPRENEURIAL THINKING

Defining Entrepreneurship

Which description of 'entrepreneur' suits you best?

- I think I would be most comfortable using my entrepreneurial skills as an employee of a company that was doing something I really believed in.

- I am passionate about a particularly daunting social problem and want to make meaning by creating and managing a venture to achieve sustainable social change.

- I want to make meaning by creating a venture that measures performance in profit and return, rather than in social capital.

- I am firmly planted in the not-for-profit mind-set and want to make meaning in the new venture I launch, but I'm not a social entrepreneur.

Carl Schramm, president of the Ewing Marion Kauffman Foundation, the world's largest foundation devoted to entrepreneurship, believes that entrepreneurs have a positive influence on the American economy by creating ways to reinvent and innovate the rules of life. "Entrepreneurs teach us about human needs we did not know existed, create jobs that provide security for people, and generate social welfare," he says.[24]

When we add 'music' to 'entrepreneur,' does the definition become more focused? What people come to mind when you think about music entrepreneurs?

This is my definition: A music entrepreneur is someone who uses creativity, innovation, and bold leadership to channel his or her passion for music into a new business that challenges the status quo and has value in the public marketplace.

Changing lives, changing markets, changing the world. This is the work of an entrepreneur. Each of us has the power to dream, create, nurture, and build something of value from our great ideas, regardless of the resources we have at hand when that flash of inspiration strikes.

As noted in the Preface of the book, this is an ideal time for bold, entrepreneurial thinking in the music industry. We need fresh, new approaches to creating products and services. We are looking to students like you to help spark a renewed sense of optimism and economic growth in the music business. To begin, let's examine why you'll want to become an entrepreneurial thinker.

Characteristics of Entrepreneurial Thinking

Changing Your Mindset

Stanford psychologist Carol Dweck has spent decades researching achievement, failure, and success. In her book *Mindset: The New Psychology of Success* she convincingly demonstrates that one's frame of mind is a major influencer in determining who achieves his or her entrepreneurial potential and who does not.

Dweck asserts that people who believe intelligence is determined at birth have a *fixed mindset*. They are consumed by constantly proving to the world that they are talented and smart in all areas of their life. "Every situation calls for a confirmation of their intelligence, personality, or character," states Dweck. "Every situation is evaluated: Will I succeed or fail? Will I look smart or dumb? Will I be accepted or rejected?"[25]

People who think that it is possible to become smarter over time have what Dweck calls *growth mindsets*. These people are not afraid to try a different way of doing things or speak up with new ideas. They understand that taking chances, trying new ideas, making mistakes, and correcting them are the tools that actually help grow entrepreneurial ability.[26] In the growth mindset, people want to become better at what they do, and they seek opportunities to challenge their abilities. They see personal setbacks as opportunities to learn and grow. Entrepreneurs need a growth mindset to flourish.

Right Brain/Left Brain

Author and former White House speechwriter Daniel Pink delves deeply into the cognitive science of right brain/left brain characteristics in his powerful book *A Whole New Mind: Why Right-Brainers Will Rule the Future*. He bases his arguments on decades of data showing that the brain has two distinct hemispheres, each controlling different emotions and ways of thinking.

Pink argues that the world is moving away from an economy and society built on logical, linear, computer-like capabilities (left brain) to an economy and society built on the inventive, empathic, big-picture capabilities of the right brain. He feels we are entering a new economic era, which he calls the Conceptual Age. We will need the capacity to detect patterns and opportunities, and to combine seemingly unrelated ideas into something new if we are to succeed in the Conceptual Age.[27]

We know that we need both 'sides' of the brain to function fully, even though we may find that we resort to one type of cognitive processing over the other, particularly in stressful situations. Look at the following worksheet. In the blank center column, write one or more of your day-to-day activities that employ the specific type of cognitive processing described in the right-hand column.

TABLE 1.1 Cognitive processing characteristics

TYPE OF COGNITIVE PROCESSING	ACTIVITIES THAT USE THIS TYPE OF COGNITIVE PROCESSING	BRIEF DESCRIPTION
Linear (Left-brain)		Processes information from part to whole in a straightforward, logical progression.
Holistic (Right-brain)		Processes information from whole to part; sees the big picture first, not the details.
Sequential (Left-brain)		Processes information in order from first to last.
Random (Right-brain)		Processes information without priority, jumps from one task to another.
Concrete (Left-brain)		Processes things that can be seen or touched—real objects.
Symbolic (Right-brain)		Processes symbols as pictures; likes to use letters, words and mathematical symbols
Logical (Left-brain)		Processes information piece by piece using logic to solve a problem.
Intuitive (Right-brain)		Processes information based on whether or not it feels right to know the answer but not sure how it was derived.
Verbal (Left-brain)		Processes thoughts and ideas with words.
Non-verbal (Right-brain)		Processes thought as illustrations.
Reality-Based (Left-brain)		Processes information based on reality; focuses on rules and regulations.
Fantasy-Oriented (Right-brain)		Processes information with creativity; less focus on rules and regulations.

Note: adapted from Carolyn Hopper, *Practicing College Study Skills: Strategies for Success* (2009), frank.mtsu.edu/~studskl/.

Pink cites the 2004 research of cognitive neuroscientists M. Jung-Beemna, E.M. Bowden, and J. Haberman at Drexel and Northwestern Universities. Their work shows that flashes of insight preceding "*aha!*" moments are accompanied by a large burst of neural activity in the brain's right hemisphere. An inspiration-centered approach to innovation (those "*aha!*" moments) requires the ability and fortitude to experiment with novel combinations and to make the many mistakes that inevitably come with upending the status quo.[28]

The Wisdom of Failing

Entrepreneurial thinking requires the ability to embrace mistakes as learning opportunities. Most of us try to avoid failing. We worry that we'll look foolish in front of our friends, or we'll lose money, disappoint people, or get a bad grade. When we are afraid of making a mistake, we become cautious and timid.

Fear of failing is a creativity-crusher. It inhibits boldness and innovation. In their Harvard Business Review publication *The Wisdom of Deliberate Mistakes*, authors Paul Schoemaker and Robert Gunther explain how traditional pedagogical practices have contributed to this anti-entrepreneurial situation. We tell children stories of famous people like Thomas Edison, the inventor of the electric light bulb, to show inspiring examples of people who failed for years before achieving their goals. Yet, as Schoemaker and Gunther point out: "Good grades are usually a reward for doing things right, not for making errors."[29]

Entrepreneurial thinkers thrive in environments that nurture optimism, build self-confidence, stimulate innovation, and embrace failure as a learning opportunity. In order to reinvigorate the music industry, we must find young adults who think like entrepreneurs and fail forward.

Fail Forward

Maddock Douglas is a Chicago company that brings innovative ideas to the marketplace. Working with many Fortune 100 companies, Maddock Douglas helps its clients identify the biggest unmet needs in its industry, brainstorm game-changing new products, services, and business models, then brand and launch the best ideas into the market. Maddock Douglas gives an annual Fail Forward award. Employees are recognized for trying new ideas, even if the result is disastrous.[30]

Reflect

 Watch video: Derek Sivers, *Why You Need to Fail*.
Now answer these questions based on your life's experiences.

1. Give examples in your life when *deliberate* failure has been encouraged and rewarded. How did you view this concept? What was the outcome?

2. Give examples of *accidental* failures—when you tried something, didn't expect to fail, but did. What was your reaction? How did others react?
3. Reflect on 'no pain, no gain' as a metaphor for 'not failing, not learning' as it applies to your life, both personal and professional.
4. "If you're not failing you're not trying hard enough." Connect this quote from the video to your personal experiences with *music*.

Over the past few pages, we have built a definition of *entrepreneur* that includes generating great ideas, bold thinking, an appetite for upending the status quo, an inspiration-centered approach to innovation, economic value, a growth mindset, and the ability to learn from failure. Now let's look at the value of entrepreneurial thinking to your future career.

Why You Need to Think Like an Entrepreneur

There is significant research showing the positive impact of entrepreneurs and new job creation in the greater world economy. That's great information, but it's not the point of this book. I want to show you that entrepreneurship is more than a business practice that creates jobs. Even if you never start your own company, or work in the music industry, learning to think like an entrepreneur can be your personal one-way ticket out of anxiety about your future career, particularly in tough economic times.

The ability to recognize opportunities and move quickly to exploit them will serve you well whether you start your own business or work for someone else, whether you lead others or only yourself. Entrepreneurial thinking will expand your repertoire of ideas and options, both for the marketplace and for your professional development.

Reflect

 Watch videos: "Leadership Lessons from Dancing Guy" and "Japanese addresses: No street names. Block numbers."

When you have watched these two videos by CD Baby founder Derek Sivers, discuss your reactions. Do you see yourself as a leader, a first follower, or something else altogether? Can you begin to see how looking at the world in a different way can change your perspective on the status quo?

Most of us begin our working lives as employees, receiving wages or salaries while learning the ins and outs of the industry and creating value for our employer.

New and existing companies want to hire people who have an open mindset and can tackle problems with creative energy and confidence. All businesses must grow to survive, and it's a company's innovation, creativity, opportunity recognition, and the ability to move quickly and anticipate market conditions that fuels growth. Therefore, individuals who think like entrepreneurs are highly desirable as employees in firms with forward-thinking leaders.

The entrepreneurial education you receive in this book will help you decide whether or not launching your own company is right for you—now or in the future. Every artist, band, and business begins with individuals taking small steps to achieve personal goals and fulfill their passion. In the process of learning to think like an entrepreneur, you may discover opportunities in the marketplace that are so compelling that you decide to start your own business before the book ends. That choice is yours.

No matter how you apply your entrepreneurial thinking skills—to an existing business or to your own company one day—you will have a high degree of control over your career direction. There is an urgent need in our uncertain economy for individuals who can see opportunities where others see only intractable problems. As a creative problem solver and opportunity recognizer, you will be a highly valued, go-to person in your workplace.

Many of us with long careers in the music industry are looking to students like you for inspiration. A decade-long turmoil in our marketplace has created deep flux and instability. Yet from an entrepreneurial point of view, this is the perfect storm of *opportunity*.

As a member of the Millennial generation you embrace technology and are more comfortable with change than older generations. You're in college, and that means you're exposed and open to new ideas and different approaches to life. You respect and understand the past, but since you are new to the music industry, you are able to stand free of the bonds of tradition. Your personal tastes in music, your thoughts about work, morals, and ethics, as well as the balance you strive to maintain between art and commerce are fueling the growth and transitions in the next-generation music industry.

For people like you, this is an extraordinary time to be part of the music industry. With an entrepreneurial mindset you will discover new ways of interacting with a venerable industry, keeping it strong by imagining and creating new products, services, and markets. How to use the new skills you are about to develop is entirely your decision. The possibilities are limitless.

A Venerable Industry in Transition

For decades the record industry *was* the music industry. Everything revolved around record labels. The health of the music industry was measured primarily by record sales. Labels' A&R (artist and repertoire) executives discovered new talent and worked with music publishers to find great songs to record. The dedicated people working at the labels spent millions of hours and hundreds of millions of dollars nurturing new artists and preparing them for sustainable careers. Nearly every artist's goal was to be signed to a label. In pre-internet days, fans discovered music by listening to the radio, going to concerts, hanging out in record stores, talking to their friends, and buying albums.

Many factors have contributed to the decade-long loss of revenue from fewer album sales. Rapid technological advances, changing consumer habits regarding music access vs. music ownership, digital music delivery, and social networking have fundamentally changed recorded music's pre-internet business models. Uncertain global economic conditions and corporate consolidations have forced companies to lay off employees and drop artists from their rosters as they struggle to maintain profitability. Some even wonder if recorded music has lost its magic as it changed from being a highly anticipated, beautifully packaged 'event' to an easy to find (and often free) computer download.

Massive marketplace changes have contributed to transitions in nearly every sector of the music industry. Recorded music, live concerts, radio, TV, video, social media, publishing, smartphones, licensing, games, retail, copyright laws, and media technologies have all combined to create a vastly different landscape for musicians, fans, and industry professionals from what existed 10–15 years ago.

Today's music industry looks like this:

Carol Del Angel/Ikon Images/Getty Images

In the past, it looked more like this:

PM Images/The Image Bank/Getty Images

Some people feel the turmoil in the music industry is fundamentally a *technological* change with artistic and economic implications. It began when the first digital compact discs became commercially available in 1982. The changes escalated with the rapid spread of digital compression files on the internet in the mid-1990s. And, many believe, the *coup de grâce* to the traditional music industry arrived in 1999 when a college student with unruly hair and the nickname "Napster" launched the first internet peer-to-peer file sharing service in 1999.

Here's another way to think about it: Perhaps this is an *artistic* about-face with technological and economic implications. Many music fans say that songwriters' creativity had been compromised because of the financial pressures of the traditional industry gatekeepers—radio and record labels. They say that, for too long, 'success' had been measured in record sales and chart position. They point to the veritable artistic renaissance now taking place, as untold thousands of musicians and artists share their music and collaborate in a global creative, online community.

Reflect

Why do you think there are so many ongoing changes in the music industry? What has prospered because of them? What has languished?

There are positive and negative effects for any industry in transition, and the music business is no exception. Thanks to the internet, social media, and changing consumer behavior regarding music consumption, it's possible today for some musicians to find a wide public by doing most of their early career-building on their own. These DIY (do-it-yourself) artists take charge of their own writing, recording, publishing, touring, licensing, sales, fan development, and marketing. It's a lot of work, and it's not for everyone.

A low barrier to entry for new artists in today's music business can have negative effects, as well. There is so much music available anytime, anywhere, and through many sources that the marketplace is crowded and noisy. This can put downward pressure on the value of music as supply far outstrips demand. With so many ways to get music for free, many artists are finding it difficult to support themselves through their art.

Another example of transitions taking place in the music industry is the widespread ownership consolidation within record labels, concert promoters, music publishers, and television and radio stations. Record stores have all but disappeared. These jolting changes create hardship for some and opportunities for others. Flexibility and an entrepreneurial mindset are key survival skills in transitional times.

Art as Business, Business as Art

The music business is a constant battle between art and commerce. It's true that everything begins with a song (the art), but if a songwriter wants to make a living at her craft, there has to be a sale (the commerce).

But to many of us, music seems more like air or water than a commercial product. We can't live without it. Our very identities are closely tied to music. Each of us has special songs or melodies that define who we are as unique individuals. How can something so vital, so intimate be called a product, as if it were a washing machine or a box of cereal?

It's worth taking a brief look at why we, as a species, are . . .

Addicted to Music

Music has enchanted humans since we first appeared on this planet. From simple drumbeats and instruments made of wood and bone to stadium shows with multimedia and pyrotechnic displays, humans have always made music. Nearly every cultural community has specific musical traditions that have evolved over time, and are proudly passed down to successive generations.

In *This Is Your Brain On Music*, session musician/sound engineer/record producer/neuroscientist Daniel J. Levitin explores the connection between music and the human brain. This fundamental human endeavor called music making has become a multi-billion dollar global industry.

Levitin explains: "music taps into primitive brain structures involved with motivation, reward, and emotion."[31] He identifies complex chemical reactions that take place in regions of the brain when a person listens to music. Some of these reactions involve a neurotransmitter called dopamine, a chemical 'messenger' that is similar to adrenaline.[32] "Dopamine affects brain processes that control movement, emotional response, and the ability to experience pleasure and pain. It is also one of the neurotransmitters that plays a major role in addiction."[33]

How does this work? Levitin found a direct correlation between positive mood changes and higher levels of dopamine. He explains that, just as the world around us unfolds in varying rhythms and speeds, our brain finds satisfaction in speeding up or slowing down to match the pace of music we hear. When a song veers away from what our brains predict will come next—a rhythmic pattern or melodic sequence— our emotional response is pleasure and amusement.[34]

One of the most fascinating sections of Levitin's book focuses on why we identify so strongly with the music that we listen to in our teen and early adult years. Musical tastes revolve around a young person's choice of communities. As we grow up and discover a world of ideas beyond those of our parents, we begin to explore different ways of seeing and thinking. Musical discovery is a highly emotional way of connecting with others. As we search for our unique identity, we form groups of friends who have traits that we admire or want to emulate. We bond with our friends through the clothes we wear, the way we spend our free time, and through the musical tastes we share. In other words, music is a powerful and defining aspect of both our individual and group identity.[35]

Levitin states: "Our brains on music are all about connections. Music we love reminds us of other songs we've heard, which then sets up a chain of emotional response to connect us with the past . . . Part of the reason we remember songs from our teenage years is because those years were times of self-discovery, and as a consequence, they were emotionally charged."[36]

Your Music, Your Brand

The music you're listening to right now is the music you'll feel connected to for the rest of your life. From an artistic point of view, this is the essence of music. It binds us to a time and a place when we moved from child to adult. From a commercial point of view, exploiting this strong emotional connection to music has enormous potential for connecting brands (products and services) to bands (the artists who wrote and performed that music) in the music marketplace. Today, branding is a key opportunity for both artists and corporations. It's a perfect example of the tug between art and commerce in the music industry. Chapter 3 explores artist branding in greater detail.

Art in the Marketplace

What fuels the music marketplace? Fans want to discover new bands. Advertisers hope to connect with potential customers. Large companies pay to enhance their image by teaming up with a specific kind of artist. School children sign up to learn how to play instruments. Unions and rights organizations support the work of their members. Producers and artists work together to create new songs.

Music is one of the leading creative industries propelling the media and entertainment sector that is now worth somewhere between U.S.$1.4 and $1.8 trillion. Music has become an increasingly important economic driver in the digital era.[37]

Today, sales can happen in real or virtual marketplaces. Goods and services are bought and sold using currency as the economic lubricant. In the music marketplace there are many communities of buyers and sellers:

- Songwriters
- Producers
- Performers
- Fans
- Retail products trade show (winter NAMM, see Appendix)
- Film and video makers
- Broadcasters
- Advertisers
- Venue operators
- Record labels
- Online and physical retail stores
- Publishers
- Unions
- Attorneys
- Rights organizations
- Video game composers.

What else can you add to this list?

MEET THIRD RAIL

Sam, Walter, Cody, and Jared are members of a fictional indie band called Third Rail. Throughout the book Third Rail will tackle the many challenges of making music their livelihood. You will be asked to guide them as they encounter opportunities and setbacks, face crucial decisions, and experience successes and failures as a DIY band.

Third Rail Logo. Artist: Ariel Fitterman

In this story, Sam has an *'aha!'* moment when he realizes that brand identity is what set a handful of bands apart from the other bands at the music festival. The concept of 'band as brand' is an economic cornerstone for musicians today, and is discussed thoroughly in Chapter 3.

Sam and his band, the Third Rail, were driving home after five days at a summer music festival. It had been an amazing and exhausting experience, with hundreds of bands and important people in the music industry all squeezed into one small town. Third Rail's three shows at the festival had gone pretty well. People seemed genuinely interested in their music.

There were thousands of musicians like Third Rail at the festival, all trying to be heard by people who could help ratchet up their music careers. Most of the music was very good, but a few bands stuck out. On the drive back, Sam, Walter, Cody, and Jared talked for hours about those exceptional bands and what made them different. Their music was solid, you could tell they'd had experience performing and working a crowd, they had fans, and a strong online presence. Walter mentioned the bands' personality, Jared talked about their merchandise, and Cody said there was just something about their look. A few of the bands even had corporate sponsors.

Sam suddenly figured it out: those bands had become brands.

"Guys, remember what the agent told us after our second show?" Sam asked. "She said there was a lot more to the music industry than writing music and playing great shows. And she told us if we want to get serious about music as a career, we'll have to work pretty much 24/7/365 and learn to think like entrepreneurs."

From what that agent at the festival said, there were a lot of different opportunities for the band to make money. That was good, but Sam wasn't sure the band could ever master the intricacies of the music industry. What should Third Rail tackle first? Maybe they should figure out their 'brand identity,' whatever that was. Sam felt they definitely had to get more buzz on social media. But he was conflicted about whether or not Third Rail should try to use it to attract music business professionals, such as a manager, booking agent, attorney, or record label. Did a band today still need to have all those traditional partners?

The agent had said they couldn't license their music for use in commercials and TV shows unless the samples were cleared. Sam wondered how difficult that would be, and how to get started. The agent had also mentioned performing rights societies, and how Third Rail needed to choose one. But Sam couldn't remember why that was important. Did it have something to do with their live shows?

Third Rail had seen some impressive merchandise for sale at the music festival. They understood how T-shirts and other merch could generate much-needed cash, but they had no idea how to get started.

Sam felt overwhelmed. He had just come face to face with the realities, complexities, and abundant opportunities of today's turbulent music industry. At the end of the chapter you'll be asked to help the Third Rail make some decisions.

Opportunities Ahead

Entrepreneurs see opportunities where others see only problems. Take a look at these 'problems' and see how you can think creatively to turn them into opportunities:

- The collapse of a rigid infrastructure has created a marketplace where many people feel music should be free. Artists and the people who support them are scrambling to adjust to this new environment.
- The game-changing benefits of the internet have provided opportunities for every artist in the world to have a global presence. This is great for artists, and for fans who want to discover new music. But it creates a challenging, crowded, and noisy marketplace in which everyone is struggling to be heard. Some people say there is too much music available and it's impossible for anyone to sort through it all.
- There is increasing pressure on artists to tour in order to compensate for less revenue from recorded music sales. With live performance one of the few consistently strong areas of the business, bands must find a delicate balance between risking over-exposure by appearing in a market too often, while keeping their ticket prices appropriate for a public that is still hurting from the global recession.

CONCLUSION

Entrepreneurial thinking and creative problem solving are the tools you need to visualize the abundant opportunities that exist amid the turmoil in the music industry today. Music may be an emotional touchstone for all of us, but it cannot survive as an industry if people aren't willing to reach into their wallets and support it. This reality contributes to the constant struggle between music as art vs. music as commerce. Some entrepreneurs, like Brian McTear of Weathervane Music, are creating opportunities to nurture young artists through innovative collaborations between local businesses and the worldwide creative community.

In the chapters ahead, we will unpack and untangle the music industry as we reflect on the present and imagine the promise of the future. You will be amazed to discover how many opportunities there are to make your voice heard as the music industry continues to change and adapt to the demands of marketplace. You are the future of the music industry. The most important voice in the pages ahead is yours.

 Talking Back: Class Discussions

Return to the story about the Third Rail earlier in the chapter. Consider all the opportunities Sam identified. Where should they begin? Here are some issues to consider:

- Internet presence
- Songwriting
- Joining a performing rights organization
- License songs in films, videos, ads
- Clear samples in their recording
- Fan base
- Merchandise
- Business stuff
- Find a manager, lawyer, booking agent, business manager
- Sign with a label or DIY
- Find or create a community artist-incubator like Weathervane Music in Philadelphia.

- Give reasons for your answers based on what you know so far about the music industry. Think like an entrepreneur.

- Name some musicians who have corporate sponsorship. How does the relationship benefit the artist? The corporation? Do you feel that anything is being lost?

- What is the artistic difference between a jingle and a song that has been re-purposed for use in a film or commercial? Sing some examples of each.

- What tools do you use to help you navigate in the crowded online music marketplace, both as a fan looking for bands and as a band looking for fans?

Web Links

- Shaking Through
  Shakingthrough.com
- Love More
  Shakingthrough.com/sharonvanetten
- Heavy Love
  Shakingthrough.com/dreamersoftheghetto

- Phantom
Shakingthrough.com/bigtroubles

- Derek Sivers, *Why You Need to Fail*
Youtube.com/watch?v=HhxcFGuKOys

- "Leadership Lessons from Dancing Guy" and "Japanese addresses: No street names. Block numbers"
Sivers.org/ff
Sivers.org/jadr

CHAPTER 2

Creative Problem Solving

CHAPTER OVERVIEW

In this chapter you will begin to master the art of generating great ideas, the first step in learning to think like an entrepreneur. Using puzzles, games, and brainteasers, you will invigorate your linear and intuitive thinking abilities. I call this type of mental preparation 'play with a purpose.' A flexible and fluent mindset will expand your potential for innovation and creativity as you explore the music industry.

KEY TERMS

- 'Blue sky' brainstorming
- Kickstarter
- Label-centric
- Nielsen Soundscan
- Next Big Sound
- TED Talks
- The 99% solution
- WhyNot.net

An Entrepreneur's Story: Alex White, Next Big Sound

Alex White was frustrated. He was on a two-month tour with the band Sing It Loud in 2009,[1] and it was his job to oversee its internet presence. He knew music was no longer a label-centric business, and firmly believed that direct access to and engagement with fans was the best way to build a band's career. White spent hours every day sending tweets, posting updates to MySpace and Facebook, and keeping up with all the new social-media sites.[2] He kept thinking "What if I could track all the internet chatter, compile it, and analyze how fans were interacting with Sing It Loud?"

White thought this type of information might even be something that other bands, their record labels, and managers would be willing to pay for. He knew that the music industry already was paying to track and analyze sales of concert tickets through TicketMaster and other ticket services, and sales of records through Nielsen SoundScan. Wouldn't agents and managers want to see what was bubbling up on the internet before an artist or band got big? White wondered if he could build a platform to capture, analyze, and sell this data.[3]

White's ideas morphed over time into Next Big Sound, a company he founded with classmates from a Northwestern University entrepreneurship class. Next Big Sound tracks the growth and popularity of hundreds of thousands of music groups across major web properties like Facebook, YouTube, MySpace, Last.fm, Twitter, and others. Every week the company releases the NBS25, a list of the fastest rising artists on a trajectory to become the next big sound.[4] To date, Next Big Sound has raised more than $1million from venture capitalists. It was named one of Billboard's Top Ten Digital Startups in 2010.

Alex White and Next Big Sound are a classic entrepreneurship story: White pays attention to something that is bugging him, gets a great idea, asks 'What if . . .', sees that there is a market for his idea, builds a team, finds funding, and launches his company. His first step—coming up with a great idea—is where we'll begin our journey toward becoming masterful entrepreneurial thinkers. White came up with a great idea, refined it, and launched a business. In the pages ahead, you will learn how to look at the world around you with fresh eyes and an open mind to change and up-end the status quo.

INDUSTRY ESSENTIALS: CREATIVE PROBLEM SOLVING

Strap on Your Growth Mindset

Your mindset determines how you see the world around you. Feeling stressed, tense, or anxious decreases your ability to tap into your creative self. On the other hand, feeling confident, relaxed, and open to new ways of thinking will energize your outlook on life. It takes work to change your attitude, but the benefits are enormous if you can.

Entrepreneurial thinking flows best when you're having fun or doing something out of the ordinary. Ever wonder why some companies that require lots of creative thinking from their employees have a room with scooters, a pool table, puzzles, Legos®, and other toys? It's because that kind of environment wakes up our brains. We're able to tap into our playful selves, which are all too often buried underneath the pressure to behave like the adults we are. The designer Milton Glaser sums it up well: "There's a conflict between professionalism that calls for *minimizing* risk, while creativity *encourages* risk."[5]

A growth mindset opens you to a 'What if . . .?' attitude. It encourages you to question the status quo and imagine a completely new way of approaching problems. You'll find yourself asking "What if we tried it this way instead?" and "What would happen if we flipped that around?" The techniques in this chapter will help you create ideas big and small, practical and whacky, technical and artistic. Most importantly, you will abandon traditional ways of thinking and embrace an open, inquisitive approach to the world around you.

Don't just *read* this chapter—you'll have to *use* these techniques in order to master entrepreneurial thinking. You'll be flexing both the left (linear) and right (creative) sides of your brain as you work the exercises ahead.

Identifying Problems and Recognizing Opportunity

There's nothing more powerful than a creative mind with a powerful idea and the passion to make it a reality. Great ideas can bring about life-changing inventions, such as the cure for polio, the car, the internet, and the plane. Ideas can bring about game-changing technological disruption, such as railroads, radio, and smartphones. Some ideas even bring about massive social change, as did the invention and widespread use of the cotton gin in the antebellum American South.

Think back over your morning. Did anything annoy you? Was there something that didn't work properly? What frustrated you because it was inefficient, poorly designed, or difficult to use? These are all excellent places to begin identifying problems that may turn out to be opportunities for entrepreneurial thinking.

After you've thought of a few problems from your morning, compete this exercise and save your work:

- Write down the problem in a simple sentence of 15 or fewer words.

- Then write down for whom (besides you) this is a problem and why.

- If this is a massive problem, it may be too large to tackle as one piece. Break it into its component parts and work on each part separately.

A good source to explore for inspiration and idea-generation is TED, a non-profit organization devoted to Ideas Worth Spreading. TED started out in 1984 as a conference bringing together people from three worlds: Technology, Entertainment, and Design. Since then its scope has become ever broader. On TED.com, you will find TEDTalks, the best talks and performances from TED conferences available to the world, for free. If you're looking for great ideas, TED is a great place to begin. There are more than 900 TEDTalks available on the website, with more added each week.[6]

No problem-solving and opportunity recognition warm-up session is complete without looking in on WhyNot.net, a site that shows "how to use everyday ingenuity to solve problems big and small."[7] Professors Ian Ayers and Barry Nalebuff from Yale University, authors of the book *Why Not?*, have created a worldwide idea exchange, complete with ideas by topic, a "Recent Hits" section, and links to other idea-generating sites like HalfBakery.com, a lively discussion of partly baked ideas.

Generating Great Ideas for Solving Problems

Tom&Kwikki/Shutterstock Images

Creativity Warm-Up

These exercises, adapted from the book, *Thinkertoys* by Michael Michalko, will help make your thinking more fluent and flexible. Fluency refers to the number of ideas you get. Flexibility refers to how well you can improvise, see beyond the traditional way of doing things, and play with context and perspective.[8] The more fluent and flexible your mind is, the greater the chance of coming up with great ideas.

You will need: paper, pencils or pens, and a minute timer.

1. Grab a piece of paper and a pen. Set a timer for three minutes. Look very carefully at something in your classroom—a pen, a chair, a door handle, your ID card. Besides its traditional purpose, how else could the object be used? Be creative, fanciful, and humorous in your answers. What type of cognitive processing are you using for this game? Compare your ideas with the rest of the class.

2. See how many four-word sentences you can compose in four minutes (set a timer) using each letter from the given words below as the first letter of a word in the new sentence.

Example: T–O–C–K.
The older child knocks.
Tired oxen can kick.

Given words:

D–R–U–M
F–I–S–H
R–E–A–D

3. Write a list of problems on the board. The problems can be things from your frustrating morning, from your community, or even global issues. We are going to try to solve the problems by using metaphors; that is, comparing each one to something unusual. By pulling apart and recombining the essential elements you will find unexpected connections and new relationships, which may lead to some great ideas.

Select one of your problems and ask: How is this problem similar to a Band-Aid? List the essential elements of a Band-Aid. What connections can you find between those and the elements of your problem?

Pair some of the other problems with any of these:

- The solar system
- A library
- U.S. Postal Service delivery trucks.

A Structure for Creative Problem Solving

What if . . .?

Yale professors and entrepreneurs Barry Nalebuff and Ian Ayres have written the blueprint for using simple methods and everyday ingenuity to come up with clever solutions to the world's problems. Their book *Why Not?* demonstrates how to generate great ideas by challenging a 'that's just the way things are done around here' attitude with an open-minded "What if . . .?" approach to problem solving. We'll be using adaptations of their structured methods to become experts at generating great ideas, as we take the first step in thinking like an entrepreneur.

Problem solving is a great way to look for ideas. It is a form of creativity and self-expression, allowing us to communicate and connect with one another. The satisfaction of helping people find a better way of doing things can be extremely rewarding. Now that your brain is relaxed and alert, let's begin.

Oprah Winfrey
Credit: Bruce Glikas/FilmMagic/Getty Images

Structured Problem-Solving Method 1: What would Oprah do?

Imagine you are Oprah, and have unlimited resources to solve problems. You are rich, have plenty of time, and access to the greatest geniuses in the world. How would you solve the problems listed below? Be bold. This is 'blue-sky' brainstorming. Don't judge your ideas. Don't look for a realistic solution. Remove as many constraints as possible on your imagination.

- Problem 1: The only time I can go to the gym is after work, and the gym is always very crowded.

- Problem 2: People in developing countries lack adequate and affordable health care.

- Problem 3: Use one of the problems you experienced this morning.

Write down your ideas. Compare them with those of your classmates. Did you come up with some great solutions?

Structured Problem Solving-Method 2: The 99% Solution[9]

It's creative and fun to come up with solutions when we take money, time, and skill out of the equation. But as practical entrepreneurs we know that there are real constraints in the marketplace. There's no point in bringing a product to market that will be affordable only to the handful of people in the world who are wealthy beyond measure.

We need to figure out a way to get most of the solution at a fraction of the cost. Nalebuff and Ayers call this 'the 99% solution.' Can you think of ways to get 99% of the benefits for only 1% of the cost? For example, if Oprah wants to create new programs for her TV network, she has the financial ability to hire well-known and expensive scriptwriters, producers, and actors. How can we get almost the same result at a fraction of the cost?

What if we try this: A young filmmaker has a great concept for a new film or TV show but lacks deep-pocketed financial backing. Could he achieve 99% of the benefits for only 1% (or so) of the cost if he filmed his talented-but-not-yet-famous actor friends in a bare-bones film set with a green screen, and created the video episodes for the web? What other ideas can you suggest?

Structured Problem-Solving Method 3: Where Else Could This Work?

Another way to generate great ideas is to start with a solution that is working in one context, analyze why it's working, and then see if it could work in a completely different context.

Here's an example of a solution to the problem of high energy bills:

In order to conserve electricity, many workplaces have installed motion-sensitive lights that turn off in five minutes if there's been no movement in the room.

What are the components that make this solution work?

- The need to conserve valuable and expensive resources (electricity).

- The benefits of using the resource (it allows us to see in the dark).

- An understanding of human nature (many of us simply forget to turn off lights).

Could this solution work in a different context, such as safe drinking water, medicines, or gasoline?

Structured Problem-Solving Method 4: Would Flipping It Work?

Sometimes changing the order of key words in a sentence can help generate great ideas and creative solutions to completely different problems. Rearranging and flipping some of the words can produce startling images that are full of potential.

Here is a solution to a chronic urban problem:

Public transportation reduces air pollution in cities.

What images do you see when the key words in the solution above are rearranged?

Air transportation in *cities* reduces *public* pollution.

What images do you see when we use the *antonym* of a key word in the sentence?

Public air *increases* cities in pollution transportation.

Try rearranging more key words, and let your imagination run wild.

Creative Problem Solving in the Music Industry

Take an entrepreneurial look at the music industry. In your opinion, what's working well? Where are the challenges? Where are the opportunities for growth and improvement? With an entrepreneurial mindset you'll be able to see opportunities where others see only problems.

Using the skills and techniques you've learned earlier in the chapter, start with the following industry problems and generate great ideas to solve them.

Problem 1

States James Diener, CEO-President of A&M/Octone Records, "Artist acquisitions are disappointingly unprofitable more often than profitable . . . At an early stage, we have to make instinctive decisions because there is typically insufficient market feedback to rely on . . . Therefore, the successful signings must produce such a windfall that they subsidize those that are unprofitable."[10]

Step 1 Restate the problem in 10 words (or fewer), and write it down.

Step 2 Imagine you have unlimited resources to solve it. Apply blue-sky thinking to come up with great ideas.

Step 3 Apply the 99% solution. How can you solve most of the problem with only a fraction of the resources?

Step 4 Are there solutions to this general type of problem in any other industry that could be translated to the music industry?

Step 5 Try rearranging the words in your Step 4 solutions to stimulate your imagination.

Step 6 Try to solve the problem by comparing it to something unusual. Pull apart and recombine the essential elements, and look for unexpected connections and new relationships.

Problem 2

Take a just-launched digital music product or service, something you've heard or read about in the past month. Using a how-could-this-be-even-more-amazing-and-make-everyone-money mindset, add on features and services that you feel people might want. Begin your dreaming with thoughts like:

The product or service sells and grows . . . everyone embraces it . . . famous musicians use it . . . fans can't get enough of it . . . they added these new features . . . they market the features in this cool way . . . it has partnered with this company/product to offer even more features . . . much fun is had . . . money is made by all.[11]

Problem 3

Third Rail (the band from Chapter 1) is a DIY (Do It Yourself) baby band. How can they get a bigger fan base? Go to NextBigSound.com, select one of the baby bands you find, and use it as a model for Third Rail. Discuss your ideas in class.

Problem 4

The retail products industry is worth $17 billion worldwide. However, its value fluctuates with the relative strength of the global economy. Read this book's Appendix: 'A visit to 2012 Winter NAMM, the World's Largest Music Products Tradeshow'. Visit namm.org/thenammshow/2012 to get a feel for the scope of the trade show. What can NAMM and the NAMM Foundation do on a regular basis to keep this industry sector vital and economically strong?

The Five Last Bastions For Thinking
by Joey Reiman

"Thinking no longer has a place in American culture. Daydreaming is frowned upon. Fast solutions are rewarded. And the workplace is the last place where you'll find real live thinkers. Ideas don't like offices—the cubicle should be spelled CUBEBIKILL because ideas die in those cells. Time to think outside those boxes!

Here are the last five places you can do that:

- The Car: Turn off the radio and turn on those wheels in your brain. As someone who is paid for his big ideas, I think of MPG as Millions Per Gallon! On the road we are both relaxed and alert. Our brains are geared for this neutral mode. Ideas start popping up everywhere. And stop signs are gifts to let you write down those thoughts.
- The Shower: It's enclosed and private, has a great sound, and is warm. It's a womb for ideas! That's why we have so many in the shower. I actually installed a shower in my office with the letters T–H–I–N–K etched in five tiles. Baths work too. After soaking in a tub all day Archimedes conceptualized "volumetric weight." Leaping out of the bath he screamed "eureka!"
- The John: Rodin's famous statue "The Thinker" assumed the position for good reason. Sitting on the john is a time of release in more ways than one or two. This can be a time for deep contemplation rather than just a waste.

- The Park: Nietzsche would take long walks in the park to generate his super thoughts. Unfortunately many of us have NDD—Nature Deficit Disorder. But nature has all the big ideas. Imagination was born here. Get outside your head and head outside.
- The Church: I was born Jewish but when I need a big idea I go to church. Nothing beats it for divine inspiration because their architecture is built on the idea of getting as close to the heavens as humanly possible. Hence the tall spires.

When Albert Einstein was interviewed at Princeton University, he was asked how he spent his day. The professor calculated that 20% of his time was spent teaching his students and 80% was invested in looking outside his window. Ponder that!"[12]

Crowdsourcing: Revolution in Problem Solving

The Importance of Amateurs

The concept of opening up a business problem to solutions generated by amateurs began with technology and the internet. The development of Linux, a free and open source software operating system, was one of the earliest ventures into the concept of allowing anyone to use, modify, and distribute an underlying source code.[13] Since the Linux 'kernel' was first released in 1991 by Linus Torvalds, the 'crowd' has helped propel the operating system into one of the most widely used in the planet. Today, Linux can be found in laptops, smartphones, TVs, piano keyboards, in-car navigation systems, digital video recorders, and e-readers.

From T-Shirts to Tour Funding, Fans Rule

The business world is eagerly embracing the benefits of weaving together the masses of humanity linked by the internet into a productive—and mostly unpaid—workforce. Online communities share their knowledge, give support, and participate in the development of products and services that they care about. From crowd-generated ad campaigns to online record labels that let the fans sign the artists, crowdsourcing has given well-deserved dignity to the concept of amateurism.[14]

In the music world, the idea of crowdsourcing and crowdfunding are excellent examples of collective problem solving. The websites Kickstarter, RocketHub, and ArtistShare help musicians, and others, find the funding for touring, instrument purchases, and recording projects. Threadless, a company begun by Jake Nickell and Jacob DeHart in 2000, has found success in using the crowd to design and vote on styles of T-shirts and other apparel. In all of these examples, one sees a community of collective problem solvers sharing knowledge for the pure pleasure of creating something from which they and others will benefit.[15]

Another Entrepreneur's Story: Kimberley Locke and I Am Entertainment

Kimberley Locke
Credit: Jonathan Leibson/FilmMagic/Getty Images

It was singing in church that got Kimberley Locke hooked on music. "I just loved to sing . . . I was a late bloomer in church. Once I discovered I had a gift then I loved it."[16] Growing up in Tennessee, a cradle of musical talent and history, Kimberley sang wherever she got the chance. At age 11 she and three childhood friends formed a quartet named Shadz of U, which performed at local churches.[17] Locke continued to sing through high school, becoming well known in the region for her vocal abilities, boundless energy, and optimistic view of life.

Surprising her family and friends, Locke did not pursue music in college. Instead, she chose to attend Belmont University for her degree in business management.

"I'm grateful for my musical gift, and I love to sing. But it's business that really turns me on," she says. "I like the dance that's involved in business—solving problems, negotiating, making decisions. I like being in control of my own career. I love making things happen."

Locke was thinking about going to law school when a friend suggested she audition for the 2003 season of American Idol. After finishing third behind Ruben Studdard and Clay Aiken, her life took a new direction. Suddenly she had a six-album deal with Curb Records, a modeling contract with Ford Models, and a two-year commitment with clothing retailer Lane Bryant.

Locke has enjoyed a very successful career as a recording artist since those early days, with eight Top 20 Adult Contemporary hits and four No. 1 dance hits across various Billboard charts. Her No. 1 club hit, a remake of the Freda Payne classic "Band of Gold," was included on Billboard's "Top 50 Dance Songs of the Decade" list in 2009.[18] Locke also has appeared in numerous television shows, including VH1's "Celebrity Fit Club" and ABC's "The View," and is a frequent host of Red Carpet events for "E!"

From her years in the music industry, Locke learned that "an artist's musicianship is only a nugget of what they can do," she explains. Artists forget—or are encouraged to ignore—the fact that they have a business side to their brain. Says Locke, "I want to encourage artists to exercise that part of who they are because you have to know business to make the art work."

She decided in 2011 that the time was right to launch a business based on an idea she'd been thinking about for more than a year. She put together a budget and a business plan and charged ahead on her venture full steam while trying to decide if she needed an investor. Locke explains: "In putting together a project that marries both the business and the creative, I've learned to strike while the iron is hot. You can't stop creating because you're waiting on financing."

Locke was hesitant to bring in an investor because of her experience with recording contracts. "When labels invest in your work, you have to give up your intellectual property and share your profits, which takes away from your profits," explains Locke. "That's just the way it is in business. But I wasn't sure I wanted to do that with my new venture."

When an investor did come forward with an offer, she realized that "I'd gotten things from Point A to Point G on my own," states Locke. So she did a cost/benefit analysis of giving up some of her ownership vs. the value the investor would bring. Ultimately, she decided to use her own money and remain in charge of her company.

Locke officially launched I Am Entertainment (IAE) in early 2011. The company provides consulting services to artists who need help creating and carrying out their big-picture career strategy. "I'm especially interested in working with young artists who, like me, were suddenly thrust into the spotlight, making more money than we'd ever dreamed," she explained. "No one is there to help you figure out how to control your spending so there's something left down the road. Everybody's taking from you, pulling you in a hundred different directions. Through IAE I'll help artists prioritize, get organized, stay focused, and learn to use the business side of their brain."

IAE is a consulting business, not a management or booking agency. In her IAE role, Locke will serve as a member of the artist's professional team of strategic thinkers.

Locke saw an unmet need in the marketplace that no one else was filling. She brings a unique value proposition to the company as both an artist and a businessperson, with years of experience in music and television. "The tag line for IAE is 'by artists, for artists,'" Locke states.

One of the first deals she did after launching IAE was to create "Making the Curve," which she will host and executive produce. "'Making the Curve' is a web-based reality show about putting together a plus-size pop singing group," states Locke. "The media portrays the ideal woman as thin, flawless, and young. But that's not reality. Most of us don't look like that, so we develop an inferiority complex about ourselves. 'Making the Curve' is a show about music, but it's more than that. It's about changing these women's lives and showing the world that plus-size women are beautiful and have valuable contributions to make in life."

In shaping the themes of her projects, Locke draws from her personal credo. "I believe that anybody can be helped if they are in a conscious state of mind and want to live life fully," states Locke. "Sometimes things happen in our lives that cause us to lose our spirit, our sense of direction. I work with people who need to get focused on re-starting their lives, whether their specific issue is a spouse, their home, or even some extra pounds they need to shed."

Locke's goal is to help people see what they need to do and give them the confidence and energy to make changes so they can reawaken the spark in their lives.

Locke is not one to step back when she's handed a challenge. It was a five-year journey for her to undo the eating habits she'd acquired living in the South. "I grew up eating everything fried, even the vegetables," she states. "I'd gained my extra pounds, just like everybody, but I was determined to be healthy."

Over those five years Locke slowly replaced each bad habit with one good habit. "It can seem overwhelming at first, so you have to break your big goal into manageable pieces, and work on them one at a time," Locke explains.

This attitude is prevalent in all of Locke's endeavors. She has a long list of projects that are in varying states of readiness. In addition to lifelong goals such as performing a one-woman show in Carnegie Hall like her idol Judy Garland, Locke has on the drawing board a series of cooking and fitness videos and a signature clothing line.

Locke is frank about how hard it is to achieve one's goals. "I'd be lying to you if I told you I wasn't scared of my next challenge," she says. "But fear only brings more fear. I live my life by the law of attractions: you attract to you what you put out into the world. I call it 'thought with a purpose.'"

Everything that Locke needed to launch IAE has come her way because of her strong faith and positive thinking. "It came together quickly because I was able to put the right team together," she explained. "I saw the opportunity and jumped on it. I don't just follow my dreams—I chase them!"

Locke possesses many of the entrepreneurial characteristics discussed in Chapter 1, and adds a new one: the power of "thought with a purpose." Do you agree with Locke's belief that "you attract to you what you put out into the world"? Have you experienced this personally? How can entrepreneurial thinkers learn to adopt this way of thinking?

Opportunities Ahead

The music industry has abundant opportunities for entrepreneurial thinkers. What area of the industry interests you the most? What are the problems you see in that sector? Use the skills and techniques you learned in this chapter to tackle one or two specific issues that you think may have the potential to grow into a business opportunity.

CONCLUSION

Learning to think like an entrepreneur can have an enormous impact on your life and the economic vitality of your community. Entrepreneurial thinking will be useful even if you don't use it to start a new venture. Every day we face problems large and small that need creative solutions. Having a growth mindset will help you be fluent and flexible in looking at the world in a new light.

The entrepreneurial thinking methods we've explored in this chapter will be helpful throughout the rest of the book, and in your future career. Think of the music industry as one big suggestion box, and contribute your fresh insight often.

 Talking Back: Class Discussions

Find a few online communities that are working on collective problem solving in an area that is meaningful to you. Reflect on what draws these people together. How are they rewarded for the work they do? How has their work helped solve the problems they set out to address? Is the business making money? If so, how is it shared?

CHAPTER 3

Brand You

CHAPTER OVERVIEW

In this chapter you will examine the historic evolution of today's music artists and how they are increasingly being referred to as brands, with significant market value beyond the tradition of pure musical creation and performance. Professor Ray Sylvester, a faculty member in music brand and marketing management at Buckinghamshire New University, U.K., provides a guest chapter on the changing nature and value of the music product and the development of the personal music brand of an artist. At the conclusion of the chapter, you will understand the complex web of communication that exists for an artist to successfully market her personal music brand.

KEY TERMS

- 'Clicks' over 'bricks'
- Direct distribution marketing
- Economies of scale
- Elements of an artist's personal music brand
- Multiple rights deal
- Post-war youth culture
- Supply chain
- The four core elements of an artistic product

An Entrepreneur's Story:
John Janick and Fueled By Ramen

John Janick understood the power of branding from an early age. Growing up in a small Florida town in the 1990s, it wasn't easy finding the punk and underground rock music he craved. He quickly learned that there were certain labels he could rely on to have the best bands. This being pre-internet, Janick ordered his music directly from the labels, and received CDs by mail. He learned first hand how strong brands help customers find what they need so they can buy with confidence.[1]

As a college student at the University of Florida in Gainesville, Janick saw an opportunity to help his friends find great music. Teaming up with Vinnie Fiorello, the drummer from the band Less Than

Jake, Janick tapped into his marketing savvy and entrepreneurial spirit to launch a record label featuring the music and artists he admired. They named the label Fueled By Ramen, in homage to the cheap noodle dinners that kept them going late into the night.

Janick moved the label to Tampa, Florida after he completed graduate school. Fueled By Ramen grew quickly using the marketing tools of the day—touring, mail order, internet, and street teams—to promote its brand. One of their early successes was Jimmy Eat World's EP which was released between their second and third albums, and had their first alt radio big single. By 2003 Fueled By Ramen had signed Fall Out Boy.

From the earliest days, Janick was laser-focused on creating a close-knit family of Fueled By Ramen staff, artists, and fans. He saw the benefits of taking an active role in all aspects of the artists' professional life.

Explains Janick: "When everybody works together with a single vision, it can be a powerful route to success for the band."

Fueled By Ramen pioneered the multiple-rights contract, or 360-deal, which provides comprehensive career support for the artist in exchange for revenue from all areas of the artist's career.

"In Fueled By Ramen's case, those rights were all collapsed from the start," says Janick. "They grew organically from the band's relationship with our staff. It just made sense for the artist, and the vibe and commitment of Fueled By Ramen. We became the artist's extended family."

"Everyone at Fueled By Ramen is involved with the artist from day one," states Janick. "We work hard to support their vision in a very hands-on way. It takes time for an artist to develop, and we make a long-term commitment."

Based on the artist's career goals, Janick and his staff look for and create branding opportunities that involve all areas of the artists' music, including recordings, touring, merch, and radio.

In another innovative move, Janick started a joint venture in 2005 with Pete Wentz of Fall Out Boy. Their Decaydance imprint signed Panic At The Disco, Cobra Starship, and Gym Class Heroes, selling millions of records along the way. Decaydance is now a separate independent label based in New York City.

Fueled By Ramen chose to distribute their records through ADA, the independent distribution arm of the Warner Music Group. Janick's extraordinary success caught the attention of Atlantic Records, one of Warner's best-known imprints. Janick and Atlantic began working together on band development projects for, among others, Panic at the Disco, Paramore, and The Academy Is . . .

"I maintained Fueled By Ramen's family culture, in partnership with Atlantic," says Janick. "The artists' manager and agent, Fueled By Ramen staff, and Atlantic all worked together in a unified way to support the artists' vision."

It was a good match all around. Under Janick's steady hand, Paramore has become a touring and record-selling powerhouse. And in 2007 Janick moved Fueled By Ramen to Manhattan to form a permanent partnership with Atlantic.

How does a cozy but hard-driving indie label keep its culture intact in the same physical space as their massive corporate parent?

"I wasn't interested in Fueled By Ramen serving as a farm team for major labels, developing artists from their earliest days only to lose them to a bigger company when they get to a certain point in their careers," explains Janick. "I wanted to maintain our company culture while having access to resources for artists when I decided it was time to pull the trigger on their next career move."

Janick's deal with Atlantic is the best of both worlds for him and his artists. It's not an upstream deal, where artists have to leave Fueled By Ramen when they attain certain sales benchmarks. Rather, an artist's Fueled By Ramen family expands to include Atlantic, which takes its lead from Janick in supporting each Fueled By Ramen artist.

"I meet at least weekly with my Atlantic colleagues to discuss and implement our key marketing and branding decisions for Fueled By Ramen artists," explains Janick. "For example, if I feel it's time to pull the trigger on a massive push in radio for one of our artists, we have Atlantic's powerful resources at our disposal to help us."

Best of all, Janick's artists do not leave the close-knit Fueled By Ramen family. "We are preserving our brand identity while serving the full range of our artists' career needs," states Janick.

The fact that this partnership seems to be working may have something to do with Atlantic's entrepreneurial roots. Founded in 1947 by Ahmet Ertegun and Herb Abramson, Atlantic was one of the most influential American independent labels until its sale in 1967 to Warner Brothers-Seven Arts. It is best known for its pioneering recordings of jazz, R&B, and rock 'n' roll, and its distinctive "Atlantic Sound." As an indie, Atlantic nurtured the careers of such greats as Ruth Brown, Big Joe Turner, Charles Mingus, John Coltrane, Ray Charles, Aretha Franklin, Robert Flack, and Professor Longhair.[2]

Janick says: "I look at the people I work with as entrepreneurs. If you treat them like this is *their* company, they'll act like it is. That's a major ingredient in the secret sauce of Fueled By Ramen."

Another benefit to having the deep resources of Atlantic at his disposal? States Janick, "The label can keep its artists as they grow—it's good for the artist and the brand."

Since Chapter 1, Sam and Third Rail have been debating the importance of branding in developing the band. They understand that everything about Third Rail—their songs, look, what they tweet and blog, their live shows and merch—have to be packaged with a single, articulate message to fans. They're still not sure how to create an identity that feels authentic. How can humans be products?

One of the best answers I've heard to that question was given by Ray Sylvester at the 2011 Music and Entertainment Industry Educators Association (MEIEA) annual summit. Prof. Sylvester is a faculty member in music brand and marketing management at Buckinghamshire New University, U.K. I've asked him to offer his insights and expertise by writing the chapter on artistic branding.

INDUSTRY ESSENTIALS: BRAND YOU

Guest Contributor: Ray Sylvester, Professor of Music Marketing, Buckinghamshire New University, U.K.

Popular Music and the Birth of the Music Artist

The conflict between art vs. commerce is put to the test by the question: Can a music artist be seen as a brand? We are all familiar with and impacted by the terms 'brand'

and 'branding': Think cars, sneakers, and computers and you will immediately associate them with specific brands. However, going back to the question above, can we integrate the notion of a brand and the branding process with a music artist? Can both a human being—the creative—and a commercial business exist as one entity?

History is full of evidence that music has always been at the heart of civilization. It was used to establish and create strong community culture, bringing people together within their distinct geographical environments.

The influence of popular music took on new significance in the first half of the 20th century, when technology allowed music to be broadcast and recorded, and transport enabled it to be distributed to new markets. The spread of music from local, to regional, to national, and eventually to global territories, resulted in an increased appreciation and consumption of music. Figure 3.1 demonstrates the reach of music as a result of new technology and distribution capabilities.

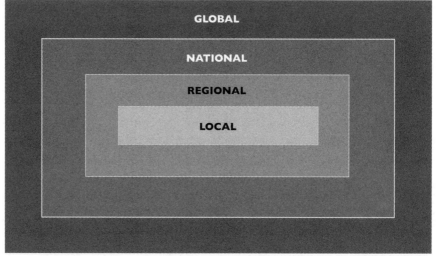

© Ray Sylvester (2011)

FIGURE 3.1 *Global, National, Regional, Local*

The post-World War II 1940s and 1950s saw an incredible boom in American production output to satisfy demand both at home and in the reconstruction of Europe and Asia. Large numbers of rural Americans migrated to cities in order meet the need for workforces. As a result, a unique convergence and subsequent integration of people and cultures occurred.

The arrival of television brought a new post-war youth culture, with an irrepressible demand to discover music of the new era. Freed from the socio-cultural traditions of the past, rock 'n' roll was at the vanguard of this revolution. A fusion of previously separate music cultures, this new genre created a pool of popular music stars, including Elvis Presley and Chuck Berry. The music artist or pop star was born.

The Artist and the Business of Selling Music

The music business was built on the ability of record labels to identify, fund, and promote commercially viable artists. The demand for artists was created and stimulated through media promotion, such as live events, radio, and TV. Record labels satisfied fans' appetite for recordings of performances through the distribution of a tangible format such as vinyl, tapes, and CDs. Therefore, individual music fans purchased and owned their favorite artist as a physical recording.

Figure 3.2 illustrates how recorded music formats have evolved from the pre-millennial to the millennial periods to create the recorded music business we know today.

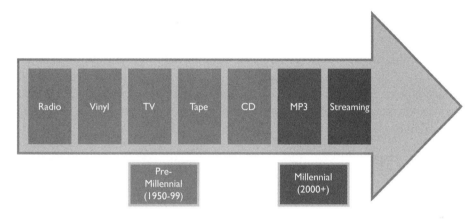

FIGURE 3.2 *An evolution of recorded music formats*

Figure 3.3 provides an illustration of the record labels' 'supply chain' mechanism that dominated the pre-millennial (1950–1999) phase of the popular music market. Here the artist depended on, and was controlled by, the constraints imposed by the system for physical recorded music format distribution.[3]

(Adapted from Graham et al. 2004)

FIGURE 3.3 *The traditional music 'supply chain'*

The search for viable artistic talent (artist and repertoire—A&R) became a priority of record labels seeking to produce and market the most profitable roster of artists. Any new artist to emerge would ultimately need to join the record company supply chain system. Throughout the pre-millennial period artists were completely dependent upon record labels to record, market, and distribute their music if they wanted to reach a global audience and sell millions of albums.

Understanding the Commercial Translation of the Artist as a Music Product

How can a living person be a product? Quite simply, *the person* is not a product. However, the person's *creativity* became a product in the form of a recorded music format. To this end there were several key characteristics that existed to enable the pre-millennial music business to maintain commercial control over artists, and thrive. These elements have been described as the 'core product'[4] elements of music, namely, the performer, the performance, and the music composition. Additionally the 'total marketable package'[5] represents the physical recorded music product format. Their characteristics are:

1. The performer—*the artist's actual persona and image.*

2. The performance—*the musical expression of the artist.*

3. The music composition and lyrics (song)—*the intellectual property (IP).*

4. The total marketable package—*the recorded music product format (vinyl, CD).*

Using the definitions above, the artist is, of course, the performer; she is the traditional recognized source of the musical performance. The artist derives value and an income directly through her live and recorded music performance.

However, the significant proportion of income comes from the copyright ownership of the song and in the manufacture of the recorded music product. The owners of the song receive royalties, paid out on the performance and the sales of physical recorded music product.

Historically, the song has been owned or partially owned by the record label because it was the source of revenue generation for a recording. Unfortunately, many artists unwittingly gave to the labels the intellectual property rights to their songs. In addition, physical recorded music products had manufacturing economies of scale (i.e., the more copies of a CD that were made, the lower the cost per CD) that gave significant profit margins. Therefore, the 'productizing' of artists enabled record labels to own the majority stake in and control of the income generation. Figure 3.4 demonstrates how the key elements of the traditional music product produced different levels of income.

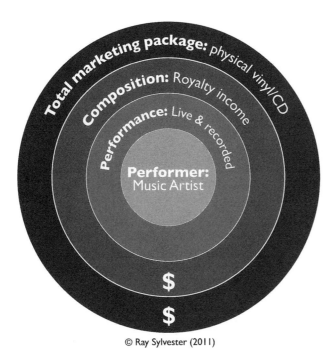

© Ray Sylvester (2011)

FIGURE 3.4 *The traditional distribution of income derived from music sales*

The Changing Value of the Music Artist and the Nature of the Music Product

Since the turn of the century, record labels have had their dominant position challenged by the digitalization of recorded music.[6] Figure 3.5 demonstrates how digital technology has significantly impacted the distribution of the traditional physical product that was the standard in the pre-millennial phase of the popular music business.

(Adapted from Graham et al. 2004)

FIGURE 3.5 *The 'direct distribution' music supply chain of the millennium*

Today, the music production control and distribution barriers once in place for the music artist are gone. The artist can now operate independently of a record label, creating and distributing directly to the music consumer, who in turn possesses much more choice and purchasing power. However, the preference for digital product (clicks) over physical product (bricks) has meant that the recorded music business has been significantly hit by a reduction of control and income from traditional physical sales-related royalties.

The way that music artists create and subsequently exchange value and receive commercial returns in the marketplace is changing. Record labels, now commonly known as entertainment companies, have been forced to identify new income channels. The 360-degree deal is an attempt by the entertainment (record) companies to partner and profit from every part of the artist's business practice. Labels are trying to move from their traditional business of control of singular royalty rights to the management and control of multiple rights.

These multiple rights deals seek to obtain a significant interest and income from the artist's concerts, merchandising, licensing to TV, films, games and direct sales from artist websites. A multiple rights deal certainly can work for an artist with an established reputation; the deal can provide immediate returns for a record label to offset the lucrative artist advance. It is clear that future income must go beyond the traditional recording of music artists, as the 'physical product' recordings have lost value in real terms. Music fans can now acquire music more cheaply through digital music product and streaming sites such as iTunes and Pandora.

The Artist's Brand Evolution

There have always been people who gained fame or notoriety for a particular performance talent or reputation. In the music industry, musical talent was identified and harnessed by record labels to manufacture and market recorded music products to an adoring global fan base.

Table 3.1 provides an overview of some of the best-selling music artists of all time.

TABLE 3.1 *Music artists and musical performance talent*

ARTIST/BAND	MUSIC PERFORMANCE TALENT	SALES
Elvis Presley (1954–1977)	Singer (King of Rock 'n' Roll)	Circa I billion
The Beatles (1954–1977)	Singing—Songwriting (The Fab Four)	Circa I billion
Michael Jackson (1971–2009)	Singer, Dancer (King of Pop)	Circa 750m
Madonna (1979–present)	Singer (Queen of Pop)	Circa 300m

© Ray Sylvester (2011)

These artists found fame and fortune because of their music *performance* talents. Collectively, they have sold billions of records. Therefore, despite their fame—and consistent with Figure 3.4—the artists' primary income source was linked to their physical recorded music sales.

Today, the artist receives an increasing amount of attention beyond his or her explicit performance talent. The explosion and significance of social media has spawned a global 24/7 surveillance culture interested in not only the music of an artist, but also in his private life and associated lifestyles. This new-media fan base is hungry to obtain artists' products and services beyond their traditional live and recorded music performance. The change is paradoxical; while the sales and value of the recorded music product and related royalty rights have gone down, the selling and value of the music artist and their total performance has gone up.

Understanding the Artist as a Brand

Tom Peters stated "You're branded, branded, branded, branded"[7] in 1997 when he coined the term 'personal brand.' He encouraged all individuals to manage themselves like companies and market their identity as a brand. While this has and could be arguably challenged, it has spawned a multi-million dollar industry. Just do a web search for personal branding and you will find an abundance of resources including, books, magazines, courses, and personal brand gurus ready to help you on your personal brand journey.

What value does personal branding have to the new music business environment? We know that many artists have become rich and famous due to their particular music performance talent—achieved through their participation in the pre-millennial record label-controlled supply chain identified in Figure 3.3. However, since the millennium, many artists on record label rosters have been dropped, due to declining profits from the falling price of recorded music.

So how do DIY artists get started today? They need to balance their *creative* music nature with a *commercial* brand nature. Chris Anderson's book *The Long Tail*[8] identified how the digital age has made it possible to find profitable niche commercial markets in a world once dominated by larger corporate hit makers. This demonstrates the possibility of artists developing themselves as individual music entrepreneurs who can now manage and market their own Personal Music Brand to a global marketplace.

Figure 3.6 describes the elements of an artist's Personal Music Brand.

The personal music brand is made up of three inseparable elements:

1. The 'Private self' relates to an individual's mental, emotional, and personal lifestyle.

2. The 'Professional self' relates to an individual's occupational competencies.

3. The 'Physical self' relates to an individual's body shape, gender, and ethnicity.

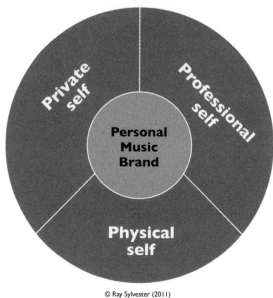

FIGURE 3.6 *The Personal Music Brand*

In today's social media age, an artist and her personal music brand cannot hide from an increasingly inquisitive public. This is in stark contrast to the pre-millennial period, when record labels hid anything about an artist that was not seen as advantageous to recorded music product sales. In the complex socio-cultural times of the past, some labels even hid the ethnicity of African American artists to ensure maximum record sales.

A personal music brand has to represent the authentic nature of the artist; if the public identifies any misrepresentation, it can significantly impact the commercial viability of the artist. A personal music brand is a strategic combination of cultural messages that provide meaning and connection to an audience. The messages successfully and consistently represent the expectations people have when engaging with the artist. Reputation is one of the most important elements in building and developing a personal music brand, as it represents the relationship and current market value of a music artist.

Due to the change in the traditional distribution of income, the evolution of the personal music brand is now the pivotal core to an artist's success in the increasingly consumer-driven marketplace. Therefore the traditional income from the singular focus of recorded music sales has been replaced by a focus upon a multiple income profile that is generated by the '*personal music brand*', the '*publics*' and the subsequent '*portfolio*' of related products. This can be simply known as the 3Ps of a music artist brand.

The 3Ps of a Music Artist Brand

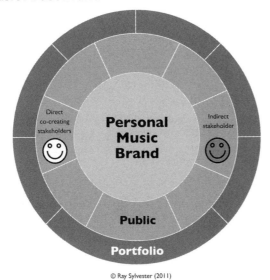

© Ray Sylvester (2011)

FIGURE 3.7 *The 3 Ps of a music artist brand*

The 3Ps of the music artist brand can be broken down as follows (Figure 3.7 and Table 3.2):

1. The Personal Music Brand: *the private, physical and professional self.*

2. The Publics:

   • *Direct co-creating stakeholders: fans, manager/agent/attorney, social media, corporate partners/sponsors, etc.*
   • *Indirect stakeholders: parents, socio-cultural trends, government policy, etc.*

3. The Portfolio: *the commercial brand representations of the artist; music brand (live and recorded), extended brand (i.e. fashion) and partnered (i.e. endorsements).*

The Music Brand Community

A brand community[9] is a group of consumers who purchase the same product. Therefore, a music brand community can be seen as a collection of like-minded music fans who share a common desire to consume a particular music brand. The music brand community is built upon principles that powerfully connect and engage fans to an artist brand. Music brand community members can be said to be:

• Committed: *They will be loyal fans.*

• Culturally savvy: *They know and understand the cultural music brand.*

• Co-creators: *They are regular communicators with and contributors to the music brand.*

TABLE 3.2 *Case example: Beyoncé Knowles' brand*

	PRIVATE SELF	PHYSICAL SELF	PROFESSIONAL SELF
Personal Music Band	Born Houston, Texas, USA Child prodigy Suffered & overcame depression Married to Jay Z Philanthropist	30 years old Female African American Curvaceous (Bootylicious) Young, sexy, and street savvy Fashion style	Since 1997: Singer Songwriter Dancer Actress Choreographer Fashion designer Model
Publics	Direct: Urban R & B, Pop, Hip-Hop Gospel music fans, fan blogs, records, film companies & fans, fashion & fragrance customers, gamers	Indirect: Health, beauty & fashion, media, film goers, African American media (Ebony, Essence, BET)	
Portfolio	Music brands: 3 Destiny's Child albums (*No, No, No, The Writing's on the Wall, Survivor*) 4 Solo albums (*Dangerously in Love, B'Day, I am Sasha Fierce, 4*) Numerous Duets: Lady Gaga, Shakira, Jay Z 16 Grammy awards	Brand extensions: 10 TV & Films (*Carmen, Goldmember, The Fighting Temptations, The Pink Panther, Dreamgirls, Cadillac Records, Obessed, A Star is Born* Fashion (House of Dereon) Fragrance (Heat, Heat Rush, Pulse)	Brand Partnerships: Pepsi L'Oréal Tommy Hilfiger Nintendo DS Vizio

© Ray Sylvester (2011)

As seen in Figure 3.8, Everett Rogers popularized an understanding of product adoption by establishing five different consumer group categories in his book *Diffusion of Innovations*.[10] In the book *Purple Cow*,[11] Seth Godin considers this process of product adoption and suggests that companies should only focus their resources and attention on the two most committed and loyal consumer groups. As a result, it could be suggested that music entrepreneurs should focus their branding and promotion of artists upon their most impassioned fans, namely, the innovators and the early minority. According to Rogers, these fans approximately represent 2.5% and 13.5% respectively. Consequently Pareto's '80:20 rule' could be applied to a music brand community—*Up to 20% of music fans provide up to 80% of financial returns*. This demonstrates the critical distinction between a music brand community strategy and that of the traditional physical music product market.

The Music Artist Brand Communication Model

Artists and music entrepreneurs have to understand the complex web of communication that exists for an artist to successfully market his personal music brand. Figure 3.9 identifies the key aspects of communication between an artist and his music brand community.

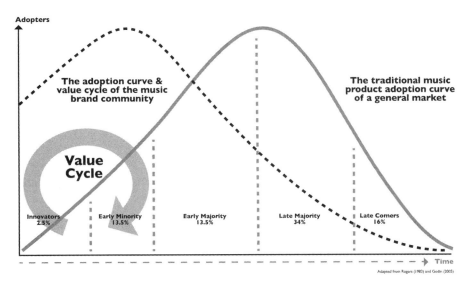

Adopters

The adoption curve &
value cycle of the music
brand community

The traditional music
product adoption curve
of a general market

**Value
Cycle**

| Innovators 2.5% | Early Minority 13.5% | Early Majority 13.5% | Late Majority 34% | Late Comers 16% |

Time

Adapted from Rogers (1983) and Godin (2005)

FIGURE 3.8 *The music brand and music product adoption processes*

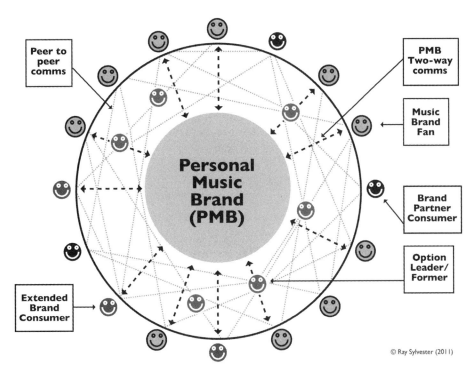

Peer to
peer
comms

PMB
Two-way
comms

Music
Brand
Fan

**Personal
Music
Brand
(PMB)**

Brand
Partner
Consumer

Option
Leader/
Former

Extended
Brand
Consumer

© Ray Sylvester (2011)

FIGURE 3.9 *Personal Music Brand communication model*

If we use the example of Beyoncé shown in Table 3.2 we can identify the following elements:

- Two-way communication with music brand community.

- Brand community opinion *leaders* and paid opinion *formers* support brand.

- Music brand fans will specifically purchase music products.

- Extended brand consumers will purchase products such as fashion and fragrances.

- Brand partner consumers consume products because of endorsement, that is, Pepsi.

Beyoncé
Credit: Kevin Mazur/WireImage/Getty Images

CONCLUSION

The personal music brand of artists—who are, after all, mere mortals—is essentially organic and subject to continual change. The personal music brand is subject to challenges, such as social-cultural change and competitive rivalry. Therefore, artists and music entrepreneurs must maintain vigilance and stay dedicated to being culturally relevant and engaged with their respective music brand community. Failure to do so could prove very costly.

Figure 3.10 provides a summary of the changes that have taken place from the pre-millennial birth of the modern popular recorded music market to the millennial music brand community that has emerged to dominate today.

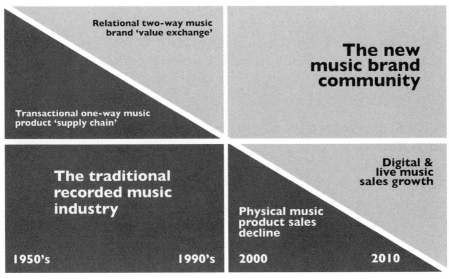

Product led music markets   © Ray Sylvester (2011)

FIGURE 3.10 *Community-partnered music markets*

Final Note: This chapter is a conceptual journey into the fast moving nature of modern music branding and therefore is equally subject to challenge and change.

Opportunities Ahead

Choose two artists—one whom you feel has a strong brand and the other who has not. Evaluate the elements of the artist's strong brand identity according to what you learned in this chapter. What can you apply to the artist who has a weak brand identity? What specific suggestions do you have to strengthen the artist's brand?

 Talking Back: Class Discussions

Make a branding checklist for Third Rail, as you did for the band above. Working with your colleagues, craft a detailed plan that will help Sam, Cody, Jared, and Walter build a strong Third Rail brand.

PART 2

Contacts and Contracts

CHAPTER 4

Copyright Law and the Music Industry

CHAPTER OVERVIEW

This chapter focuses on the development of U.S. copyright law. It introduces the two copyrights in music, copyright duration, registration of copyright, major revisions to copyright law, and a few exceptions to the exclusive rights of copyright holders.

The chapter includes stories of entrepreneurs and artists who feel that the laws enacted decades ago to *create* incentives for innovation actually may be *obstructing* artistic freedom and economic growth in the digital age. Please add your voice to this debate.

KEY TERMS

- Copyright infringement
- Creative Commons license
- Digital Audio Home Recording Act of 1992
- Digital Millenium Copyright Act of 1998
- Exclusive rights of copyright owners
- Fair Use
- Fairness in Music Licensing Act of 1998
- First Sale Doctrine
- Intellectual property
- No Electronic Theft, or "NET" Act of 1997
- Phonogram
- PIPA and SOPA
- Public domain
- Registration of copyright
- Sampling
- Sonny Bono Copyright Term Extension Act
- Work for hire

An Entrepreneur's Story: Patrick Sullivan and RightsFlow

Patrick Sullivan, a young New York entrepreneur, had deep professional experience in the field of rights management before founding his company, RightsFlow. After receiving a master's degree in Music Business from NYU, Sullivan worked for three of the largest companies in the rights management sector: the Harry Fox Agency, the NMPA, and The Orchard. From his daily responsibilities helping clients find and license music for their projects, he understood firsthand how challenging the process of procuring a mechanical license could be.

Sullivan identified an opportunity to move into this established market, even with such strong competition as his former employers. In a March 2011 interview with Billboard's Ed Christman, Sullivan explained: "For music users, licensing can be a painful issue. So our business was built from their point of view, to help the user manage that responsibility and not from the licensor point of view. RightsFlow handles publishing royalty accounting on behalf of music licensees, instead of rights holders."[1] He wanted to make copyright and publishing easy for everyone.[2]

When Sullivan and co-founder Ben Cockerham launched RightsFlow in 2007, they essentially flipped the existing rights management business model. RightsFlow upended the status quo by putting the copyright *user* at its core, rather than the rights owner.

What exactly does RightsFlow do? It is a licensing and royalty service provider for artists, record labels, distributors, and online music companies. It houses more than 30 million songs from 10,000 labels. Basically, RightsFlow has already done the heavy lifting for music users by obtaining permission from the copyright holders to issue mechanical licenses on their behalf. This gives the user the right to manufacture, distribute, and sell their recorded product legally. The user may select from a variety of licenses, such as physical CDs, ringtones, streaming, and permanent digital downloads. RightsFlow enables its more than 12,000 clients to obtain licenses from publishers and songwriters all over the world—including major, independent, and artist-controlled works. [3]

RightsFlow also powers Limelight (SongClearance.com), its online mechanical licensing utility. Limelight's goal is to provide the simplest way to clear any cover song for individual musicians, bands, choirs, and small- to mid-size labels.[4] When licensing from SongClearance.com, a user has only three things to do:

- Enter Song Information
- Pay $15 and Royalty Fees
- Get Mechanical License.

In December 2011, YouTube's parent company, Google, acquired RightsFlow. The technology developed by RightsFlow will help YouTube quickly identify and control the amount of unlicensed music uploaded to the site. In addition, RightsFlow will compute the royalties owed to copyright holders and smooth the payment process.[5]

In just four years, Sullivan achieved his goal of making copyright and licensing easy to understand and accessible to thousands of musicians. And with its new YouTube partnership, Sullivan and RightsFlow are in a position help hundreds of thousands more people use music legally.

As Patrick Sullivan has shown with RightsFlow, it is possible to simplify the process of getting permission to use a work that is under copyright protection. In the pages ahead, you will see how copyright law began, and how it has become more complex over the intervening years. As you begin to master the basics of music copyright, you, too, may see entrepreneurial opportunities to help people use music easily and legally.

INDUSTRY ESSENTIALS: DEVELOPMENT OF U.S. COPYRIGHT LAW

Introduction: Intellectual Property—Creations of the Mind

Most books about the music industry begin with a chapter on copyright for a good reason: almost every aspect of the music industry is underpinned by copyright law. To understand how the music industry functions you need a foundation in the basics of copyright law.

For those of us who are not attorneys, or planning to become attorneys, mastering the intricacies of copyright law is an imperfect and sometimes daunting process. In order to help music business students make sense of this dense and complex field, I have found that looking at copyright in the broader context of intellectual property rights and global trade agreements is a good place to begin.

The term 'intellectual property' is used to describe a variety of rights for works that originate as creations of the mind. Copyrights, trademarks, patents, industry designs, and sometimes trade secrets are common types of intellectual property rights. In most countries, these works will be protected by a set of exclusive rights if certain, specific conditions are met.

Intellectual property laws were created to provide financial encouragement for creative thinkers and inventors to bring new ideas and products to the commercial and artistic marketplaces. The World Intellectual Property Organization (WIPO) website describes it as follows:

"Intellectual property shall include rights relating to:

- literary, artistic and scientific works
- performances of performing artists, phonograms,* and broadcasts
- inventions in all fields of human endeavor
- scientific discoveries
- industrial designs
- trademarks, service marks and commercial names and designations

---

* Phonogram means sounds fixed in some form (disc, tape, vinyl, etc.) that are exclusively aural. It does not include, for example, the sound tracks of films of Broadway shows.

- protection against unfair competition
- and all other rights resulting from intellectual activity in the industrial, scientific, literary or artistic fields."[6]

What Is Copyright?

Copyright is one of two categories of intellectual property law; the other being industrial property. The purpose of copyright and related rights is twofold:

- To encourage innovation and creativity in society by providing a way for creators to lead a dignified economic existence

- To give the public widespread, affordable access to works such as music, art, choreography, films, scientific discoveries, inventions, poems, plays, reference works, architecture, advertisements, maps, and computer drawings.[7]

The Exclusive Rights of Copyright Owners

The following general overview of copyright is adapted from information found on the U.S. Copyright Office website.[8]

What Is Copyright?

Copyright literally means the right to copy. It is a form of protection grounded in the U.S. Constitution and granted by law for original works of authorship fixed in a tangible medium of expression. Copyright covers both published and unpublished works.

What Does Copyright Protect?

Copyright protects original works of authorship including literary, dramatic, musical, and artistic works, such as poetry, novels, movies, songs, computer software, and architecture. Copyright does not protect facts, ideas, systems, or methods of operation, although it may protect the way these things are expressed. 'Copyright' has come to mean that body of exclusive rights granted by law to authors for protection of their work. The owner of copyright has the exclusive right to reproduce, distribute, and, in the case of certain works, publicly perform or display the work; to prepare derivative works; in the case of sound recordings,† to perform the work publicly by means of a digital audio transmission; or to license others to engage in the same acts under specific terms and conditions.

When Is My Work Protected?

Your work is under copyright protection the moment it is created and fixed in a tangible form that is perceptible either directly or with the aid of a machine or device.[9]

---

† Sound recordings are "works that result from the fixation of a series of musical, spoken, or other sounds, but not including the sounds accompanying a motion picture or other audiovisual work" (U.S. Copyright Office).

Copyright issues related to the music industry receive a lot of press. We read about well-known artists, producers, and songwriters involved in high-stakes copyright lawsuits, such as the one involving producers of the Broadway musical *Spiderman: Turn Off The Dark*, whose music was written by Bono and The Edge. You or someone you know may have received a letter from YouTube asking you to remove copyright-protected music from a video you've posted without a license. Once popular sites like Lime Wire and Pirate Bay were shut down because they were used for illegal file-sharing activities.

In our daily lives we see the wide reach of copyright law. For example, the symbol © ('C' in a circle) plus an author's name is commonly found in books, along with a warning such as: "All rights are reserved. No part of this book may be reproduced in any form or by any electronic or mechanical means including information storage and retrieval systems without permission in writing from the publisher, except by a reviewer, who may quote brief passages in a review."[10]

A similar warning from the FBI appears at the beginning of videos that you own or rent for home viewing. The warning very clearly states the penalties (fine, imprisonment, or both) that could befall a viewer who is cited for copyright infringement.

Throughout this chapter we'll explore the economic and cultural implications of a system of laws put into place hundreds of years ago that, ultimately, will determine if you may include a sampled drumbeat on your next hip-hop recording. We'll look at existing laws and customs, primarily in the U.S. but also in other parts of the world. We'll also examine some important legal cases that have helped shape today's music industry.

You will be asked to think about the fundamental values of cultures and societies in relation to the economic impact of intellectual property and global trade. And we'll examine a question that many people are asking today: Is it possible that laws designed more than three centuries ago to *create* economic incentives for innovation by protecting creators' rights are today *obstructing* innovation and economic growth?[11]

We will unpack these issues in the pages ahead.

Historical Background

We will soon be deep in the thicket of licensing and rights ownership in the current music industry, which is based on copyright law, customs, and common practices. Things can get very complicated very quickly. So, as we're mastering the basics of this body of knowledge, we'll pause occasionally to look back at the origins of copyright law and remember its historic context and the intentions of those early lawmakers.

The United States was still a British colony when King George III established the new idea of authors' ownership of copyright. This innovative concept ultimately became the basis of American intellectual property law.

The Statute of Anne granted a fixed 14-year term of ownership, renewable for another 14-year term. It also established that, after a copyright-protected work was purchased, the original owner no longer had any control over how it would be used. The concept of the public domain, where works no longer under copyright protection were available for anyone to use without charge or fear of copyright infringement, was established in the Statute of Anne.

In drafting the U.S. Constitution (1787, Article I, Section 8, Clause 8), the First Congress gave Congress the power "to promote the progress of science and useful arts, by securing for limited times to authors and inventors the exclusive right to their respective writings and discoveries."

This single sentence gives us a very clear idea of the founding fathers' intentions regarding the value of intellectual property both to the creators (exclusive rights) and to society in general (to promote progress).

A few years later, the "U.S. Copyright Act of 1790, An Act for the Encouragement of Learning, by Securing the Copies of Maps, Charts, and Books to the Authors and Proprietors of Such Copies," was adopted. It was modeled on the 1710 British Statute of Anne. The U.S. Act of 1790 granted American authors the right to print, reprint, or publish their work for a period of 14 years and to renew for another 14. The law was intended to provide an incentive to authors, artists, and scientists to create original works. It gave creators an economic monopoly on their works for a period of time. The founders felt this would stimulate creativity and, ultimately, contribute to the advancement of "science and the useful arts" through wide public access to works in the "public domain."[12]

The first copyright laws of the U.S. protected books, maps, and charts from unauthorized printing and vending. Over time, and continuing through today, there have been additions to and reforms of the copyright law. Many of these reforms are discussed later in the chapter. Various forms of creative expression were added to the list of protected works, including prints (added in 1802), music (1831), dramatic compositions (1856), photographs and photographic negatives (1865), and works of art (1870). Unauthorized public performance of music was added in January 1897. Motion pictures were added as a protected work in 1912. Recording and performing rights were extended to non-dramatic literary works in 1953 (this includes fiction, non-fiction, poetry, textbooks, reference works, directories, catalogs, advertising copy, compilations of information, and computer programs).[13] Sound recordings were granted limited copyright protection if fixed and first published on or after February 15, 1972. Protection was granted to architectural works in December 1990.[14]

U.S. Copyright Office

The U.S. Copyright Office is the best place to begin to acquire a basic understanding of copyright law. Located in Washington, D.C., its mission is to promote creativity by administering and sustaining an effective national copyright system. It is headed by the Register of Copyrights, Maria Pallante (serving as Interim Register in 2012). While the purpose of the copyright system has always been to promote creativity in society, the functions of the Copyright Office have grown over time to include:

U.S. Copyright Office, Washington, D.C.
Credit: Danita Delimont/Gallo Images/Getty Images

- Administering the copyright law

- Creating and maintaining a public record through registration of claims and recordation of documents, including those related to compulsory licenses

- Providing technical assistance to the Congress and to executive branch agencies

- Providing information services to the public

- Supporting the Library of Congress by obtaining and making available deposits for the Library's collections

- Serving as a resource to the domestic and international copyright communities.

Copyright activities, including deposit and registration, weren't centralized in the Library of Congress until 1870. Indexing of the record of registrations also began at that time. By 1891, a record of all the works that had been registered was published in book form and entitled Catalog of Copyright Entries. The Copyright Office became a separate department of the Library of Congress in 1897. Copyright law was codified into positive law as Title 17 of the U.S. Code.[15]

Songwriters and the Copyright Office

There are many compelling reasons for a professional songwriter to register her music promptly and accurately with the Copyright Office. Here are answers to frequently asked questions, excerpted from the Copyright Office website.

Do I have to register with the Copyright Office to be protected?
No. In general, registration is voluntary. Copyright exists from the moment the work is created. You will have to register, however, if you wish to bring a lawsuit for infringement of a U.S. work.

Why should I register my work if copyright protection is automatic?
Registration is recommended for a number of reasons. Many choose to register their works because they wish to have the facts of their copyright on the public record and have a certificate of registration. Registered works may be eligible for statutory damages and attorney's fees in successful litigation. Finally, if registration occurs within five years of publication, it is considered *prima facie* evidence in a court of law. See Circular 1, *Copyright Basics*, section "Copyright Registration" and Circular 38b, *Highlights of Copyright Amendments Contained in the Uruguay Round Agreements Act (URAA)*, on non-U.S. works.

I've heard about a 'poor man's copyright.' What is it?
The practice of sending a copy of your own work to yourself is sometimes called a 'poor man's copyright.' There is no provision in the copyright law regarding any such type of protection, and it is not a substitute for registration.[16]

It's now possible for writers to register works online through the electronic Copyright Office (eCO). To register a work, writers will submit a completed application form, a non-refundable filing fee ($35 for online registration or $50 for registrations using Form CO), and a non-returnable copy or copies of the work to be registered.

 Watch video: A helpful tutorial on submitting works to the eCO.

When a writer registers her claim to a copyright in a work with the U.S. Copyright Office, she is making a public record. All the information provided on the copyright registration is available to the public via the internet. There is no legal requirement that the author be identified by her real name on the application form. Writers may file under a fictitious name by checking the "Pseudonymous" box when giving information about the authors.[17]

Here is a list of forms available for registering specific types of works:

TX   literary works
PA   performing arts works, including motion pictures
SR   sound recording
SE   single serials.

Whose Music Is It, Anyway?

It may surprise you to learn that many songwriters do not own the copyright to their compositions. Here are some of the reasons:

- Songwriters as employees—Copyright law states that an employer owns the copyright to the music written by his employees. These compositions are known as 'works for hire.'

- Commissioned works—If a songwriter is asked to write a work for a person or an organization, the rights will be owned by the person or entity that engaged the songwriter to compose the work.

- Assignment of copyright—Copyrights can be sold, given away, divided up, and bequeathed. For example, Cody owns 25% of each Third Rail song. Cody can decide to give his sister half of his copyright to a song as a birthday gift. For that particular song only, there would be five owners: Sam at 25%, Walter at 25%, Jared at 25%, Cody at 12.5%, and Cody's sister at 12.5%.

- Multiple writers—Every Third Rail song has four co-writers, and each owns 25% of the copyright to their songs.

Major Revisions to U.S. Copyright Law

There have been four major revisions to the U.S. Copyright Act of 1790. The list below highlights some of the key components of each revision that are pertinent to our discussions in this chapter:

- First revision, 1831:

  - Music is added to the list of creative works protected against unauthorized printing and sales.

  - First term of copyright is extended from 14 years to 28 years, with option for one 14-year renewal term if specific conditions were met.[18]

- Second revision, 1870:

  - Authors are granted the right to create certain derivative works including translations and dramatizations.[19]

- Third revision, 1909:

  - From this date forward, the term of protection for works begins on date of publication.

  - The *renewal* term of copyright protection is extended from 14 to 28 years, if specific conditions are met. This brings total possible copyright protection to a first term of 28 years plus one renewal term of 28 years, for a total of 56 years. (Reminder: the total possible copyright protection term in the first Copyright Act was 28 years.)[20]

- Fourth revision, 1976:

    ◦ The term of protection for works created on or after the effective date of this revision (January 1, 1978) is set at life of the author plus 50 years after the author's death, with no options for renewal.[21]

- September 1962:

    ◦ The first of nine special acts extending the terms of renewal copyrights is introduced, pending congressional action on general copyright law revision.[22]

- June 1992:

    ◦ Renewal registration becomes optional for works that are created before Jan. 1, 1978.

    ◦ Automatic renewal is granted to works copyrighted between January 1, 1964 and December 31, 1977.[23]

- October 1998:

    ◦ The Sonny Bono Copyright Term Extension Act adds 20 years to the term of copyright protection for most works. Copyright duration now stands at life of the author plus 70 years. For an anonymous work, a pseudonymous work, or a work made for hire, copyright endures for a term of 95 years from the year of its first publication or a term of 120 years from the year of its creation, whichever expires first.

    ◦ This Sonny Bono Copyright Term Extension Act includes the Fairness in Music Licensing Act of 1998, which excludes certain types, configuration, and sizes of establishments from the requirement to obtain a performance license when music is played.[24]

For works first published prior to 1978, the term will vary depending on several factors. To determine the length of copyright protection for a particular work, consult chapter 3 of the Copyright Act (title 17 of the *United States Code*).[25]

The First Sale Doctrine provides that someone who has legally purchased a particular recording may rent, lease, or lend it without the consent of the copyright rights holder.[26]

In 1984, Congress passed legislation that became known as the Record Rental Amendment. This is an exception to the First Sale Doctrine, and grants the owner of copyright in a sound recording the right to authorize or prohibit the rental, lease, or lending of phonorecords for direct or indirect commercial purposes.[27] In other words, in giving rights owners of sound recordings control over commercial rental of their works, the legislation diminished the rights of the person who has purchased the sound recording. The sound recording purchaser still has the right to *resell* the recording; he no longer has the right to *rent* or lend the recording. The law excludes libraries and other non-profit organizations from the restriction.

The legislation was prompted by concerns that commercial lending could encourage unauthorized copying and displace sales, thereby diminishing the incentive for creation of new sound recordings. The 1993 North American Free Trade Agreement Implementation Act (NAFTA), among other things, made permanent the prohibition of sound recordings rental.[28]

The Digital Audio Home Recording Act (DART) of 1992 is an example of Congress' efforts to mitigate the economic impact of illegal copying of rights-protected works by levying a tariff on manufacturers and importers of digital audio recording devices and media who distribute products in the United States. The money collected from these tariffs is deposited into two royalty funds (Sound Recordings Fund and Musical Works Fund) and are paid to copyright owners who file a claim and meet certain conditions. DART also clarified the legality of home taping of analog and digital sound recordings for private non-commercial use.[29]

While a student at the Massachusetts Institute of Technology (MIT) in 1994, David LaMacchia had operated internet commercial bulletin boards for the free uploading and downloading of various commercial software products. In the resulting lawsuit, *United States v. LaMacchia*, the copyright owners of the software products claimed financial losses in the millions of dollars due to the illegal trading. Mr. LaMacchia was indicted for wire fraud, since the law at that time required that a commercial motive be apparent to prosecute willful copyright infringers. Ultimately, the case was dismissed, with the court ruling that copyright infringement cannot be prosecuted under the wire fraud statute.[30]

The No Electronic Theft, or "NET" Act of 1997 was a response to the growing awareness of the financial damage that illegal downloading was causing to the intellectual property community. The NET Act closed the legal loophole illustrated in *United States v. LaMacchia* by making two main changes. First, it clarified that the 'private financial gain' element of criminal infringement "includes barter—that is, situations where the illegal copies are traded for items of value such as other copyrighted works, not only where they are sold for money."[31] Second, it redefined criminal infringement to include "willful infringement by reproduction or distribution, including by electronic means, that lacks a commercial motive but has a substantial commercial effect."[32] The NET Act made uploading and downloading of digital files on the internet punishable for maximum penalties of five years in prison and up to $250,000 in fines in some circumstances.

The Digital Millenium Copyright Act of 1998 (DMCA) provided for the implementation of two WIPO treaties: WIPO Copyright Treaty (WCT), applicable to authors, and the WIPO Performances and Phonograms Treaty (WPPT), applicable to performers and producers of phonograms. The DMCA also limited certain online infringement liability for internet service providers (ISPs), providing what is known as a 'safe harbor' for online service providers, including ISPs. This means that online service providers are protected from copyright infringement if they promptly remove, or block access to, allegedly infringing material on their sites when informed by a copyright holder that such material is available on their site.[33]

Resource: Find a copy of the Act on the U.S. Copyright Office website.

Keeping Track of 'Copyright Creep,' or the Ever-Lengthening Term of Copyright Protection

The average lifespan was 73.5 years for an American male or female of any race who was born in 1978.[34] Using the statistical averages provided, compute the following:

- In what year is it likely that a work could enter the public domain if it was written and published in 1998 by an American who was born in 1978?
- What is the total number of years that work will receive copyright protection?
- How does that compare with the total number of years of copyright protection that was granted in the original Act of 1790?

 Let's hear your opinion

- What is the effect on public domain works when copyright duration is lengthened?
- What are the economic benefits of increasing the length of copyright protection?
- Are these two competing ideas—protection and open access—in balance today?

Understanding the Two Copyrights in Music

When it comes to music, there's a copyright for the song itself (the music and lyrics, also called the underlying composition) and a separate copyright for the recording of a particular performance of the song. This concept can easily become confusing. It can be helpful to use the U.S. Copyright Office symbols and registration form designations in referring to one or the other of the music copyrights.

- For the song itself (underlying composition):
    - PA—This is the name of the Copyright Office *form* used to register performing arts works, including motion pictures. A songwriter will complete and submit Form PA, with payment and a copy of the song, to the Copyright Office in order to register her work.
    - © (the letter C in a circle), or the word 'copyright'—This is the symbol used by the Copyright Office as the type of *notice* for 'visually perceptible copies' of a work (the underlying composition).[‡] A songwriter will use ©, or the word 'copyright' on a printed copy of her song.

‡ Musical, dramatic, and literary works often are fixed in a sound recording, rather than fixed in a 'visually perceptible copy.' For example, audio recordings are considered 'phonorecords' and not 'copies.' In this case, the ℗ (P in a circle symbol) is the only form of notice that is needed. The © (C in a circle notice) is not used on sound recordings to indicate protection of the underlying composition. (copyright.gov)

- For the sound recording of the song:
  - SR—This is the name of the Copyright Office *form* used to register sound recordings. A record label will complete and submit Form SR, with payment and a copy of the song, to the Copyright Office in order to register the recording of a song.
  - ℗ (the letter P in a circle)—This is the symbol used by the Copyright Office as the form of *notice* for phonorecords embodying a sound recording. You will see this symbol on CDs (e.g., ℗ 2012 Radbill Records Inc.)

If a songwriter owns the copyright to both the underlying composition and the recording, she has the artistic and economic freedom to decide who can or cannot license her songs. (There are a few exceptions.) She has this exclusive right for the period of time her work is under copyright protection, so long as she doesn't assign, sell, or give the copyright to somebody else.

The two copyrights in music create some pretty interesting and complex relationships between songwriters, publishers, record labels, and music users, as this story demonstrates.

Fun with the Two Copyrights

A songwriter named Amanda has her own publishing company. One of her songs is recorded by Keith Urban and becomes a hit. Amanda owns the copyright to the underlying composition (the song itself) but Mr. Urban's record label owns the rights to the recording of the song.

If Procter and Gamble (P&G) wants to use Mr. Urban's recording of Amanda's song in a Tide commercial, P&G will need to get Amanda's permission *and* the permission of Mr. Urban's label. Without both copyright owners' agreement, the deal is off. If P&G wants to use the song but have it recorded by a different band for the Tide commercial, P&G needs only Amanda's permission. Amanda owns the rights to the underlying composition, but not to the recording of her song.

Here's another way to look at it: If Third Rail recorded a song they had not written ('covered' a song), the band members would own the copyright to the recording but not to the underlying composition. Third Rail needs a license to record the cover song, and will pay the rights holder of the underlying composition for the right to reproduce and distribute his work in Third Rail's recording.

Here are more examples of situations where there are two separate copyrights for what might appear to be the same work.

Ownership of a CD and the right to use it publicly are two separate issues. When you purchase a CD, you are in effect given a license only for private use of the CD in your home. The license does not carry with it the right to perform the CD outside the home, unless the site where the CD is performed is properly licensed for performance.

The same is true for films. Neither the rental nor the purchase of a movie carries with it the right to show the movie publicly outside the home, unless the site where the movie is used is properly licensed for public exhibition.[35] The legal compliance requirement does not change if admission is free, if the facility or organization is commercial or non-profit, or if there is a governmental agency involved. However, there is an educational exemption that allows a film or CD to be performed in certain types of teaching.[36]

Why is this the case? Because the copyright holder retains exclusive public performance rights to the recording or the film.

Fair Use: An Exception to an Exclusive Right

'Fair use' is an exception to and a limitation of the copyright owner's exclusive right to reproduce her work, or permit others to do so. Examples of fair use include using small portions of a work in commentary, teaching, news reporting, and research.

Fair use is called a 'gray area' of the law, meaning that there is no bright line in the law that says '*this* is fair use, but *that* is copyright infringement.' Over the years a doctrine of fair use has been developed from court decisions, but new technology and artistic usage of work continues to make this a very tricky area for musicians to navigate.

DJ Girl Talk
Credit: Jon Attenborough/WireImage/Getty Images

Gregg Gillis, the DJ artist known as Girl Talk, believes the work he creates based on samples of other artists' recordings falls under the copyright doctrine of fair use. However, based on a strict interpretation of the law, his use of unlicensed samples may be considered to be copyright infringement.

Mr. Gillis is an artist who is testing the legal boundary between fair use and copyright infringement. He contends that his sampled material actually increases awareness of and interest in the artists he samples. Furthermore, he claims that if he were to get permission to sample the works and pay for the licenses to do so, he would have to charge "$1,000 for a copy of the album, or maybe $10,000."[37]

Mr. Gillis explains: "'I like making the music because I grew up with hip-hop and I like hearing samples. But I also feel that it's not creating competition for the artists . . . If anything, it's the opposite. I'm always hearing from kids on Facebook who are like: 'I've gotten so into the Electric Light Orchestra after I heard that sample you used.'"[38]

Contrary to popular belief, in music there is no specific number of notes that may be copied from a previously existing work or reproduced without the copyright owner's permission. A songwriter runs the risk of being accused of copyright infringement if she accidentally or intentionally uses part of a protected work without permission, even if she acknowledges its source. Here's the best advice: get a license from the copyright owner before you use his material. If you can't get permission, don't use it.

What Is a Sample? HarryFox.com explains . . .

"A sample is typically the use of an excerpt of a sound recording embodying a copyrighted composition inserted in another sound recording. This process is often referred to as digital sampling and requires licenses for the use of the portion of the composition and the sound recording that was reused in the new sound recording. In some instances, artists re-record the portion of the composition used in the new recording and, therefore, only need to obtain a license for the use of the sampled composition."[39]

Flipping the Focus: In Support of the Public Domain

The public domain is commonly used to mean any work of intellectual property that is not protected by copyright or patent, and therefore is open to the public for general use and appropriation.

Let's return to a question posed earlier in this chapter: "Is it possible that laws designed more than three centuries ago to *create* economic incentives for innovation by protecting creators' rights are today *obstructing* innovation and economic growth?"[40] Some people feel that the economic benefits to rights owners from stricter and longer copyright protection is overshadowing the benefits to society in general of works in the public domain.

Duke Law School's Center for the Study of the Public Domain promotes research and scholarship on the contributions of the public domain to speech, culture, science, and innovation. It is focusing attention on the realm of *unprotected* intellectual property in order to spark debate about the balance needed in our intellectual property system.[41]

Scott Maxwell/LuMaxArt/Shutterstock Images

Creative Commons—A 'Some Rights Reserved' Approach to Copyright

Creative Commons is a non-profit organization that is working to balance current copyright laws and creative work on the internet.

CreativeCommons.org provides a set of copyright licenses and other tools that give individual creators and corporations a simple, standardized way to keep their copyright while allowing certain uses of their work—a 'some rights reserved' approach to copyright. Creative Commons has collected a vast pool of content—a digital commons—that can be copied, distributed, edited, remixed, and built upon, all within the boundaries of international copyright law.[42]

Lisa Green, chief of staff for Creative Commons, stresses that the importance of Creative Commons is as an add-on to copyright and not a replacement for it. "It relies on the teeth of copyright," she explains. "In fact, it's the existence of copyright law that makes Creative Commons enforceable."[43]

Joi Ito, the chair of Creative Commons, makes the point that as products become more complex, more people need to share intellectual property. "The sharing happens first within companies and then between companies. As the net makes more connections possible, it's possible to innovate . . . by sharing the intellectual property more widely."[44]

PIPA and SOPA: Power to the People

On January 18, 2012, Wikipedia staged a 24-hour blackout to protest proposed legislation under consideration in the U.S. House and Senate that websites such as Google, Facebook, and others felt would make it difficult if not impossible for them to operate. The two bills, the Protect Intellectual Property Act (PIPA) and the Stop Online Piracy Act (SOPA), were supported by the recording and motion picture

Stan Honda/AFP/Getty Images

industries, which have been battered financially by illegal file sharing. If passed, PIPA and SOPA would have required Google, Wikipedia, Amazon, and other internet service providers to block access to foreign websites that infringe on copyrights. The 24-hour blackout was successful in tabling PIPA and SOPA, at least for now.[45]

Opportunities Ahead

Sit back and recharge your right brain. It can be challenging to find opportunities for entrepreneurial thinking in the music copyright sector. For inspiration, watch some of the videos on "Creativity & Culture, Science & Innovation," from Duke University's Center for the Study of the Public Domain (law.duke.edu/cspd/video/). You'll find talks by professors at law schools including Duke, Harvard, UCLA, Kansas, American, Cardozo, MIT, Baltimore, Michigan, and Columbia, and from organizations including Creative Commons, Knowledge Ecology International, and Research on Innovation.

CONCLUSION

The term 'intellectual property' is used to describe a variety of rights for works that originate as creations of the mind. Copyrights, trademarks, patents, industry designs, and sometimes trade secrets are common types of intellectual property rights. In most countries, these works will be protected by a set of exclusive rights if certain, specific conditions are met.

It is important to have a strong foundation in the basics of copyright law in order to study and work in the music industry. Copyright and neighboring rights (discussed in the next chapter) protect the rights of authors, performers, producers, and broadcasters, and contribute to the cultural and economic development of nations.

The U.S. music industry has developed in specific ways based on decades of copyright law interpretation and litigation. As entrepreneurial thinkers, it's our job to look for opportunities even in such a heavily regulated area as copyright law.

 Talking Back: Class Discussions

Explore these resources for research and discussion about copyright:

- "Copyright and Fair Use," Stanford University Libraries. Contains copyright case opinion summaries, copyright news, legislation, and a lively blog.
- "Music Copyright Infringement Resource," sponsored by UCLA and Columbia Law Schools. A website packed with information about music copyright infringement cases from the mid-nineteenth century forward.

Web Links

- Copyright Office
  Copyright.gov/eco/eco-tutorial.pdf
- Copyright Office
  Copyright.gov/legislation/dmca.pdf
- Copyright and Fair Use
  Fairuse.stanford.edu/
- Music Copyright Infringement Resource
  Cip.law.ucla.edu/Pages/default.aspx

CHAPTER 5

International Copyright and Trade Agreements

CHAPTER OVERVIEW

This chapter provides an overview of copyright law within the context of intellectual property as it has developed around the world. It explores international copyright and trade agreements and their impact on U.S. copyright law. The challenge faced by lawmakers to keep copyright laws current with the rapid technological changes of recent years is examined. Copyright reform in the U.K. is an illustration of an of-the-moment example of entrepreneurial thinking and problem solving on a huge scale.

KEY TERMS

- Berne Convention
- Digital Millennium Copyright Act (DMCA) of 1998
- Neighboring rights
- Professor Ian Hargreaves
- Rome Convention
- Termination rights
- TRIPS agreement
- Uruguay Round
- WIPO
- WIPO Copyright Treaty (WCT)
- WIPO Performances and Phonograms Treaty (WPPT)
- World Trade Organization

INDUSTRY ESSENTIALS: INTERNATIONAL CONVENTIONS AND INTELLECTUAL PROPERTY PROTECTION

Introduction

Intellectual property (IP) law is made up of two areas: 'industrial' property, which deals with inventions and patents, and 'copyright,' which focuses on literary and artistic creations.[1] IP law is applied differently in these two areas.

Copyright law protects the *expression* of an artistic idea, not the idea itself. For example, the words and music in a blues song (the *expression* of an idea) are protected, but the song's 12-bar, I–IV–V chord structure is not protected. That's because the universally recognized structure of a traditional blues song is considered a building block—an *idea*—for all blues songs. Copyright law protects the owner against unauthorized use of the expression of her artistic work; it does not protect the idea.

By contrast, industrial property law protects the *idea* itself. There is a lengthy and vigorous review of an inventor's design before a patent is issued, granting the inventor exclusive rights to his design for 20 years in the U.S. When the term of protection ends, the idea becomes part of the public domain, free for everyone to use.

Songwriters: If you want to register your new song with the U.S. Copyright Office, all you have to do is submit the appropriate form, a copy of the work, and payment. The Copyright Office does not review the song to see if it is actually an expression of an *original* idea. The test for that occurs in the courts, but only if someone feels your song infringes on his copyright-protected work.

What Is "Property" and Why Are There Laws to Protect It?

Tangible Property

You own a bike. The bike is visible, tangible, and moveable. The bike is yours to use as you please forever, so long as you do not break any existing laws, such as using it to smash store windows or running over small children. You alone can decide to give the bike away or loan it to your friends. You could even disassemble the bike and use its parts to create completely new products, such as a Ferris wheel for squirrels.

You have the exclusive right to do as you please with your bike because of the laws in place in your country that recognize and protect the legal ownership of property. How would you react if someone used your bike without your permission? What legal recourse do you have if your bike is stolen?

Intellectual Property

Let's say you've had your heart broken and your mind is full of melancholy thoughts. You decide to express yourself by writing a blues song.

If your song meets a few specific criteria, you just may have successfully created a piece of *intellectual* property that is protected by copyright law. The criteria are:

- The music and lyrics are your original creation

- The song is of sufficient length and substance to be considered a 'work'

- The song is fixed in a tangible form that is perceptible either directly or with the aid of a machine or device.[2]

The song is a product of your intellect, your mind. In the U.S., you will have a bundle of exclusive rights that allow you to profit from using your song for a specific period of time. Those rights—called copyright law—will protect your intellectual property so that you alone may reap the value of your work. At least for a while.

Tangible property (a bike) differs from intellectual property (a song) in obvious and important ways. Today, most countries have laws that protect their citizen's intellectual *and* tangible property. But for centuries the concept of legal protection of intellectual property was the subject of vigorous global debate. Did intellectual property (IP) belong to the creator, or to the public? It was not until the Age of Enlightenment (mid-17th century through the 18th century) that laws concerning intellectual property were introduced in England, France, and the U.S.[3]

Most nations want to encourage the intellectual creativity of its citizens in order to advance the country's social, cultural, and economic goals. A way to do this is to give the creator exclusive rights that allow her to reap the economic benefits of her creation.

But countries must balance this economic exclusivity with their desire to allow all of society to have free and legal access to the works to use as the foundation for future creations. So they limit the amount of time that the individual creator may control how his work may be used. After the period of exclusive copyright protection ends, the creator's work falls into the public domain, where it is available for all to use without permission and without charge.

Copyright laws give creators exclusive rights to their work—but only for a while.

Duration of Protection

You can see that IP laws attempt to balance the economic rights of individuals and society. As you might expect, there's a big difference between the time periods of exclusive use for *ideas* (industrial property) compared to the *expression* of ideas (intellectual property).

Copyright duration in the U.S. lasts much longer than the 20 years given to an industrial property patent. As stated in Chapter 4, for works written after January 1, 1978, a songwriter, playwright, sculptor, or painter (and other artistic creators) will have exclusive economic rights to his or her work for their lifetime plus 70 years. For a musical work that is commissioned by a person or organization, and for a work that is created by an employee of a company—called 'work for hire'—the duration of copyright is 120 years from the date it was created, or 95 years from publication, whichever expires first.

The 1976 U.S. Copyright Law granted a 35-year 'Termination Rights' opportunity for songwriters, recording artists, and other artists, allowing them to regain control of their work after 35 years (a two-year advance application is required). The Termination Rights provision applies to most songs created after 1977. When the term of copyright protection ends, the expression of the songwriter's artistic idea falls into the public domain.

> What's the difference? Creation means the date the work was completed. Publication means the date it was first offered for sale to the public.

Historical Background

Countries have exchanged ideas, goods, and services for centuries. A closer look at the development of international trade legislation allows us to pull back the curtain and see how the issues of the day varied from country to country and decade to decade.

By the early 19th century, many countries had copyright and neighboring rights laws in place to protect the intellectual property of its citizens when in their home country. But it wasn't until the 1870s that discussions concerning international protection of intellectual property began in earnest. The catalyst for this movement was the 1873 International Exhibition of Inventions in Vienna. Exhibitors outside of Austria refused to attend for fear that their inventions and ideas would be stolen and exploited by other countries.[4]

Paris Convention

In order to ensure that its creators and rights owners were protected in other countries as well as their native land, the Paris Convention for the Protection of Industrial Property (inventions, trademarks, and industrial designs) convened in 1883, and entered into force in 1884 after being signed by 14 countries.[5]

> Resource: Read the full text of the Paris Convention.

Intellectual property is a valuable export—and thus revenue producer—for many countries, particularly the 'developed nations.' While the discussion of and action upon international agreements regarding intellectual property protection across borders is an ongoing dialogue, the actual creation of laws and their enforcement is a highly political process. As in any negotiation, the outcome is influenced by the relative strength of those at the bargaining table.

International treaty conventions often go on for many years. The word 'convention' in the context of international negotiations has a different meaning from what we think of today as a gathering over several days of people who accomplish most of their goals on site and return home. As you might expect, meetings involving international agreement on any topic requires discussion, patience, sensitivity to vast cultural, economic, and legal differences, lobbying, and perseverance.

As you will see reading forward, many of the intellectual property international conventions remained in the discussion-and-lobbying mode for years. After a convention ultimately emerges with a document that reflects a consensus on terms and is signed by the participants, the completed document must be ratified by each participant's home country. If some of the convention document's terms conflict with a country's own laws, that country's lawmakers will have to modify its laws in order to become a party to it. The convention agreement goes into force only after it has been ratified by a specific percentage (often 50% or more) of the nations whose representatives signed it. Given the complexity of and differences in global cultures and legal systems, and the length of time it takes countries to ratify treaties after a convention, it often takes years for these agreements to enter into force.

International copyright agreements greatly simplify the conditions under which its member countries offer protection to foreign works. However, there does not exist an 'international copyright' that offers identical protection to rights owners throughout the world. The national laws of each country still prevail in cases involving unauthorized use.[6]

Berne and Universal Copyright Conventions

Shortly after the Paris Convention for the Protection of Industrial Property was put into force in 1884, the issue of international copyright protection was addressed at the Berne (Switzerland) Convention for the Protection of Literary and Artistic Works in 1886. The aim of the Berne Convention was to help its member nations obtain international protection of their right to control, and receive payment for, the use of their creative works such as:

- novels, short stories, poems, plays

- songs, operas, musicals, sonatas

- drawings, paintings, sculptures, architectural works.[7]

The Berne Convention is based on the concept that countries should give the same amount of copyright protection to foreign citizens' works as the countries give their own citizens' works. For example, if a French copyright owner sues for an infringement occurring in another country that is also a member of the Berne Convention, the foreign country's copyright law will be applied.[8] This is important because it recognizes the rights of sovereign nations to create their own laws while acknowledging the importance of global protection of intellectual properly.[9]

Not every country wishing to participate in some form of multilateral copyright protection agreed with all aspects of the Berne Convention. In the 1950s, the Soviet Union and many developing nations believed that the terms of the agreement favored the copyright-exporting nations. So, under the auspices of the United Nations Educational, Scientific, and Cultural Organization (UNESCO), these countries adopted an alternative to the Berne Convention: the Universal Copyright Convention.

The Universal Copyright Convention for the Protection of Producers of Phonograms Against Unauthorized Duplication of Their Phonograms, or UCC as it is known, was adopted in Geneva at September 1952 and entered into force in September 1955. (Note the similarity in its title to the 1971 Geneva Phonograms Convention, which is discussed later in this chapter.) The UCC includes language that discourages Berne Convention members from leaving Berne and joining the UCC instead. The UCC has lost significance over the years as more and more countries become—or hope to become—members of the World Trade Organization, which requires adherence to the Agreement on Trade-Related Aspects of Intellectual Property Rights (TRIPS).[10] TRIPS will be discussed in greater detail later in this chapter.

> Resource: Read the full text of the Universal Copyright Convention.

The Berne Convention has been revised many times since it was completed in Paris in 1896. It now has more than 150 member countries, and is administered by the World Intellectual Property Organization (WIPO). As an interesting side note, and to show how long it can take for countries to ratify an international agreement, the U.S. did not become a party to the Berne Convention until 1989.

> Resource: Read the full text of the Berne Convention.

Buenos Aires Convention

The Buenos Aires Convention is a copyright treaty signed at Buenos Aires in April 1910 by the U.S. and countries in Central and South America. Since all of the signatories to the Buenos Aires Convention have adopted the Berne Convention, the Buenos Aires Convention has little current significance.

I mention Buenos Aires only in passing because it introduced the phrase 'all rights reserved' next to the copyright notice as a commonly accepted method of identifying the full spectrum of the copyright owners' legal rights. The phrase is still seen today, although it carries no legal significance. However, it has come to be associated with Creative Commons, a global non-profit organization that advocates for a more nuanced approach to copyright restrictions in the digital age. Creative Commons uses the phrase "*some* rights reserved" as a pointer to its Creative Commons license, which gives rights owners options regarding how they allow others to use their work.

> Resource: Visit the Creative Commons website. Creative Commons will be discussed later in this chapter.

Rome Convention

You'll recall that we've discussed the two copyrights in music: one for the underlying composition and the other for the sound recording. It was the Rome Convention for the Protection of Performers, Producers of Phonograms and Broadcasting Organizations, adopted in 1961, which first provided international recognition of copyright protection for record producers, separate and distinct from the rights of the composer and performer.

The technology to produce music cassette tapes and small tape recorders was developed in the late 1950s, and by the mid-1960s pre-recorded music cassettes were popular in Europe and the U.S.[11] Treaty countries to the Rome Convention are protected against unauthorized copying of their recordings, and have a right to payment for broadcast of their recordings, subject to certain exceptions.[12]

Resource: Read the full text of the Rome Convention.

Geneva Phonograms Convention

The widespread use of music cassettes and tape players through the end of the 1960s made it much easier for consumers to copy vinyl records without paying for a license. An additional treaty was adopted in 1971 to deal with the growing problem of illegal duplication of recorded music. The Geneva Phonograms Convention for the Protection of Producers of Phonograms Against Unauthorized Duplication of their Phonograms obliges the signatory countries to protect each other's phonogram producers against "the making, distribution, and importation of unlicensed copies of his phonogram."[13]

Resource: Seventy-two countries are parties to this treaty. Read the full text.

Moving into the Digital Era

The struggle to keep copyright laws current with technology is not a new challenge. In the late 15th century a game-changing invention called the printing press gave unprecedented access to information at rapid speed and (relatively) low cost. Prior to this, documents were copied by hand, a lengthy and laborious task that made the cost of books out of reach for most people. At the time, neither a book nor its author had copyright protection.

The idea of their subjects being able to put ideas into printed form and share them with anyone who could read was alarming to many monarchs of the time. The British government restricted printing to a group of approved publishers who also had the right to censor what was printed. This situation remained in place until 1710, when the Statute of Anne was enacted in Britain.

Copyright law is the bedrock of the music industry in the U.S., the U.K., Europe, and many other countries. Strong legal systems are in place to enforce these laws, with unpleasant consequences for those who run afoul of them. At the same time, technological innovations such as music file compression, digital media and devices, and the internet—as well as changes in consumer behavior concerning the discovery and consumption of music—contribute to uncertainty about and even flagrant violation of the traditional boundaries of the law. But as we can clearly see from the hardships that have befallen the global recording industry, tough enforcement alone doesn't solve the copyright infringement dilemma in our digital age.

Given the differences in the culture of lawmaking compared to the culture of technological innovation, it is not surprising that international laws lag behind the technologies that give us the ability to communicate and exchange ideas rapidly around the globe.

Stevie Wonder at WIPO
Credit: Fabrice Coffrini/AFP/Getty Images

World Intellectual Property Organization

The World Intellectual Property Organization (WIPO) was established in 1967 by the WIPO Convention. It was charged with promoting the protection of IP throughout the world in cooperation among states and in collaboration with other international organizations. In 1974, WIPO became a specialized agency of the United Nations. Currently, WIPO serves 184 member states and administers 24 treaties. It is based in Geneva, Switzerland.[14]

In the early 1990s, WIPO initiated an international dialogue resulting in two treaties, both special agreements under the Berne Convention, which brought copyright protection into the digital age: the WIPO Copyright Treaty (WCT) for authors, and the WIPO Performances and Phonograms Treaty (WPPT) for performers and phonogram producers. The WCT and WPPT were adopted by the international community in 1996, and implemented in the U.S. in the Digital Millennium Copyright Act (DMCA) of 1998.

The WCT and WPPT update previous treaties by granting rights regarding distribution activities and computer programs; protecting against unauthorized internet use; and protecting technological measures used on copyright material and rights-management information against hacking, removal or alteration.[15] As another example of the length of time it can take to put an international agreement into force, the WIPO Treaties were signed by more than 60 countries at the Diplomatic Conference in Geneva in December 1996. Thirty ratifications were necessary to bring each Treaty into force, a goal that was finally achieved in 2002.[16]

Resource: Read the full text of WCT and WPPT.

The discussion in this chapter of international treaties involving intellectual property rights is very brief. WIPO is an excellent source of full texts, summaries, and lists of countries that ratified the international intellectual property treaties and agreements. For students who wish to explore the topic in depth, I recommend the general WIPO website (wipo.int/portal/index.html.en) and these two sources in particular:

- "Summaries of Conventions, Treaties and Agreements Administered by WIPO": www.wipo.int/freepublications/en/intproperty/.../wipo_pub_442.pdf

- An illustrated and very user-friendly timeline of major world events and WIPO treaties from 1883 to 2002: wipo.int/treaties/en/general/.

The U.S. does not have reciprocal copyright relationships with every country.

Resource: For a list of countries and the nature of their copyright relations with the United States, see Circular 38a, *International Copyright Relations of the United States*, from the U.S. Copyright Office.

Delegates attending a WTO ministerial conference
Credit: Fabrice Coffrini/AFP/Getty Images

The World Trade Organization and the TRIPS Agreement

The extent of protection and enforcement regarding intellectual property rights varies widely around the world. As communication, transportation, and technological advances bring the world into closer and easier contact, the differences in rights protections become a source of tension in international economic relations. New internationally adopted trade rules for intellectual property rights are seen as a way to introduce more order and predictability, and allow disputes to be settled more systematically.[17]

Beginning in the 1980s, the U.S. began incorporating copyright protections into multinational trade-based agreements. The linking of intellectual property protection and international trade appears to acknowledge that the failure to adequately protect intellectual property internationally can be seen as an unfair trade practice.[18]

Intellectual property trading issues are an important part of the work of the World Trade Organization (WTO). Established in January 1995, the WTO's basic mission is to help its member governments sort out the trade problems they face with each other.[19] The World Trade Organization agreements, negotiated and signed by the bulk of the world's trading nations, provide the legal ground rules for international commerce. These agreements bind governments to trade policies that affect how producers of goods and services, exporters, and importers conduct their business on a daily basis.[20]

The WTO's Agreement on Trade-Related Aspects of Intellectual Property Rights

(TRIPS), negotiated near the end of the 1986–1994 Uruguay Round of the General Agreement on Tariffs and Trade (GATT), introduced intellectual property rules into the global trading system for the first time. The TRIPS Agreement is an attempt to narrow the gaps in the way rights are protected around the world, and to bring them under common international rules.[21]

The TRIPS agreement requires all members to comply with the key provisions of the Berne Convention. TRIPS mirrors the Rome Convention protections against unauthorized copying of sound recordings, and provides a specific right to authorize or prohibit commercial rental of these works. It also provides a detailed set of requirements relating to the enforcement of rights that require remedies and procedures to effectively deter illegal use of protected works.[22]

TRIPS is a minimum standards agreement, meaning that members may provide more extensive protection of intellectual property if they wish.[23] In yet another demonstration of how complex it can be to negotiate international trade treaties, the TRIPS agreement came into effect in three phases: in 1995 for developed countries; in January 2000 for developing countries; and in January 2005 for least-developed countries.

Resource: Read an overview of the TRIPS Agreement.

Since coming into force, TRIPS has received a good deal of criticism from developing countries, non-governmental organizations, and academics, particularly in the area of public health.[24] While at first glance this may seem to have little to do with the music industry, the controversy surrounding TRIPS sheds light on a consistent dilemma in the area of protection of intellectual property: Is it possible that the laws intended to encourage creativity and innovation by giving rights holders a temporary monopoly on commercial exploitation of their work actually restrict the use of knowledge? How do the differences in the fundamental values of cultures and societies impact this discussion?

Some highly respected individuals, among them Joseph E. Stiglitz, former chief economist of the World Bank and a recipient of the Nobel Memorial Prize in Economic Sciences, speak bluntly about what they see as gross inequities caused by TRIPS. Here is an excerpt from an article entitled "Trade Agreements and Health in Developing Countries," published by Professor Stiglitz in *The Lancet*, January 31, 2009: "The fundamental problem with the intellectual property (patent) system is simple: it is based on restricting the use of knowledge. There is no extra cost associated with an additional person gaining the benefits of knowledge. Restricting knowledge is thus inefficient, but the patent system also grants (temporary) monopoly power, which gives rise to enormous economic inefficiencies."[25]

yui/Shutterstock Images

Copyright Reform in the U.K.

On August 3, 2011 headlines around the world read: "U.K. Announces Massive Copyright Reform: Scraps Website Blocking, Allows CD Copying, Music Parodies."[26]

Acknowledging the crucial importance of intellectual property as an economic driver and catalyst for growth, the British prime minister, David Cameron, announced that the U.K. government had accepted all of the recommendations contained in the May 2011 report, "Digital Opportunity: A review of intellectual property and growth" by Professor Ian Hargreaves. Cameron had commissioned the report and selected Hargreaves, an Oxford-trained digital communications scholar and professor at Cardiff University, Wales, to chair the committee.

During its five months of deliberation, Professor Hargreaves and his committee sought and received comments from a wide swath of the U.K. population. Upon accepting the recommendations of Hargreaves' report, Cameron and his government declared their intention to reform and open up their intellectual property systems "to allow innovative businesses to develop new products and services."[27] Hargreaves' report "proposes a clear change in the strategic direction of IP policy . . . this change is modest in ambition and wholly achievable."[28]

Here is an of-the-moment example of entrepreneurial thinking and problem solving on a huge scale. It underscores the concept that copyright law affects all parts of a society in today's digital world. However, it remains to be seen whether or not all of the accepted recommendations in Professor Hargreaves' report actually will be put into place, given the reality of politics and pressures from the various parties involved.

Resource: Read the entire report, "Digital Opportunity: A review of intellectual property and growth."

Opportunities Ahead

A substantial portion of the revenue generated in the U.S. comes from exporting intellectual property. IP-intensive industries accounted for approximately 60% of total U.S. exports rising from $665 billion in 2000 to $910 billion in 2007.[29] Let's apply what you've learned in this chapter to some situations that are common to music entrepreneurs.

Scenario 1: I am a U.S. record label owner who has created a compilation CD of reggae music played by regional bands. Through Bandit A&R I have discovered a company in Sweden who is interested in licensing some songs from reggae bands. I contact the Swedish company and they're interested in hearing the songs on my CD. I put the music on SoundCloud, and the company decides it wants to license two of the songs. What are some of the copyright issues that must be addressed to license these songs in Sweden?

Scenario 2: I have just developed a new set of headphones that lets people tap their headphones together and automatically have access to each other's personal playlists. A company in Germany wants to license this technology. What are the intellectual property issues that must be addressed?[30]

CONCLUSION

Intellectual property (IP) law is made up of two areas: 'industrial' property, which deals with inventions and patents, and 'copyright,' which focuses on literary and artistic creations. Most nations want to encourage the intellectual creativity of its citizens in order to advance the country's social, cultural, and economic goals. Intellectual property laws attempt to balance the economic rights of individuals and society.

Since the early 19th century, countries have gathered to discuss the complex issues of international trade and intellectual property. These conventions, such as the Paris Convention and the Berne Convention, can last for many years. International dialogue and, ultimately, agreement on any legal topic requires discussion, patience, sensitivity to vast cultural, economic, and legal differences, lobbying, and perseverance. Two organizations that work in this area are the World Intellectual Property Organization (WIPO) and the World Trade Organization (WTO).

 Talking Back: Class Discussions

Listen to these two songs. Compare, contrast, and discuss.

John Fogerty, lead singer of Creedence Clearwater Revival (CCR) was sued in 1994 by Fantasy Records for plagiarizing himself in his song "The Old Man Down The Road." In other words, Fantasy Records thought "The Old Man Down the Road" (which Fogerty recorded as a solo act) sounded too much like CCR's song "Run Through the Jungle" (to which Fantasy owned the rights). Even though Fogerty won the case, for years afterward he refused to perform and record anything from the CCR catalog to avoid having to pay royalties for playing his own songs.[31]

Web Links

- The Paris Convention
  wipo.int/treaties/en/ip/paris/trtdocs_wo020.html
- Universal Copyright Convention
  portal.unesco.org/en/ev.php-URL_ID=15241&URL_DO=DO_TOPIC&URL_SECTION=201.html
- Berne Convention
  wipo.int/treaties/en/ip/berne/trtdocs_wo001.html
- Creative Commons
  creativecommons.org/
- The Rome Convention
  wipo.int/treaties/en/ip/rome/
- WIPO Performances and Phonograms Treaty
  wipo.int/treaties/en/ip/phonograms/trtdocs_wo023.html
- WCT and WPPT
  wipo.int/treaties/en/ip/wppt/summary_wppt.html
  wipo.int/treaties/en/ip/wct
- International Copyright Relations of the United State
  copyright.gov/circs/circ38a.pdf
- The TRIPS Agreement
  wto.org/english/tratop_e/trips_e/intel2_e.htm
- Digital Opportunity: A review of intellectual property and growth
  ipo.gov.uk/ipreview-finalreport.pdf

CHAPTER 6

The Role of the Music Publisher

CHAPTER OVERVIEW

This chapter focuses on the role of the publisher in the music industry. For most professional songwriters, a music publisher is an important part of her team. The work of a music publisher revolves around owning and exploiting the rights to songs and compositions. The chapter concludes with the fictional indie band, Third Rail, debating the ethical and legal ramifications of clearing samples in cover songs they've recorded.

KEY TERMS

- AIMP
- Assignment of copyright
- Audit
- Catalogue
- Creation vs. publication of a work
- Derivative work
- Exploit a work
- First use
- *Grand Upright Music Ltd. v. Warner Bros. Records*
- Harry Fox Agency
- License
- Music supervisor
- NMPA
- Recording company reserve fund
- Royalty statement
- Sample
- Synchronization license
- Tin Pan Alley

An Entrepreneur's Story: Aaron Bisman and JDub Records

"I have to share some unfortunate news. After almost nine years in operation, JDub's Board of Directors has decided to wind down the organization."[1]

So began Aaron Bisman's letter in the summer of 2011 to friends, fans, and supporters of JDub Records, the company he founded in 2002. In that time he built an innovative record label/concert production/consultancy business that impacted hundreds of thousands of people and launched at least one musician who attained pop star status.[2]

"We were never a normal record label, nor were we ever just a record company,"[3] Bisman explains.

Starting a record label was the furthest thing from Bisman's mind when he returned from spending his junior year studying in Israel. "When I got back to NYU, one of my roommates was creating mash-ups of Hassidic melodies, original music, and down-tempo hip-hop," explains Bisman. "It sounded unlike anything I'd heard before, and I was decently well versed in Jewish music. It sparked a litany of questions: if one college kid was coming up with music like this in his dorm room, who else was exploring similar sounds and why? Where should this music be performed, how would you market it, who would come and why would they show up for 'new Jewish music?'"[4]

Bisman and his roommate, Ben Hesse, began tossing around ideas about how to find more artists making this kind of music, and brainstorm what they could do to build a community around it. When Bisman heard about a possible funding opportunity, he knew it was time to turn his ideas into a plan.

"I spent six months fleshing out my thoughts, trying to figure out how to design a non-profit organization that could run a record label," states Bisman. "I was learning about the music industry and had some experience working at [indie label] Ropeadope, and Hieroglyphics, but I didn't have a clue about writing a grant proposal and being interviewed by people who might give me $60K."

He hired an interview coach, polished the proposal, and ultimately made a successful pitch to the Jewish Venture Group, a funding organization that invests in visionary leaders whose work will significantly impact the Jewish world.[5] Bisman's half-year of thinking and planning resulted in the launch of JDub Records, whose mission is to forge vibrant connections to Judaism through music, media, and cultural events. JDub sought to combine thousands of years of Jewish musical traditions with contemporary sounds, and provide a platform for the music to engage audiences both Jewish and non-Jewish.[6]

"The company was the conflation of many things I wanted to do with my life," explains Bisman. "Discovering, nurturing, and promoting proud Jewish voices to invigorate the wider Jewish community was one part. Another was helping individuals find their way back to their cultural roots, and adding *their* voices to the ongoing dialogue of what it means to be Jewish in the world today." JDub's innovation was to model what a new Jewish organization could look like and achieve.

Bisman continues: "After one of our concerts a young guy came up to me and said he'd never felt very connected to Judaism. He told me that tonight, while listening to the music, he'd suddenly understood how his family's traditions fit into a modern world, and how it deepened his sense of personal identity. To us [at JDub], this kind of 'aha!' moment between the artists, the music, and the community was a validation of our vision and our hard work."

Bisman is a social entrepreneur, an innovator who addresses pressing societal needs through the work of his company. JDub is a non-profit organization as well, meaning that it must rely on a combination of philanthropic support and sales of its products and services to survive.

JDub was well on its way to accomplishing the first goal of social entrepreneurs, that of making significant progress toward resolving a pressing social issue for a specific community. The recording industry, still strong during JDub's early years, helped them meet the second goal of social entrepreneurship's 'double bottom line': making money to pay the bills and grow the company.

Matisyahu
Credit: Vallery Jean/FilmMagic/Getty Images

JDub earned about half of its annual budget from album sales, concert tickets, and consulting fees. The other half came from foundation grants and individual donations. One of the strongest-selling artists on JDub's roster was Matisyahu, whom Bisman signed when the artist was still an unknown Hassidic hip-hop and reggae musician who rapped on Jewish themes.

Three of JDub's most visible events were bringing 3,500 people together for The Unity Sessions at Celebrate Brooklyn; producing six simultaneous Hanukkah concerts across the country including at Webster Hall in New York, The Independent in San Francisco, and The Echoplex in Los Angeles; and coordinating a collaboration between Matisyahu and Trey Anastasio of Phish at Bonnaroo in 2005.

So what happened? How could an organization this successful and creative shut its doors?

Bisman explains: "The decision to close was entirely financial. Between the recording industry in a shambles, a prolonged global recession, and philanthropic sources drying up, we couldn't sustain our business model. I looked at the options for staying open but didn't find any that would allow us to retain our true essence. It wasn't easy, but I feel at peace with our decision."

JDub is taking the next few months to wind down its activities before officially closing. Bisman is trying to find new homes for their artists, sell JDub's catalogue and other assets, and complete their consulting contracts.

"JDub's stakeholders should feel nothing except 'mission accomplished,'" writes Felicia Herman, executive director of the Natan Fund, JDub's longest-standing funder. "In addition to the hundreds of thousands of people JDub touched directly through its events and albums, JDub also changed the communal conversation, and made the community aware of the need to adapt to 21st-century American realities."[7]

Clearly, longevity isn't the only way to measure the impact of social entrepreneurship ventures. The mission JDub accomplished in introducing scores of Jewish musicians to a broad public, while sparking reflection and dialogue about an ancient peoples' role in a wired world, has already spread well beyond one company's work. JDub, the tangible manifestation of Aaron Bisman's vision, may soon be gone but it has set in motion societal changes that will be felt for years to come.

The idea of embracing setbacks and failures as opportunities to learn is a recurring theme in developing an entrepreneurial mindset. If you had been faced with Bisman's choices, what would you have done? Was there any other way to turn around JDub? What will happen to the copyrights that the company owns after it is no longer in business? Do you think Aaron Bisman 'failed forward'?

INDUSTRY ESSENTIALS: THE ROLE OF THE MUSIC PUBLISHER

Vector-illustration-/Shutterstock Images

Quick Review of Music Copyright

As discussed in Chapters 4 and 5, each song has two separate and distinct copyrights: the rights to the underlying composition (the music and lyrics), and the rights to the recording of the composition. Traditionally, a music publisher owns the *underlying composition* rights, and a record label owns the rights to the *recording* of the song.

The U.S. Copyright Office uses © as the registration mark for the underlying composition, and Ⓟ as the registration mark for sound recordings.

These rights derive from the 1909 U.S. Copyright Law, which recognized a performance right and a mechanical reproduction right. Performance rights refer to the right to publicly play the song, which is broadly defined and includes live concerts, radio and TV broadcasts, and recorded music playing in bars, restaurants, gyms, and retail stores, among others. Mechanical rights refer to the act of 'fixing' a song in a medium such as tape, vinyl, or plastic, and making copies of it.

The rights owner of the underlying composition must grant permission for a potential user to perform a song and record it. Permission comes in the form of a license, which generates revenue for the publisher and the writer.

Rights ownership and licenses can get confusing pretty quickly. The following brief example may help.

While a record label may own the rights to a *recording* of the song (the Ⓟ), it usually does not own the rights to the underlying composition (the ©); those are owned by a publisher—either a band with its own publishing company or a third-party publisher. So, if an ad agency wants to license a specific artist's recording of a song for use in a commercial, the agency will need permission from *both* the rights owner of the underlying composition (usually a publisher) and the rights owner of the recording (usually a record label). These licenses are negotiated directly with the rights owners, and fees are determined by whatever the market will bear. Both the publisher and the label (the rights holders of the two copyrights) have to agree to grant a license in order for the ad agency to use the recording. If the artist or song are very popular, the rates will be higher than they will be for an artist or writer who is less well known. (The ad agency may decide to re-record the song, using a different, less expensive artist. In that case, the agency would need only a license from the publisher for the underlying composition.) You can see that using a specific recording in a commercial (or film, video, etc.) could get complicated and expensive.

Introduction to Music Publishing

In music publishing we are focusing on the rights associated with the underlying composition—the music and lyrics (the ©). Songwriters and music publishers play a leading role in this sector of the music industry. In nearly every conceivable use of a song, the user is required by law to get a license and pay the rights owner of the underlying composition of the song. Since the songs' rights owners are usually music publishers, you can see how important a publisher becomes in a songwriter's career.

A publisher's job is to find revenue-generating ways to use a writer's music, keep track of the revenue earned through the song's usage, and distribute a portion of the money to the writer. Publishers earn money from the licenses they grant to others for use of a writer's songs. Examples of common uses include songs in advertisements, films, video games, concerts, recordings, and TV shows.

In exchange for receiving a publisher's professional assistance, a songwriter traditionally transfers ownership (assigns) the copyright of his songs to the publisher. This means that the publisher owns the copyright to the underlying composition (the ©), and enjoys the benefits of copyright protection as granted by law.

Inside a Music Publishing Company

Large, full-service publishing companies can be a one-stop solution for a songwriter who wants her songs to produce revenue. Major publishers have the infrastructure (skilled employees, systems, and processes) to take care of all aspects of the complex legal and accounting paperwork associated with copyright ownership and exploitation.

A large music publishing company usually has a professional staff that can provide a wide range of services. Traditionally, a company is organized into departments with specific functions, such as creative, promotion, mechanical licensing, synchronization licensing, foreign, finance, business and legal affairs, copyright, royalty, and information technology. Music publishing staff understand the laws of copyright that pertain to music and licensing. They will have a large network of potential clients with whom they are in frequent communication, pitching songs in their catalogue for placement in, for example, a film or TV show.

A publishing company's creative staff understands the needs of each potential music user and recommends music from the publishing company's catalogue that makes sense for the user's project and budget. The creative staff are skilled negotiators who understand the value of their catalogue, the financial resources of the potential user, and the going industry rates for music usage. They must constantly be looking for new ways to use music in order to expand the revenue streams of the writers and their company.

Some of the work of publishers is administrative in nature. Paperwork may seem less exciting than pitching songs to a major movie producer. In fact, it's the attention to detail that forms the foundation of the publishing industry, ensuring that the correct amount of money is flowing to the creators. The many daily tasks of a publisher must be executed with care and accuracy. These include such things as proper copyright registration; filing complete and correct information with PROs and mechanical rights organizations; making sure royalty statements from record labels are accurate; auditing record labels (hiring an accountant to check the label's financial records) when errors are suspected or detected; tracking revenues that are due from music users; following up on every detail involved in negotiating a license; keeping up with the complex and changing copyright laws; and helping to develop and use new technologies to streamline administrative tasks.

Smaller, independent companies generally have fewer resources, and may offer only some of the services of a major. However, many writers feel that indie music publishers may give them a higher level of support and personal attention than a large company of mega stars could provide.

There are approximately 1,520 music publishers in the U.S.[8] Publishing companies range in size from a composer who exploits only his own music to giants affiliated with major record labels, such as Warner/Chappell and Universal Music Publishing. Warner/Chappell is more than 200 years old, and owns songs (the music and lyrics) by legendary songwriters such as Cole Porter, and George and Ira Gershwin, as well as contemporary stars Green Day, Muse, and Timbaland. Universal Music Publishing's catalogue includes hits from top recording artists, producers, and songwriters such as Eminem, Justin Bieber, Coldplay, U2, Elton John, Mariah Carey, Adele, Bon Jovi, Paul Simon, Florence and the Machine, and Justin Timberlake.[9]

Adele at the 54th Annual Grammy Awards
Credit: Kevork Djansezian/Getty Images Entertainment/Getty Images

Muse performing on main stage in Lisbon, Portugal
Credit: C Flanigan/WireImage/Getty Images

Florence Welch, Florence + the Machine
Credit: Jamie McCarthy/WireImage/Getty Images

Some publishing companies are large but not connected with a major label. Two examples of large indies are Memory Lane Music Group and Canadian publisher Olé Music. Memory Lane's catalogue includes standards such as "Santa Claus Is Comin' to Town" (by Haven Gillespie and J. Fred Coots) and "What a Wonderful World" (by George David Weiss and Robert Thiele), as well as music by hip-hop, Top 40, and jazz writers. (See more information at MemoryLaneMusicGroup.com.)

Olé Music owns copyrights such as Taylor Swift singles "Fearless," "White Horse," and "Teardrops on My Guitar," Rascal Flatts' "Why Wait," Kelly Clarkson's "Miss Independent," and Tim McGraw's "Something Like That." (See more information at MajorlyIndie.com.)

The Major Functions of a Music Publisher

If songs and songwriters are the music industry's lifeblood, how do music publishers help keep the music business alive and well? While no two music publishers are

Taylor Swift
Credit: Rick Diamond/Getty Images Entertainment/Getty Images

identical, there are some basic building blocks that define the publishing industry. Below is a general overview of their most common tasks.

Find and support up-and-coming songwriters. A publisher's main focus is to encourage the creation of commercially viable music that can be licensed to earn money for both the writer and the publisher. Publishers often support new songwriters by providing co-writing opportunities, access to recording studios to create demos, and financial advances to help writers pay their bills so they can focus on songwriting. This type of support is very important to a writer's career. Co-writing in particular is helpful to young songwriters who are building their catalogue of songs, honing their professional and creative skills, and making connections to other writers in the industry.

Verify copyright protection for the songs it owns. Publishers make sure that copyrights and ownership of songs are correctly registered with the Copyright Office and all pertinent royalty collection agencies. These may include the Harry Fox Agency; the American performing rights organizations ASCAP, BMI, and

SESAC; and foreign performing rights organizations such as GEMA (Germany), SOCAN (Canada), and PRS for Music (U.K.).

Find revenue-generating uses for the songs it owns. While some songwriters' music is so popular that the publisher is swamped with requests to license their songs, other publishers must be pro-active in finding placements for the music in their catalogues. A publisher makes money only when the songs it owns are licensed and producing revenue. One of the areas of expertise that a songwriter taps into when signed to a publisher is the publisher's large network of people who work in the fields that use music, such as film, television, record labels, and advertising agencies.

Negotiate licenses and fees for use of its songs. Publishers' creative staff spend a lot of time pitching songs to potential users, and hammering out deals that will result in licenses and royalty payments.

Keep track of all monies owed from licensing the music in its catalogue. This administrative function is important, complex, and time-consuming. It involves careful accounting and follow-up on all licenses issued by the publisher, plus royalty payments from collecting societies like ASCAP (for a 'performance' of the underlying composition in all areas except recordings that are transmitted through non-interactive digital audio), and the Harry Fox Agency (for issuing a mechanical license, and sync licenses prior to June 2002).

When a songwriter signs with a performing rights organization (PRO), she is in fact giving the PRO the right to issue performance licenses for her songs. In exchange, the PRO will collect and distribute the revenue that is generated. No copyright ownership changes hands when a writer signs with ASCAP, BMI, or SESAC.

Although publishers usually are paid four times a year (quarterly) by the companies that have licensed music from its catalogue, in some cases it can take five months to more than two years for money to reach the publisher. Record labels' mechanical royalty reserve accounts are one reason for this delay. Here's why: For each song recorded and reproduced (as in a CD, tape, or digital download), labels are required to pay a fee, called a mechanical royalty, to the rights owner of the underlying composition. For songs that are in a tangible format, such as CDs, labels typically hold back 20% or more of the royalties they owe the song's rights owner. That's because labels accept returns of records that do not sell quickly. The retailer may send back unsold albums and receive a refund from the label. Mechanical royalties are only due on sold merchandise, not shipped merchandise, because of this return policy. Labels don't want to overpay the publisher so they hold back (reserve) a large percentage of the money they may owe from mechanicals. After retailers ship back unsold merchandise, the labels will compute how much they actually owe the publisher in mechanicals. Labels do not have reserve funds for digital sales.

Here's an example to help illustrate this point: A label presses and ships 100,000 copies of a CD that includes a song owned by your publishing company. The label owes the publishing company 9.1 cents for each copy of the song. It looks like the label owes the publisher 100,000 × 9.1 cents, or $9,100.00. The label decides to hold 60% of that amount in reserve until it is certain how many of the shipped CDs sell. That means the label will send the publisher 40% of $9,100, or $3,640, reserving the difference of $5,460 until it sees how many unsold CDs are returned by retailers. After giving the retailers a specific time period in which to return unsold CDs, the label will then compute how much more money it owes the publisher from its reserve account.

Let's say 90,000 records sold. The label owes the publisher a total of 90,000 × .091 = $8,190. The label has already paid the publisher $3,640. So the label will clear (liquidate) the reserve fund and send another check to the publisher for $8,190 less $3,640, or $4,500. Most labels do not clear their reserve funds until 18–24 months after the first shipment.

Since the label sends out checks to publishers 60–90 days after the close of each quarter, it can be years before the publisher gets its money and, in turn, before the writer gets his share. You can see why the advances that a new songwriter receives from his publisher can be so important to stabilizing his financial condition and allowing him to focus on writing.

Reflect

Why do you think record labels allow retailers to return unsold merchandise? This policy has been in place for decades. Consider both the labels' and the retailers' points of view.

Sales of physical recordings are steadily decreasing, while digital sales continue to grow. What impact could this have on publishers' and songwriters' royalties?

Oversee printed music production and distribution. Printed and digital musical scores are an important but less profitable business area for publishers than they were in previous years. In the early 20th century, sheet music sales were driven by easily accessible and inexpensive printed music (remember the music in your grandmother's piano bench?), demands of a large population of amateur musicians, and the success of publishers called song pluggers in the days of New York City's Tin Pan Alley. Song pluggers pitched their publishing company's music to well-known and up-and-coming performers of the day. Printed music was a substantial part of a publisher's business in those days, but today it has shrunk in importance, accounting for less than 10% of most publishers' total annual revenue.[10] Most music publishers do not produce their own sheet music but license print rights to third-party sheet music companies such as Hal Leonard or Alfred.[11]

Stay informed about and promote new legislation. Laws often can protect the rights of creators, in the U.S. and around the world. Two industry membership organizations that support music publishers in this effort are the National Music Publishers

Association (NMPA), and the Association of Independent Music Publishers (AIMP). To learn more about both organizations, see: NMPA.org and AMIP.org.

Protect copyrights of songs against infringement. This is achieved through legal channels such as litigation or settlement of claims. When an unauthorized use of the publisher's music or lyrics occurs, such as uncleared samples in a recording or unlicensed lyrics on a website, the publisher may take legal action itself and/or seek assistance from the NMPA, the AIMP, or outside counsel.

Do-It-Yourself (DIY) Music Publishing: A Third Rail Story

Third Rail Logo. Artist: Ariel Fitterman

Third Rail and their mentor, Alix, are meeting to talk about making some money from their songs.

"If you want to earn money from your music, you'll have to give others permission to use it," Alix tells them.

The guys look confused. Alix goes on: "Think of all the ways you hear music in your average day. If that music is under copyright protection and legally transmitted, someone has paid to use it by licensing it."

"Yeah, it's about time I got paid," Walter says.

Jared and Sam look at each other and shake their heads.

"So, if you want to hear your songs recorded by a well-known artist, or used in a TV commercial or film, you'll have to be able to help people legally use it," Alix said. "That's why you'll need to set up a publishing company."

The guys groan and Cody says, "Wait, I thought we just had to get signed to a publisher and they would take care of all the legal. I'm a guitar player! I don't want to set up a company."

"It's not that hard to set up your own publishing company," says Alix. "Most bands that write their own music have a publishing company. But don't get worked up about this. I'll talk you through it and you can decide if you want to do it yourselves or try to get signed to a third-party publisher."

By the end of the chapter, you'll be able to help Third Rail make their decision.

How Songwriters and Publishers Earn Money

Recent and significant changes in technology and consumer behavior are creating many new uses for music. Video games, interactive media, webcasting, online social networking, and commercial branding are a few of the newer opportunities for music licensing. Add to that the more traditional sources of music licensing—feature films, shorts, documentaries, movies made for home video and TV, corporate videos, advertisements and commercials, toys, printed music, instructional music DVDs, recordings in all formats, ringtones, television, and live theater—and it becomes clear why music publishing is such a large and prosperous sector of the music industry.

The U.S. music publishing industry earned approximately $4.9 billion in 2011 from licensing its music. The three highest revenue-producing areas were mechanical royalties (49.5%), performance royalties (22.5%), and synchronization royalties (20%).[12]

Mechanical Licenses

Having a well-known artist license one of your songs for a recording is a traditional and still lucrative way to earn money and recognition as a songwriter. For example, if Adele recorded a Third Rail song on her next album, Third Rail's publishing company (the rights owner) would be paid mechanical royalties by Adele's record company. Third Rail's publishing company also will earn money if Adele's recording of the song plays on radio and TV. If Adele's recording is a hit, Cody, Jared, Sam, and Walter will become better known as songwriters, and may be sought out by other artists who want to record their music. Music supervisors may seek out Third Rail to license a song for use in a film or an episode of *Gray's Anatomy*. All of these uses (exploitations) of their music will earn Third Rail money.

Using a writer's song in a recording requires the rights owner's permission in the form of a mechanical license. This is the legal document that a copyright user must receive in order to "reproduce and distribute" someone else's work. The copyright user will pay the copyright owner a specific penny rate for each reproduction of the work. That rate is determined by a copyright board and is overseen by the Library of Congress. It's called a statutory rate because it is based on copyright laws (statutes) enacted by Congress.

Resource: Consult the Harry Fox website to find a mechanical royalty calculator and current rates for all uses.

First use (A Review): This is a quirk in copyright law concerning mechanical licenses that you need to know about.

The first recording of a song is a big deal in copyright law. A copyright owner has the right to "reproduce and distribute" his work. This means only the rights owner can decide who makes the first recording.

However, after the first recording, the law states that the rights owner is *compelled* to allow others to record the song—without getting permission—as long as the user pays the rights owner the current statutory mechanical royalty rate.

A mechanical license doesn't change anything concerning copyright ownership of the underlying composition, or of the new recording. Rights ownership remains the same after a mechanical license is issued. For example, a band called Frostbite may decide to record (cover) a previously recorded Red Hot Chili Peppers song under a compulsory license. Frostbite won't have to ask permission, but they will have to pay Red Hot Chili Pepper's publisher for every copy they make of the song. Red Hot Chili Peppers' publisher still owns the underlying composition, and Frostbite (or its record label) owns the rights to the recording of the song.

Chad Smith of the Red Hot Chili Peppers
Credit: Jordi Vidal/Redferns/Getty Images

Some musicians react negatively to the idea of being forced to allow people to record their music. Why did the U.S. Congress make an exception to one of the exclusive rights of copyright holders?

The compulsory license was created in the 1909 Copyright Revision Act.[13] One explanation for its creation is that it was written into the law in order to prevent a monopolistic market in piano rolls by members of the Music Publishing Association and the Aeolian Company, the largest maker of player pianos at the time.[14] The first player pianos came onto the market in the late 19th century. Recorded music was just getting started in the early days of the 20th century. The statutory rate was set at two cents in the 1909 Act and did not change until the Copyright Act of 1976 went into effect, when the rate was adjusted upward to 2.75 cents.[15]

Another possible explanation for legislating a compulsory license may relate to the rationale for having copyright laws in the first place. Compulsory licensing supports the social purpose of copyright by ensuring that ideas can be shared easily across society, while honoring the underlying economic incentive for creators.

Reflect

What do you think? Discuss the plusses and minuses of the mechanical license from an artistic and an economic perspective.

When a record label issues a recording, it must license the underlying composition and pay the rights owner of the song. Music publishers, usually the song's owner, will collect royalty payments directly from the labels or from the Harry Fox Agency (HFA). Created in 1927 by the National Music Publishers Association (NMPA), the Harry Fox Agency serves as the publishers' non-exclusive agent for mechanical licenses. Outside of the U.S., collection societies perform this function for publishers.

The Harry Fox Agency issues mechanical licenses on behalf of the publisher, collects the money, and pays the publisher (less a small administrative fee). The publisher then sends the writer her share of the revenues. Mechanical licensing rates are set by the U.S. Copyright Royalty Board. In 2012 the rates are 9.1 cents for songs under five minutes in length, and 1.75 cents per minute for songs longer than five minutes.

In case you're wondering, the mechanical royalty rates are set by a panel of three independent copyright royalty judges, known as the Copyright Royalty Board, and appointed by the Librarian of Congress. The rate has increased over the years at a very slow pace. If the rate increases had kept pace with inflation, today's rate would be more than 40 cents per song.

Publishers' income from mechanical royalties is deeply affected by a clause in a recording contract known as the controlled composition clause. Recording companies try to reduce the amount of mechanical royalties they pay for using songs that are written or 'controlled' by the recording artist. In this context, 'controlled' means songs that are owned by the writer/artist's publishing company or some other entity that is not the record label. Reduced mechanical royalties mean less money for the publisher and the writer. As you can imagine, this is a controversial topic for publishers and writer/artists. The typical controlled composition clause calls for the writer/artist to receive 75% of the statutory rate.

In addition to recordings, uses that require a mechanical license include permanent downloads, interactive streaming, ringtones, and ringbacks. Master ringtones/ringbacks, on-demand (interactive) streaming and limited downloads are subject to the current statutory royalty rate.[16]

How much money are we talking about?

Copyright users may be able to negotiate a *lower* ('reduced') rate with the copyright owner, but legally a user can't be forced to pay more than the prevailing statutory rate. (Note: A rights holder *may* charge more than the prevailing statutory rate if he is negotiating a first use; that is, when he is considering a request from someone to be the first to record the work. In this situation, the statutory rate does not apply. It is only *after* the first use that the rates set by Congress are applicable. As in any negotiation, both parties must agree on the final terms of the offer.)

Let's do the math: The compulsory mechanical royalty rate was two cents in 1970. If a record maker paid the full rate per song and made 150,000 copies, how much would it owe the copyright owner?

If a record label presses 10,000 copies of a recording in 2012 that includes a cover of a three-minute Third Rail song, how much will the label owe Sam and the band if they do not negotiate a lower rate? If the user also sells 75,000 permanent downloads of the song they've licensed from Third Rail, how much will they owe for the downloads? And how much will they owe in total (downloads + CDs)?

Reflect

You may wonder—Why a *maximum* rate? And why did Congress single out only musical recordings for this exception to the exclusive right to reproduce and distribute? For some answers, research the copyright history links on the textbook website.

Performance Royalties

A songwriter has many important decisions to make when seeking professional partners to help him earn money from his creative work. In addition to finding a music publisher, a writer will affiliate with one of the three American performing rights organizations: ASCAP, BMI, or SESAC.

There are four key differences between a writer's performing rights organization (PRO) and his publisher:

- PROs are not publishers. PROs serve as the publisher's *agent* for performance licenses. Performing rights organizations license, collect, and distribute money earned through performance licenses ('Small Performances'). They send the performance royalties (less a small administrative fee) to their writer members and to their publisher members.

- Writers do not give up any of their copyrights when signing with a PRO. This is in contrast to a traditional agreement between a publisher and writer, where the writer may be required to assign his copyright to the publisher.

- PROs pay the writers directly; they do not send the writer's share to the publisher for a later split. The writer's PRO will apportion the revenues as directed by the writer's publishing contract, and then send two separate checks: one to the writer for the writer's share and one to the publisher for the publisher's share. This allows the writer to receive his performance royalty check without first being processed by his publisher. This is the only instance in the collection of publishing royalties in which the writer is paid separately from the publisher. In all other cases, the publisher collects the income and pays the writer his share.[17]

- A writer may join whichever PRO she chooses. Her contract with a PRO will last two or three years, depending on the PRO. After that time, the writer may decide to remain where she is or move to a different PRO, depending upon many factors including her relationship with the staff at the PRO and how confident she is about their ability to support her career. In a traditional contract, a writer is bound to her publisher throughout the publisher's ownership of her songs, often for the full duration of copyright protection, which could be decades.

You remember from Chapter 4 that the right to perform a work is an exclusive right granted by copyright law. When a writer selects his PRO (he can only affiliate with one at a time), he is granting the PRO the right to issue licenses and collect money from the performances of his music. In addition to live shows, 'performances' can include music used in TV, radio, the internet, and business establishments.

Publishers usually affiliate with all three PROs, in essence giving them permission to license the performance rights and collect the revenue for all of the works in its catalogues. This arrangement makes things a lot easier for potential licensees, such as television and radio stations, which use a lot of music by many different composers. Rather than trying to find the rights owner for each song it wants to play, a radio station, for example, will get a blanket license from the PROs. Blanket licenses cover all the works in each publisher's catalogue, giving the licensee the legal right to use any song in a performance without fear of copyright infringement. See Chapter 8 for detailed information about PROs.

Synchronization Licenses

When previously recorded music is used in conjunction with a moving image, it requires permission from both the owner of the underlying composition (the ©) and the owner of the recording (the ℗) if a master recording is used. The permission is granted in what's known as a synchronization license. To date the smallest revenue producer for publishers and writers, synchronization (synch) licenses are a significant growth area for rights holders. Synch licenses are needed for music used in TV commercials, TV shows, advertising campaigns, video and film, video games, and Karaoke machines—anywhere that music is combined with a moving image.

For example, if a film director wants to use Stevie Wonder's recording of "Superstition" from his 2002 album *The Definitive Collection* in a movie, the director must get permission in the form of a synch license from both the rights holder of the underlying composition and the rights holder of the recording. Rarely are these the same person or company. In nearly all cases, there will be a fee to license the music. The director and the rights holders will negotiate a rate for the ways in which the director wants to use the music. This could include how the song is used in the film, whether or not it is used in advertisements for the film, shown in movie theatres, on television, on the internet, in airplanes, and so on. The duration of the license and the territory the license covers (regions or countries outside the U.S.) are also negotiated.

It's possible that one or both of the rights holders will decline to grant the synch license, or that the fee to use Mr. Wonder's song is outside of the film director's budget. If money is the sticking point, the director could consider re-recording the song by a less-expensive artist as long as the song is not a sound-alike recording. The director still needs a synch license from the publisher, but the price for using the recording may drop significantly.

A synch license gives the film director the right to include a song in his film. But a synch license alone is not sufficient to show the film in public. In addition to a synch license, a TV station will need a performance license to show the film.

Here's an example of what one song might have earned by being licensed and performed on the TV shows *Oprah* and *Glee* on the same day.

Glee perform in London
Credit: Matt Kent/WireImage/Getty Images

Songwriter Stephen Schwartz's song "For Good," from the play *Wicked*, aired on two high-profile shows on the same day in May 2011. It was sung by Kristin Chenoweth, the actress who played Glinda in the play, on the next-to-last *Oprah Winfrey Show* to air on ABC. By coincidence, later that day two of the stars of the show *Glee* sang "For Good" in the *Glee Finale* on Fox Television.[18]

Music publishing sources estimated that the song earned approximately $23,000 from synchronization (synch) licenses on May 24. A synch license allows the user to pair a visual image with sound. Since synch licensing fees are negotiated between the copyright user and owner (or their representatives), there are many factors that affect the price. Some copyright owners may agree to a lower rate because they really want the visibility of that particular performance, which could bring them more business in the future. Some may raise their rate because they know their song is immensely popular and there is a lot of competition by advertisers to use it.

The *Oprah Winfrey Show* had an enormous viewing audience that day, and therefore was in a strong negotiating position when it came to determining the rate it would pay. After all, Oprah could choose any song she wanted. And she could probably afford any song she chose.

Oprah's production studio, Harpo Studios, probably paid a synch fee of $1,500–$3,000 to license the song. *Glee*, on the other hand, usually pays an average of $20,000 per synch fee. It's important to note that *Glee* clears rights for music use that are much broader than those initially cleared by the *Oprah Winfrey Show*. This is one reason that *Glee*'s sync fee is significantly higher than Oprah's.[19]

A Few More Ways for Publishers to License Their Music

- Publish sheet music, folios (collections of songs), and books or films about the creators of music or the songs themselves.

- Create libraries of pre-cleared music sounds, drum beats, loops, and music for use in film, television, advertising, recordings, and interactive media. This kind of music is also known as production or stock music. Many production music companies are owned by the major labels' publishing companies, such as Universal (owns Killer Tracks). SmashTrax Music is an independent stock music company, and worth checking out at *SmashTrax.com.*

- Compile and market special collections, projects, and events that involve the songs in their catalogue. Ideas might include a postage stamp series featuring specific composers, or a deluxe box record set with photos of manuscripts and songs from a specific time period in a songwriter's career.

- Grant licenses for derivative works to be made from its songs. For example, if Volkswagen wants to use a Third Rail song in a TV ad campaign but is planning to make substantial changes in the lyrics to fit the images, Volkswagen will need permission in the form of a derivative license from the rights holder to the underlying composition. The licensing fee and terms of use for the song will be negotiated.

- License music for use in a corporate ad campaign. This has become a major source of revenue for publishers and bands.

- Grant sampling licenses (for the underlying composition) to artists who want to use previously recorded music in a new recording.

Reflect

Name the artists and bands you have discovered by hearing them first on an ad or TV show.

Third Rail Logo. Artist: Ariel Fitterman

Clearing Your Samples: A Publishing Pre-Requisite
Third Rail is grappling with this issue right now.

Alix asks the guys in Third Rail: "Did you use any samples in your songs? Before you can publish, record, or sell your music, it has to be original to you or properly licensed."

Walter frowns. "What do you mean, 'clear' a sample? I thought the artists would be happy to have their stuff in our song. Look at DJ Girl Talk. He seems to be doing OK without clearing his samples."

Cody gives Walter an exasperated look. He explains to Alix that they have samples in two songs. "We looped about 10 seconds from a track in A Tribe Called Quest's album *The Low End Theory*. The other is about four seconds of "The Spark" off The Roots' album *Things Fall Apart.*"

Alix tells the band they'll need permission from the copyright owners of both the underlying composition (traditionally a publisher) and the master recording (traditionally a record label) in order to use the samples in their recording.

But Third Rail isn't interested in what Alix has to say. Cody remarks: "You can't really recognize the originals because we added so much distortion. I don't think it'll be a big deal."

"Yeah," agrees Sam. "It's too much of a hassle to try to find the copyright owners, and it'll probably cost too much. We'll just take our chances and hope we don't get caught."

Some bands don't bother to clear samples. They may not understand their legal obligation, or they may not care. But legally it's considered a copyright infringement of both the sound recording and the underlying composition if samples are used in a record without the copyright owners' permission. Copyright infringement lawsuits can be lengthy and expensive. It's not worth it—get the samples cleared or re-record the song without the sample.

Reflect

DJ Girl Talk, Pretty Lights, and other artists are upfront about not getting clearance for the music they sample. Why do you think they're not being sued for copyright infringement (at least at the time of this writing)?

The U.S.A. is the cradle of music sampling and, owing to its strict interpretation of copyright laws, a hotbed of sampling lawsuits. One of the earliest music sampling cases was *Grand Upright Music Ltd. v. Warner Bros. Records* in 1991. Rapper Biz Markie, signed to Warner Bros. Records, had sampled without permission Gilbert O'Sullivan's song "Alone Again (Naturally)" on a track of his album *I Need A Haircut*. In delivering his decision to Warner Bros. to cease distribution of Markie's album, Judge Kevin Thomas Duffy began with a biblical quote: "Thou shalt not steal." Judge Duffy's decision signaled the strict interpretation of sampling laws by U.S. courts, and changed the business structure of hip-hop music. From then on, labels insisted that their artists clear all samples before releasing the record.[20]

Biz Markie
Credit: Steve Pyke/Premium Archive/Getty Images

TABLE 6.1 *Overview of common ways to license music*

SONG USE	TYPE OF LICENSE	SOURCE OF LICENSE(S)	COST OF LICENSE
First use of a song	First use—mechanical	Publisher	Negotiated
Cover song on recording	Mechanical—compulsory	Mechanical licensing Agent (HFA, RightsFlow)	Statutory rate unless lower rate is negotiated
Film, video, documentary	Synchronization	Publisher for music & lyrics Record label—only if requesting a specific recording	Negotiated
Corporate training DVD	Synchronization	Publisher for music & lyrics Record label—only if requesting a specific recording	Negotiated
Terrestrial radio & TV (small performances)	Performance—blanket OR Direct License with rights holder	Performing rights Organizations or label	Negotiated
Ringtones, ringbacks	Mechanical	Publisher for music & lyrics Record label—only if requesting a specific recording	Negotiated
Mastertones	Mechanical	Harry Fox Agency or publisher	Statutory rate set by Copyright Royalty Board
Electronic greeting cards	Mechanical	Publisher for music & lyrics Record label when requesting a specific recording	Negotiated
Non-interactive digital streaming radio	Performance	PROs	Negotiated
Interactive digital streaming radio	Mechanical	Harry Fox Agency	Statutory
Download available for purchase on web	Mechanical	Mechanical licensing Agent (HFA, RightsFlow)	Statutory rate set by Copyright Royalty Board
Printed music, folios, special collections	Print	Publisher	Negotiated

SONG USE	TYPE OF LICENSE	SOURCE OF LICENSE(S)	COST OF LICENSE
Theatrical stage productions (grand rights)	Performance	Publisher or rights holder such as Samuel French, Tams Witmark Music Library, Rodgers & Hammerstein	Negotiated
Derivative work	Derivative	Publisher	Negotiated
Lyrics licensed to print greeting cards, books, magazines	Lyric reprint	Publisher	Negotiated
Music Business services (Muzak, airlines)	Mechanical	Publisher for music & lyrics Record label—only if requesting a specific recording	Negotiated
Video games	Synchronization	Publisher for music & lyrics Record label—only if requesting a specific recording	Negotiated
Radio ads	Commercial sync license (and master rights if using existing recording)	Publisher for music & lyrics (Label for master rights)	Negotiated
Television ads	Synchronization	Publisher for music & lyrics Record label—only if requesting a specific recording	Negotiated

Opportunities Ahead

Notice how many licenses require negotiations to determine a fee. Experienced publishers are skilled negotiators. How could an artist who is self-publishing learn how to negotiate effectively?

CONCLUSION

Copyright law is the underlying bedrock of the music industry, and rights owner-ship is the key to economic and artistic control of musical works. Music publishers play a major role in discovering and nurturing new songwriters. In exchange for signing with a music publisher and receiving the benefit of its expertise in exploit-ing her music, a writer may be required to assign some or all of her copyrights to the publisher for the duration of the song's copyright protection.

Publishers earn money for their writers and their company by placing songs in film and video, TV, record labels, advertising, games, internet applications, greeting cards, mobile phone applications, and all types of interactive entertainment. Publishers also have the infrastructure to take care of the legal and accounting paperwork associated with licensing songs and paying their songwriters.

 Talking Back: Class Discussions

Even though they're resisting, you need to persuade Third Rail to clear the samples in their songs. Walk them through the process described below, and see if it produces the results you want.

To find a U.S. publisher, begin with the performing rights organizations, ASCAP, BMI, and SESAC. Use their searchable databases. You could also try Harry Fox Agency. If the song is from a writer outside the U.S., find the collection society for that country and search its database. (See Chapter 8 on Performing Rights Societies.) If you can't find the information online, call the company and ask for the song indexing department. Remember, a songwriter can only be registered with one performing rights society, so you may need to contact all of them before you find the artist and her publishing company.

When you find the publisher's name, contact the company and ask for a sample license. This is where the situation can get challenging. As an unknown indie band or unsigned artist, you do not have much bargaining power, particularly when dealing with rights holders such as major labels, publishers, and large independents. You will be required to pay an upfront fee that may be well beyond your budget. Be realistic about your chances and have a back-up plan in mind if you can't afford the sample license.

Next, you'll need to find the copyright owner of the master recording, which traditionally is a record label. You could try asking the publisher if they know, or search for the recording on iTunes or other online services. Again, be prepared for the possibility that a sample license cost is higher than your budget.

You may run into challenges because one of more or the companies has gone out of business, or sold their rights to another company. Remember the story of JDub Records at the beginning of this chapter? Sometimes the rights have reverted to the songwriter or her heirs. If you're still willing to put in the time, the next step would be to find a copyright clearance expert and let them work their magic—for a fee, of course.

What do you think Third Rail should do if . . .

- They can't find all the rights holders for permission?
- They can't afford the licensing fee?

Web Links

- Harry Fox
  HarryFox.com/public/RoyaltyRateCalculator.jsp

CHAPTER 7

Songwriters and Music Publishers

CHAPTER OVERVIEW

This chapter provides an overview for songwriters who are thinking about entering into a publishing contract. The six types of publisher contracts are reviewed in detail. You will help Third Rail decide if they should seek out a third-party or become a DIY publisher.

KEY TERMS

- A&R function of a publisher
- Advance
- *Campbell v. Acuff-Rose Music*
- Co-writing
- Development Deal
- Harry Fox Agency
- NMPA
- Recoupable
- Rights transfer
- Royalty stream
- Sampling
- Scope of work
- Termination rights
- Types of publishing contracts
- Writer's draw

INDUSTRY ESSENTIALS: SONGWRITERS AND MUSIC PUBLISHERS

The Relationship

In contrast to how a writer chooses a PRO, the formal relationship between a publisher and a writer is made jointly: the publisher indicates an interest in signing a writer by entering into conversations about a potential relationship. If the writer and the publisher agree on terms, a contract is prepared and reviewed by the writer's attorney. Once both parties have signed, the contract is in force.

The signing of the contract indicates the beginning of a long-term relationship. This is very different from the writer's contract with the PRO because, in many cases, the writer has agreed to transfer his copyright ownership to the publisher for a minimum of 35 years.

Wait a minute: *35* years? Don't copyrights last for the life of the longest-living author plus *70* years? The 1976 U.S. Copyright Law granted a 35-year 'Termination Rights' opportunity for songwriters, recording artists, and other artists, allowing them to regain control of their work after 35 years. (There are a few strings attached, such as the artists must apply to terminate at least two years in advance.) The Termination Rights provision applies to most songs created after 1978. This issue has become a source of concern for both publishers and record labels as they face the prospect of losing valuable works, beginning in 2013.*

Reflect

Think of all the hits that were composed around 1978 by songwriters such as Tom Petty, Bryan Adams, Loretta Lynn, Kris Kristofferson, Tom Waits, and Charlie Daniels.[1] Many of those songs have just reached the window of opportunity to terminate rights with their publishers. What is the potential impact for the publishers that may lose the rights to well-known songs? What are some strategies that publishers might consider to avoid losing those songs?

You can see why it is essential for a songwriter to explore her options, in consultation with her attorney, before signing with a publisher. It is likely that the writer will give up (assign) full ownership of her copyright for a long period of time. In addition, she also must trust that the publisher is enthusiastic about her music, and has the necessary industry knowledge and connections to earn the maximum amount of money possible by exploiting her music.

Assigning one's copyright is no small matter. So what does the writer receive in exchange for transferring his copyright ownership to a publisher? Among other things, he receives a share of the monies earned when his songs are licensed for use. This means that when the publisher is successful at placing the song—the underlying composition—in, say, a recording, an ad, or a film, the licensing fee will be paid to the publisher, who then sends the writer his share, retaining the other half to cover the expenses of running the publishing company plus making a profit. The traditional publisher/writer split is 50/50 of all monies that are earned through the

---

* The actual date that a terminating party recaptures its rights is dependent upon when it filed termination, the conditions of which are stipulated under the Copyright law (section 203a).

Loretta Lynn performing at Bonnaroo 2011
Credit: FilmMagic/FilmMagic/Getty Images

Inductee Tom Waits performs onstage at the 26th annual Rock and Roll
Hall of Fame Induction Ceremony in New York City
Jeff Kravitz/FilmMagic/Getty Images

publisher's exploitation of the writer's music. The precise revenue split is one of the many items to be discussed and agreed upon in the publishing contract.

Looking back at the long list of what a music publisher does, it's clear how important it is for a writer to proceed carefully when thinking about signing a publishing agreement. As in the choice of one's life partner, the best partnerships are based on trust, mutual respect, and confidence that both parties have similar goals.

Main Points to Be Considered in a Publishing Negotiation

The relationship. Before signing a contract, a songwriter and publisher will discuss the type of relationship that makes sense for both parties. The acquisition of rights to the songwriter's work, and what services and revenue splits the songwriter may receive in return, are key points in any agreement.

Contract duration. How long will the contract be in force? What is the process for and consequences of an early termination or a contract extension?

Rights transfer. When a copyright owner transfers her rights to a third party, such as a publisher, all the rights and privileges that pertain to copyright ownership transfer as well. (Reminder: We are talking about the rights to the underlying composition, not the recording of the song.) In a traditional publishing contract the writer assigns (transfers) her copyright ownership to the publisher for the duration of the copyright period as defined by federal law. (Note: There are publishing deals, described later in this chapter, that do not include copyright ownership transfer.)

The rights to the underlying composition that transfer with the copyright to the new owner (the publisher, in this case) include the right to reproduce, modify, distribute, perform, and display the work. With a nod to the rapidly changing environment in which music and media operate today, a contract will almost always include phrases that include rights in future, unnamed uses, current and future technologies, and even 'beyond the known universe.'

Writers may try to include a clause in the contract that gives them some control over how their songs may be used. For example, a well-known writer may be able to negotiate a clause stating her songs may not be used in advertisements unless she personally approves it. Writers who are less well known probably won't be successful in negotiating this clause.

Reflect

Reflect on the competing issues in the struggle between art and commerce in this scenario: The writer may feel strongly that she doesn't want her songs to be used to promote products she doesn't like, or causes she does not support. On the other hand, the publisher wants to license the music in its catalogue as often as possible because it makes money only when someone is using and paying to license its songs.

Advances. An advance is money paid to the writer by the publisher. Issues to discuss in a negotiation include the size of the advance, the payment periods, and whether or not the advance is recoupable against future royalty earnings.

Co-writing. It is very common in today's music industry for songwriters to collaborate. While this may complicate the rights-ownership landscape, most publishers accept co-writing as a fact of life. For example, when a writer who has an exclusive agreement with a publisher works with a writer who self-publishes, the publisher will request its signed writer to make her best efforts to obtain the co-writer's share for the publisher, rather than for the co-writer's own publishing company. As the frequency of collaborative writing increases, this clause becomes challenging for publishers to enforce.

First-use mechanical licenses. Copyright law gives the rights owner the exclusive right to decide who makes the first copy of his or her song. Thus, when a writer assigns his copyright to a publisher, the first-use right transfers to the publisher. First-use mechanical licenses are not subject to the statutory rates that guide the recording of cover songs *after* their first recording and publication. Publishers will negotiate first-use licenses on the open market, meaning that the cost to record the song for the first time will vary depending upon the reputation of the writer, his prior success, how strongly the potential song licensee desires to use the song, and other factors.

Making changes to a work. Copyright law gives the rights owner the exclusive right to make derivative works from a song. If a potential licensee wants to make substantial changes to a song's lyrics or music (beyond a key change or recording a pop song as a jazz arrangement, for example), the potential user will seek a license to make a derivative of the work. As stated earlier in the chapter, this is a negotiated license, meaning it is not governed by a statutory rate. If the desired terms are not met, the rights owner can refuse to grant a license to make the derivative work.

Weird Al Yankovic, a Grammy-winning American singer-songwriter, producer, and comedian, has built a career making humorous parodies of hit songs and contemporary culture. To record and distribute his music, Mr. Yankovic must first negotiate the terms of a derivative license with the rights owners of the song in order to avoid infringing on the owner's exclusive rights to make a derivative of the work.

The complexity of copyright issues involving parody and fair use is reflected in the number of high-profile lawsuits in the music industry. Here are two cases that are worth exploring.

Campbell v. Acuff-Rose Music, 510 U.S. 569 (1994). The rap group 2 Live Crew borrowed the opening musical tag and the words (but not the melody) from the first line of the song "Pretty Woman" ("Oh, pretty woman, walking down the street").[2]

Resource: Read the full case.

Fisher v. Dees, 794 F.2d 432 (9th Cir. 1986). The composers of the song "When Sunny Gets Blue" (Marvin Fisher and Jack Segal) claimed that their song was infringed by Rick Dees' "When Sonny Sniffs Glue," a 29-second parody that altered the original lyric line and borrowed six bars of the song.[3]

Resource: Read the full case.

2 Live Crew
Credit: Michael Loccisano/FilmMagic/Getty Images

Ownership and promotion of demo recordings. Usually publishers own everything created by their writers, even their demo recordings. While it is not common to release a demo as an actual finished recording, it can be an intriguing opportunity for a publisher to consider, particularly after a famous recording artist dies and there is high demand for her material, especially previously unpublished songs or versions of songs.

Timeliness of royalty payments from the publisher. It is the industry standard for publishers to send royalty statements and payments to the writer twice a year. Publishers retain the money they collect on behalf of the writer for 45 days to three months *after* the closing of each six-month collection period. This means that a writer whose song was used in an advertising campaign that ran at the beginning of a six-month collection period might not receive payment for up to eight months after the commercials aired. It's clear why advances can be life-saving to writers. On the other hand, it can take three years or more for a publishing company to fully recoup (be paid back from the writer's earnings from song exploitation) the advances paid to a writer, even if money begins flowing in right away after signing the writer.

Audits. An audit allows the writer to bring in an accountant to review the publisher's books. The writer may suspect that she has not received all the royalties owed to her and wants a third-party professional to examine the publisher's accounting records. An audit clause may also include the right of the publishing company to audit the writer/artist's record label, for the same reasons.

Summary. As in any negotiation, the final contract reflects the relative strengths of the parties at the bargaining table. A new but promising songwriter may have less bargaining power than a well-established writer whose works have been popular for years and have produced significant amounts of revenue. A skilled entertainment attorney is an essential member of the writer's negotiating team, and will work on her behalf to get the best deal possible.

Six Different Types of Publishing Contracts

If talks go well, the publishing company will issue a contract to the songwriter. While each publishing company has its own contract language, drawn up by its attorneys and based on years of experience with its writers, there are six general types of agreements or relationships that the songwriter may consider, depending upon his stature and a proven track record of writing songs that are commercially viable.

The first two types of contracts listed below generally are offered to writers who have come to a publisher's attention but have not reached their full potential. Experienced and successful songwriters more commonly seek and/or are offered the third, fourth, and fifth contracts listed. The sixth type of contract is a hybrid. It's called a development deal, and pairs an experienced writer (who is often a producer and recording artist, as well) with a new writer.

- Exclusive agreement

- Individual song agreement

- Administration agreement

- Co-publishing agreement

- Joint Venture/Co-venture agreement

- Development deal.

Exclusive Agreement

In an exclusive writer/publisher contract, the writer agrees to allow only one publisher to exploit the work he creates during a specified period of time (usually no fewer than five years) and transfers 100% of the copyright to the publisher. There is often a minimum song commitment involved or certain measurable goals set, such as income generated by songs. The term continues until the minimum song commitment or income goal is met and perhaps longer if the commitment or goal is met prior to the specified length of time.[4] In exchange, the writer will receive regular (often monthly) payments, called a 'writer's draw,' against future earnings from the exploitation of the songs during the period of exclusivity. These regular payments can be an enormous help to songwriters, reducing the anxiety of waiting for royalties to be paid by copyright users such as record labels and performing rights organizations. The writer's draw is almost like a salary, except that all monies paid will be deducted from future revenue that the writer earns. This means when the publisher receives payment from a copyright user, the money goes into the writer's account to recoup, or pay back, the draws that have been paid to the writer. Typically songs created during the term of the agreement are assigned to the publisher for the life of copyright. The agreement itself (i.e., the length of time the songwriter is signed exclusively to the publisher) is for a certain number of years. Once the draw has been recouped, the publisher pays the writer her 50% of royalty earned. In effect, the publisher is taking a calculated risk that it will be successful in licensing the writer's work. The publisher must bring in enough money to cover the draws they are paying the writer, as well as make a profit, for the publisher to stay in business.

There are many benefits for a developing writer in signing an exclusive agreement. Having a steady income for the period of the agreement allows the writer to focus on her songwriting without worrying how she'll pay her rent and bills. In addition, the publisher often will provide access to recording studios for the writer to work with other writers, create new work, and record demos.

Individual Song Agreement

In this agreement a songwriter transfers to a publisher 100% of the copyright for a specific song or songs, in exchange for a nominal advance and a split of the future revenues from licensing the song(s). The writer is exclusively bound only to that publisher for those specific songs. She may work with any number of publishers on a per-song basis. Why would a songwriter do this? She may feel a particular publisher will be better qualified and more eager to promote certain of her songs. Similarly, some publishers may be interested in only specific types of songs from a writer because that is their area of expertise. Again, the business-savvy songwriter will do extensive research into each publisher to be certain she is placing her songs in the right hands. The duration of the licensing period is a factor to be discussed in the contract.

Administration Agreement

In this type of contract, a songwriter will retain the rights to his songs and pay a percentage of his earned income to a publisher, in exchange for the publisher performing any number of the common administrative functions inherent in music publishing. This type of agreement may suit the needs of writers who record their own works as artists; writers whose style of music is not conducive to being covered on albums or licensed in commercials, film, or TV; and for songwriters whose works are in high demand and who have little need for the A&R (creative) function of a publisher. The major difference—and it's a very big deal—between an administration agreement and other types of publishing contracts is that the writer does not have to give up any of her copyright in an administrative agreement.

As in other contractual arrangements, an administration agreement can be tailored to meet the needs, expertise, and financial needs of the two parties involved (publisher and writer). The most common duties found in administration agreements include:

- Filing copyright registrations

- Updating information with collecting agencies like Harry Fox Associates, ASCAP, BMI and SESAC, and foreign collecting societies

- Registering songs with the PROs and mechanical licensing companies.

For these types of services the administering publisher would receive approximately 7–10% on all income collected.

If the writer is looking for additional help from the publisher, the fee could increase to 20% and may even involve partial ownership of specific songs. Depending on the administering publisher's areas of strength, the duration of the agreement, and the level of enthusiasm for the writer's songs, an administration agreement could even include song promotion, securing new uses for the songs, demo recording, license negotiation, contract drafting, and connections to and advice about foreign territory licensing.

At this point you may be wondering why a publisher would enter into an administration agreement with a writer, as it appears that the publisher is doing the same kind of work as an exclusive or co-publishing contract, but without the major benefit of owning the copyright. For some publishers, the chance to work with a very well-known catalogue of music will allow them to burnish their reputation, which in turn may attract more high-profile writers. There are publishers who accept an administration agreement in order to strengthen their connections in a specific musical genre. Still other publishers may find that administrating a catalogue from, say, a well-known recording artist or popular television series will be so lucrative that it is a good strategic move, even if they cannot own the copyrights.

The common elements in an administration agreement, no matter how much or how little the writer wants from the publisher, include:

- Term of the agreement—how long will it last, how can it be renewed or terminated?

- Scope of work—what services will the publisher provide to the songwriter? How will that affect the administration fee charged by the publisher?

- Physical territory covered by the agreement—in what countries or areas of the world will the administering publisher work for the writer? Will there be an additional fee for working outside the writer's home country?

- Royalty payments—will they include gross income for each song, or more detailed information about how the income for each song has been distributed?

- Royalty statements—what information will be included in the statements? How often will statements be sent?

For the additional services required of the publisher—particularly song promotion that results in new uses and cover records—the writer will expect to pay an additional percentage to the publisher. The writer may decide to create incentives for the publisher to actively seek new uses of her music by building into the contract additional percentages for specific deals. For example, the contract could state that the publisher will receive an additional 5% on revenues generated by a song if the administering publisher secures a cover deal of the song with a high-selling recording artist. Another type of incentive for the publisher to be pro-active in finding new uses for a writer's music is for the writer to offer a percentage of the copyright if certain specific goals are achieved.

As you can see, an administration agreement can cover many types of services. The writer/publisher relationship can range from the complex but straightforward collecting monies and sending out royalty statements and payments, to being pro-active about finding and securing new opportunities in which to license the writer's music, thus bringing more revenue to both the administrative publisher and the writer.

Co-Publishing Agreement

A co-publishing agreement is offered primarily to well-established or highly desirable writers. In such an agreement the songwriter does *not* transfer 100% of the copyright to the publisher in exchange for receiving 50% of the revenue earned, as in the exclusive and individual song agreements. In a co-publishing arrangement, the songwriter usually receives some type of recoupable advance and retains a portion of her copyright in her own publishing company, where she will earn publishing royalties, *plus* her writer's share. In effect, the writer is receiving a portion of the money that would have gone to the publisher. Typically, a co-publishing deal will stipulate the right of the publisher to administer the writer's retained publishing interest. Why would a publisher enter into an agreement with these terms? When a writer has a proven track record of creating hits and/or easily licensed music, the publisher is taking a calculated risk that the amount of money it can earn from exploiting the music will be very substantial, and could more than make up for 'losing' part of their traditional copyright ownership.

The concept behind the splitting of revenues in a co-publishing deal can be confusing at first. This story may help you understand the process.

Performance royalties are paid to Really Big Publishing Company.

Sergey Goruppa/Shutterstock Images

Half of the money goes to Jesse the songwriter, and Really Big keeps the other half.

Andrei Shumskiy/Shutterstock Images

Jesse the writer keeps her share, but Really Big Publishing has to share its half with Jesse's Personal Publishing Company.

happydancing/Shutterstock Images

Jesse the writer now has 50% of the performance royalties . . .

50% Jesse's Writer's Share

. . . and Jesse's Personal Publishing Company has half of the publisher's share (1/2 of 50% = 25%)

25% Jesse's Personal Publishing Company's Share

So, of the original amount of performance royalties paid to Really Big Publishing Company at the beginning of this story . . .

Sergey Goruppa/Shutterstock Images

. . . Jessie has control of 75% of the royalties . . .

> 75% = Jesse's Total Royalty Share

. . . and Really Big has control of 25% of the royalties.

> 25% = Really Big Publishing Company's Share

The terms of each co-publishing contract can vary significantly from writer to writer. For example, after splitting the full royalty payment 50:50, with 50% going to the writer and 50% to the publisher, the agreement also could specify a subsequent 30:60 writer/publisher split of the *publisher's* 50%. That would mean that the writer would receive 50% of the full royalty payment *plus* 30% of the publisher's 50%. Here's another example to help you understand the concept:

$250,000   Full royalty payment for use of the copyright in a film
The publisher and writer split this 50:50, resulting in
   $125,000   Publisher's share
   $125,000   Writer's share

Then, publisher gives 30% of his $125,000 to writer's publishing company ($37,500).
  So . . .
  Writer and her publishing company end up with $162,500 ($125,000 + $37,500).
  Publisher ends up with $87,500.

A Few More Issues

There are a few more issues to resolve in a co-publishing agreement between Jesse, Jesse's Personal Publishing Company, and Really Big Publishing Company.

- Which of Jesse's compositions are covered (Current only? Past? Future?)

- Jesse may sign other songwriters to her own publishing company. What are Really Big Publishing Company's rights to songs written by those writers?

- Can Jesse place any restrictions on how Really Big may license her works?

- For how long will Really Big, Jesse, and Jesse's Personal Publishing Company share revenues for the songs that are defined in the co-publishing agreement? Will it be for the entire duration provided by copyright law, or some other amount of time?

- How will the expenses of normal business activities, such as copyright registration and creation of demo recordings, be shared between Really Big Publishing and Jesse's Personal Publishing Company?

- When and under what conditions could/will the copyright controlled by Really Big revert to Jesse's Personal Publishing Company? The reversion of rights is a key issue in all contracts involving a change of ownership in copyright. Will Really Big Publishing Company maintain the rights for the entire legal duration of copyright? Are all songs involved, or only specific songs? Will recoupment of the writer's account be a factor in reversion possibilities? Can the issue be re-explored at a later date, depending upon the success or disappointment of the songs' commercial viability?

Joint Venture/Co-Venture Agreements

Another creative partnership that publishers can enter into is called a joint or co-venture agreement. In this relationship a publishing company and a successful, well-known songwriter (or a small indie record label) find mutual benefit in working together to discover and help develop new talent. In a joint or co-venture, a publisher will gain access to new talent that is identified by the songwriter or indie label, thus adding more A&R capabilities to the creative services offered by the publisher. The songwriter (who also may be a recording artist and producer) identifies the up-and-coming writer, and is able to attract and nurture him with financial and other support from the publishing company. The writer and the publishing company co-own the rights to the music created by the up-and-coming writer. In addition, the publisher usually receives the right to administer the new compositions worldwide.

In a joint venture/co-venture agreement all parties benefit. The up-and-coming writer is mentored by a successful writer/artist/producer and is signed to the publishing company. The publishing company supports emerging talent and enlarges its catalogue of new songs that can be promoted globally. If the new songwriter becomes successful, both the publisher and the writer who signed him will benefit financially, as they co-own the rights to his songs. Depending on the nature of the contract the new writer signs with the publisher, he also may receive a percentage of royalties earned by his songs. Other issues to be considered when negotiating a joint venture/co-venture agreement are:

- Duration of the agreement

- What happens to song ownership when the contract period ends? Can the agreement be extended or suspended?

- Advances—new writers may receive advances that are either paid entirely by the publisher, or paid as a split by the co-venture partners (the experienced writer and the publisher). In addition, the experienced writer may also receive advances from the publishing company as a co-venture partner. In most cases, all advances are recoupable and are applied against earnings as they are received.

Some music publishers are open to negotiating all sorts of creative deals. For example, EMI Music Publishing signed a joint venture agreement with songwriter, musician, and record producer Rodney 'Darkchild' Jerkins. He has written, co-written, and produced hit recordings by, among many others, Lady Gaga, Katy Perry, Mary J. Blige, Michael Jackson, and Beyoncé. In this joint venture, Jerkins helps EMI discover talented new songwriters and shares the publishing with EMI and the songwriter.[5]

Development Deals

A development deal is another way for publishers to find new talent, nurture, and develop it in exchange for ownership of the copyright. The main goal of a traditional development deal is to have the songwriter recognized as a recording artist in her own right and offered a record deal by an independent or major label.

When a publishing company's A&R staff finds a songwriter whom they feel also could be a successful performing artist, the company may make the strategic move of entering into a development deal with the songwriter. There are many contractual issues to be considered, but the primary goal is for the publisher to get the writer/artist signed to a label in the time specified in the contract. The strategic thinking on the publisher's side is that they would then be in a position to benefit from *two* royalty streams from their writer: revenue from exploiting the underlying compositions in any of the ways described earlier in the chapter *plus* royalty points from sales of the album or singles. (These royalty points will be part of the writer/artist's recording contract.) Even though recorded music sales have declined significantly over the past decade, people all over the world still purchase music. And the publisher would receive a percentage (points) of each sale under the terms of a development agreement.

In any contract, and particularly in a development deal, the writer and her attorney will attempt to push for specific, measurable, and quantifiable terms. These could include:

- Duration of the contract

- The type and size of the label to which the artist wants to be signed

- A guarantee of a specific dollar amount of support from the publisher to make professional, studio-quality demos (or even full albums in some cases)

- A set time-frame in which the recording session of the demo will take place

- Advances to the writer/artist and clear language as to what financial assistance from the publisher is recoupable from future writer/artist earnings

- Funds for purchasing equipment that will help the writer/artist compose and record a great demo

The publisher will want similar reassurances that the artist/writer will fulfill her part of the bargain, and could include in the contract:

- The specific number, nature, and quality of songs to be written and recorded in the contract period

- The ownership of copyright to all songs produced during the contract

- The right to negotiate and commit the artist/writer to a record deal

- The percentage split of all monies from the recording deal

- Options for ending or extending the development deal

- The option for converting the development deal into another type of songwriter/publisher contract, such as a co-publishing agreement.

We've only touched on a summary of the most salient points to be discussed and agreed upon in a negotiation between a writer and a publishing company. As you can see, contracts are complex, requiring comprehensive review and discussion with attorneys. Contracts may often require many weeks or even months to come to closure. If both parties are confident that they want to work together, they may sign a deal memo before the contract is fully drawn up.

The deal memo is much shorter than the full contract. It outlines the most important points that have been agreed upon, and allows the parties to get to work while the attorneys from both sides complete the negotiations and prepare the full contract for review and signature. After signing a deal memo, the writer may be able to receive advances that allow him to focus on writing songs and recording demos. The publishing company can begin to work on organizing a strategy for promoting and exploiting the writers' compositions.

Despite the best of intentions, negotiations can break down even with a deal memo in place. As always, the relative strength of the two parties at the negotiation table will determine whether or not the deal moves forward to a full contract.

Reflect

The buying and selling of entire catalogues of music is not uncommon in the music industry. Many iconic publishing catalogues, such as Motown, Northern Songs, Famous Music, and the Rodgers & Hammerstein Organization, have been sold in recent years, even during the prolonged economic downturn. Find information about a specific catalogue of music that interests you and reflect on how you would exploit the songs in it if you were the owner.

Opportunities Ahead

In this section you'll use the creative problem-solving methods from Chapter 2 in order to find entrepreneurial solutions to Third Rail's problems: How can they earn money from their music to pay their rent? Would you advise them to seek out a third-party publisher or become DIY publishers? Think like an entrepreneur as you come up with creative solutions to their challenges.

- *What would Oprah do?*[6]
  Imagine that you have unlimited resources to solve the problem.
- *The 99% solution*[7]
  Now find most of the benefits for only 1% (or so) of the cost of your Oprah solutions.
- *Where else could this work?*[8]
  Find a solution in a completely different industry and apply it to the problem.
- *Would flipping it work?*[9]
  Rearrange the words in your solutions above to see if you come up with unexpected ideas for solving Third Rail's problems.

CONCLUSION

There are plusses and minuses for songwriters who self-publish. It may be relatively simple and inexpensive to become a music publisher in the Digital Era, but the downside is that the songwriter will have to do most of the work herself. Anyone working in music publishing must understanding complex music copyright laws, have a wide network of contacts in many areas of the music and entertainment industry, know how to market, sell, and keep careful accounting and licensing records.

No matter which direction a songwriter chooses to go—sign with a publisher or become one—he'll need legal advice. Publishing contracts are complex and require expert analysis by an attorney who specializes in the music industry. Legal advice when starting a publishing company or signing a contract is invaluable, and helps avoid costly errors and future legal problems. An attorney is an essential member of a professional musician's team.

 Talking Back: Class Discussions

Most young writers would jump at the chance to be signed by a reputable music publisher. How can a writer perform her due diligence (deep research) on a potential publisher?

Web Links

- *Campbell v. Acuff-Rose Music*, 510 U.S. 569 (1994)
  scholar.google.com/scholar_case?case=16686162998040575773&q=Campbell+v.+Acuff-Rose+Music,+510+U.S.+569+%281994&hl=en&as_sdt=2,39&as_vis=1
- *Fisher v. Dees*, 794 F.2d 432 (9th Cir. 1986)
  cip.law.ucla.edu/cases/1980-1989/Pages/fisherdees.aspx

CHAPTER 8

Performing Rights Societies

CHAPTER OVERVIEW

In this chapter you will see the many ways artists earn money through performances. The definition of 'performance' is very broad and includes live concerts, radio and television broadcasts, business music, and a few others. We'll take a look at the newest U.S. performing rights society, Sound Exchange, and compare it to its sister performing rights societies. Your mastery of copyright basics will guide you through the complex story of how rights societies collect and distribute money from performances around the world.

KEY TERMS

- Census and sampling
- CISAC
- Compulsory license
- Direct license vs. blanket license
- Exclusive right to publicly perform a work
- Non-dramatic musical works
- Non-interactive vs. interactive radio
- Performing rights societies
- Statutory rate
- Underlying composition

An Entrepreneur's Story: Marni Wandner and Sneak Attack Media

Marni Wandner is an accidental entrepreneur. Finding herself between jobs in 2006, Wandner said 'Why not?' to an offer from a friend who needed help with online marketing for his record label. Wandner was intrigued at the idea of focusing on just one aspect of marketing after three years of working in the recording industry doing management, marketing, and a bit of public relations. Online marketing sounded fun and creative, and would tide her over until she found a 'real' job.

"It was the perfect time to move from old media to new," states Wandner. "I didn't realize it, but becoming a specialist in online marketing was the perfect niche for me."[1]

Three months later Wandner had more clients than she could handle. Her accountant began encouraging her to start a business officially, but it wasn't an easy decision.

"I didn't have a business plan, a mentor, or an investor," Wandner explains. "I was so busy I didn't even have time to sit down and think: Do I really want to run a business? Sure, I had lots of clients, but what if this flurry of activity was a fluke? What if I start the company and then don't have any work? I was definitely scared of failing at times."

Wandner turned to family and colleagues for advice as she came closer to making a decision. By the end of 2006 she had taken the plunge and launched Sneak Attack Media, a digital promotions and creative services company based in New York City.

"It was terrifying, really," Wandner admits. "At the beginning I felt like I was flying blind. I have a tendency to climb, climb, climb— and *then* look down, instead of thinking about a challenge *before* I accept it. In this case, that was a good thing."

Wandner just kept climbing, taking on one new client after the next. Even at critical moments in the evolution of Sneak Attack, though, Wandner chose not to seek outside funding. "I really wanted to keep control," she says with a laugh. "I had a tiny bit of early start-up money, but I chose to grow Sneak Attack organically rather than share ownership with investors."

About a year after the economic recession hit the music industry, Wandner began to notice the effect of downsized companies and smaller budgets. "I hired a few more people so that we could adapt to the changing market. We had a higher volume of business but a lower budget per client," she explains. The strategy worked. Sneak Attack Media now has eight employees and an impressive list of projects and clients.

Sneak Attack promotes music primarily, but also has worked with films, brands, and books. Clients and projects have included Neil Young, Tom Petty, Lou Reed, Florence + The Machine, Laurie Anderson, Rachael Yamagata, Tori Amos, Craig Wedren, Rufus Wainwright, and more. Sneak Attack was involved in promoting the soundtracks for shows like *30 Rock* and *Californication*; and the soundtracks for films like *MacGruber, Bridesmaids, and Beginners*. "Our promotional efforts include things like online PR, social media strategy, and digital tool development," explains Wandner.

Sneak Attack's competition includes larger marketing companies like Filter Creative Group and Cornerstone Promotions, as well as Girlie Action, a PR and marketing company specializing in music and pop culture. As an entrepreneur, Wandner knows that she must position Sneak Attack Media to compete strongly in the product branding and services marketplace.

"Sneak Attack first and foremost is a service-driven company," states Wandner. "We care deeply about our clients and we take great pride in creating unique campaigns for each project we take on."

Since founding Sneak Attack, Wandner has been an active member of the New York chapter of Women in Music (WIM), and has served on the board since its relaunch in 2007. She turned to her strong network of WIM colleagues for guidance and support—and to find interns and employees—while building the company.

"WIM was started in 1985, when there truly were very few women in the executive ranks of the music industry," says Wandner. The founding WIM members reached out to their female colleagues to get them involved, encouraging them to stay in an industry that, at the time, was very much a 'boy's club.' Interestingly, Women In Music has always had male members, and today the music industry as a whole is a much more gender-balanced workplace.

Sneak Attack Media has turned into far more than a 'real job' for Wandner and her staff. Having weathered the contraction of the music industry *and* a global recession, Wandner has proven that she is far from an 'accidental' entrepreneur.

"I didn't set out to start a company, but I see that my instincts led me to the right place," says Wandner. "Being able to guide my business and work with amazing clients who benefit from our services is very fulfilling. I'm still sometimes a little surprised to find myself here, but I've grown more comfortable in my role as an entrepreneur."

Used with permission

It's not unusual for people to be working on something they really enjoy and slowly realize they've become a business owner—an entrepreneur. Heading down a path that one didn't expect to travel can be intimidating, but a growth mindset and a 'What if . . .?' attitude can help make the journey a little less bumpy and a lot more fun. In the pages ahead you'll learn a few new ways to think like an entrepreneur and put your adventurous spirit to work in the complex area of performance rights management.

INDUSTRY ESSENTIALS: PERFORMING RIGHTS SOCIETIES

teacept/Shutterstock Images

Introduction

Phoebe, the vocal half of a bluegrass duo, just heard a song from her new album on the radio. She immediately texted Earl, the banjo player, to tell him.

"Great!" Earl replied. "When do we get a check?"

Many artists have the same question as Earl does: "How will I get paid when my songs play on the radio?" As you'll see in a moment, the answer is complicated.

As copyright owners of both the underlying composition and the recording, and as performers on the sound recording, Phoebe and Earl feel they should be paid when their songs are played on radio. Copyright law states that they have the *exclusive* right to 'publicly perform' their work. No one else may perform their music unless they get permission from Phoebe and Earl.

Here's the definition of 'publicly perform' directly from the source, the U.S. Copyright Office:

To "perform" a work means to recite, render, play, dance, or act it, either directly or by means of any device or process or, in the case of a motion picture or other audio-visual work, to show its images in any sequence or to make the sounds accompanying it audible.[2]

The application of the term 'perform' is very broad. It encompasses music that is played in the course of normal business activities on: major television networks; local television; terrestrial, internet, and satellite radio stations; cable and satellite networks and systems; internet web sites; colleges and universities; night clubs, taverns and restaurants; background music services; fitness and health clubs; private clubs, hotels, conventions and trade shows; concert presenters, dance halls, shopping centers and malls; theme and amusement parks; airlines; skating rinks; retail stores; and music users in a variety of other industries.[3]

Let's talk first about the royalties that Phoebe and Earl could receive as rights holders to the underlying music, and tackle the sound recording-related royalties later on.

U.S. Rights Societies

Phoebe and Earl gave permission for their music to be 'performed' at any of the above types of businesses when they signed with ASCAP as their performing rights society.

ASCAP is one of three U.S. performing rights societies for authors and composers (referred to in this book as PROs), along with BMI and SESAC. The PROs were created to serve as the middlemen between the copyright owner (songwriters and publishers) and the copyright user. PROs negotiate performance licenses for the public performance of non-dramatic musical works on behalf of copyright owners of the underlying composition. PROs then collect the money from the businesses that they've licensed, and distribute payments to their member songwriters, composers, and publishers.

> Dramatic vs. Non-dramatic: While there is no bright line between dramatic and non-dramatic works, dramatic works are commonly defined as those that use music to enhance the story or plot. An example of a dramatic work would be the musical *West Side Story*. PROs do not license their members' work for dramatic use; the rights for this type of use are negotiated between the rights holder and the user.

There are hundreds of thousands of global businesses that want to use music to help sell their products and services. It would be impractical and costly to require copyright owners and users to find each other to negotiate licenses every time someone wanted to use a song. So the U.S. and many other countries have created performing rights societies for the express purpose of issuing licenses and collecting fees for the performance of works that are protected by copyright. PROs throughout the world have reciprocal agreements with each other to collect and pay royalties to songwriters and publishers.[4]

Rather than go through a PRO, some businesses prefer to license directly from the copyright owner. That could make sense if the business is only using one composer's music. However, most music-using businesses want to have legal access to a wide variety of musical styles, genres, composers, and songwriters. So they pay for a *blanket* performance license from all three PROs, allowing them use of every single song and composition in the PROs' catalogues.

To get a sense of how huge this industry is, Spotify's blanket license with ASCAP allows Spotify to stream more than 8.5 million musical works from ASCAP's approximately 415,000 members. Spotify's license runs through 2013.[5]

As we'll see in the next few pages, the digital revolution is upending the status quo for performing rights societies. Performing rights organizations, previously one of the most stable sectors in the music industry, are facing competition and uncertainty. This is a sure sign that there are entrepreneurial opportunities ahead.

Phoebe and Earl want to earn a living from their music so they hope to license it as often as possible. As songwriters, joining a PRO makes sense and they don't have to give up a portion of their copyright to benefit from ASCAP's services. Phoebe and Earl manage their own publishing company, Shooting Star, which is a *publisher* member of ASCAP.

When paying its members, the authors, composers, and publishers, PROs still adhere to the traditional royalty arrangement, where songwriters split their copyright ownership 50:50 with a third-party publisher. So when ASCAP sends a royalty payment to Phoebe and Earl, it will pay them 50% (the writer's share) and will pay Shooting Star 50% (the publisher's share), even though they are technically one and the same.

Resource: See the ASCAP, BMI and SESAC websites for detailed information about their member services and licenses.

Global Performing Rights Societies

Music is a global industry, and hundreds of countries support their artists and copyright owners with strong performing rights laws and practices. CISAC, the International Confederation of Societies of Authors and Composers, was founded in 1926 and works to protect *creators'* rights.[6] CISAC is a non-governmental, non-profit organization with a membership of approximately 232 authors' societies from 121 countries. Its headquarters are in Paris, with regional offices in Budapest, Santiago de Chile, Johannesburg, and Singapore.

The 2011/2012 CISAC annual report, issued in January 2012, summarized data of 230 performing rights societies around the world. Below are the highlights.[7]

Member revenues for 2010 were 7.55 billion Euros ($9.34 billion), up from 7.15 billion Euros in 2009. Table 8.1 shows how that broke down by category of licensees.

TABLE 8.1 *Breakdown of CISAC member revenues for 2010 by licensee category*

Public Performance	73.1%
Mechanical Reproduction	19.0
Other (private copying, resale rights, multimedia, karaoke, etc.)	7.9

Each country in the European Union (EU) has its own performing rights society, with distinctive traditions and policies. This makes licensing very complicated for music rights owners and users. Currently the author of a single work must have a separate copyright agreement on the work in each of the 27 EU member states. In fact, users from one country may be prevented from accessing a song if the rights to that song are managed in a different country.[8]

In order to remain globally competitive, the European Commission has mandated its member countries to provide one-stop licensing for digital music providers. Theoretically, this would permit digital service providers to procure all their music clearances from one place instead of going to each separate EU society.[9]

Here is a partial list of the songwriting/underlying musical work performing rights organizations (PROs) and copyright collection societies around the world:

Australia	APRA
Canada	SOCAN
France	SACEM
Germany	GEMA
Ireland	IMRO
Japan	JASRAC
Netherlands	BUMA
Spain	SGAE
Sweden	STIM
Trinidad & Tobago	COTT
UK	PRS for Music

Resource: Go to the BMI website for a complete list with links.

Sergey Goruppa/Shutterstock Images

How Does the Money Flow?

After collecting the fees from businesses that pay for public performance licenses, the PROs deduct a percentage (9–12%) for their administrative expenses, and pay out the balance of the money to the copyright owners—the songwriters and their publishers.

Each PRO uses a different method to calculate how much to pay its songwriters and publishers. All of the methods are complex and, some people contend, controversial. With PROs still tied to traditional radio and television airplay to determine how to distribute their licensing revenues, in general the more airplay the song receives, the greater the income generated from the song. Some songwriters and publishers feel this favors hit songs, even though the PROs collect data from many types of TV and radio stations.

According to ASCAP, the value of each radio and television performance is determined by many factors, including the amount of license fees collected in a medium (television, cable, radio, etc.), the type of performance, (a 'visual vocal' where the artist actually is seen performing, background music, theme song, jingle, etc.) and the economic significance of the licensee (how much a station pays ASCAP).[10]

In 2011, BMI collected approx $931m and disbursed approx $796m in royalties.[11] ASCAP collected $985m and distributed $824m in royalties.[12] The PROs collect music data on more than 4,000,000 hours of radio airplay and more than 15,000,000 television broadcast hours per year.[13]

Changes for Performance Rights in Sound Recordings

It All Began with an Act

In the early days of the internet, Congress recognized that legislation was needed to update copyright law. At the same time, record labels saw an opportunity to seek a performance right for the broadcast of their music. They were successful, but only in the digital medium.

The Digital Performance Right in Sound Recordings Act of 1995 (DPRA) and the Digital Millennium Copyright Act of 1998 (DMCA) granted a performance right in sound recordings for certain digital and satellite transmissions. In exchange for this new right, sound recording copyright owners are subject to a *compulsory license* for the use of their sound recordings of music, spoken word, and comedy, provided the user complies with those conditions set forth in the copyright law.[14]

A compulsory license means that, after the first recording of the work, the copyright owner is *compelled* to let others record it. In exchange for allowing the work to be recorded without explicit permission, the rights owner and recording artists must be compensated by the user according to the prevailing statutory rate, which is set by Congress.

A New Performing Rights Society Is Born

Sound Exchange, the newest American PRO, was created in 2000 by Congress to collect and distribute statutory digital performance royalties on behalf of featured recording artists, master rights owners (like record labels), and independent artists who record and own their masters. The royalties are collected from *non-interactive* satellite radio, internet radio, cable TV music channels, and similar platforms for digitally streaming sound recordings.

Non-interactive means the listener is in 'lean back' mode: he just sits back and passively listens to what the station plays. Examples of non-interactive radio include Pandora, Sirius XM, and radio stations that simulcast on the web.

By contrast, interactive, or 'on-demand,' refers to services like Spotify, where the listener can choose what he or she wants to hear.

How does Sound Exchange work? When Phoebe and Earl's recordings of their songs are streamed on certain internet radio stations, played on digital satellite radio, or used on digitally streamed cable music channels, Phoebe, Earl, *and any other performers on that recording* accrue a small royalty. This is a big deal because, in the U.S., performers and sound recording copyright owners do not receive a royalty when a recording is played on terrestrial radio and television. As the performers and the

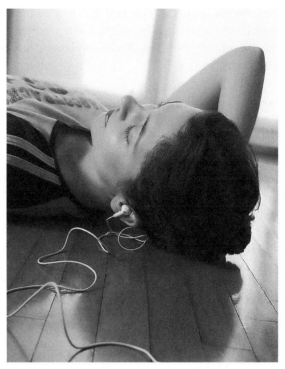

Diego Cervo/Shutterstock Images

sound recording copyright owners, Phoebe and Earl will receive royalty payments from Sound Exchange. (They will also receive two checks from ASCAP—the writer's share for Phoebe and Earl, and the publisher's share for Shooting Star.)

Are We Confused Yet?

Believe it or not, we're still trying to answer Earl's question from the beginning of the chapter, "When do we get a check?" There are a few more essential building blocks of the performing rights societies to understand, so hang in there for just a little longer.

Traditional *terrestrial* broadcasters in the U.S. are legally required to license the music and pay the rights holder of an *underlying composition*. However, the U.S. is the only developed country that does not require terrestrial TV and radio broadcasters to license the music and pay a performance royalty to the rights holder of the sound recording or to the recording artist who performs on a sound recording.

This is very confusing to most people. Why is it this way? Like any business, traditional (terrestrial) broadcasters want to keep their costs down. Terrestrial broadcasters already pay to license the underlying composition through the PROs.

But it goes deeper than that. Since the early days of commercial TV and radio, broadcasters have been successful in convincing Congress that they should not have to pay royalties to the sound recording copyright owner (usually a record label) and the recording artist. From time to time record labels and artists try to get the law changed for terrestrial broadcasting, but so far they have not prevailed.

How Sound Exchange Is Different from Its Sister PROs

Sound Exchange works on behalf of sound recording rights holders and the performers on sound recordings that are broadcast via non-interactive digital audio (i.e. Pandora) transmission. ASCAP, BMI, and SESAC work on behalf of the rights holders of the underlying musical composition when their music is performed via the many types of broadcast (except digital audio transmission) discussed earlier in the chapter.

ASCAP, BMI, and SESAC collect and distribute royalties only to their respective songwriter/composer, author, and publisher members. In contrast, Sound Exchange is required to collect royalties on recordings that are transmitted by non-interactive digital services for all performers on a recording, as well as for sound recording rights holders.[15]

Collecting Data and Making Payments

Sound Exchange receives payment accompanied by detailed electronic play logs from the digital music service providers. This data collection method is called census. It allows Sound Exchange to pay exactly what has been earned, minus a percentage for administrative costs.[16]

In contrast, ASCAP, BMI, and SESAC use the sample method of 'listening in' on radio and TV broadcasts to collect their music data, and pay according to their own proprietary royalty earning systems. BMI, for example, requests all licensed stations to log performances for a three-day period each year, with different stations logging each day of the year. This sample is then used to create a statistically reliable projection of all stations throughout the country.[17]

Check out each PRO's website for details about the newest technologies they use to calculate royalty payments to their members.

Licensing

Another important difference between the PROs and Sound Exchange is that Sound Exchange's digital streaming licenses are compulsory *statutory* licenses. This means that the copyright users pay a rate per download that is determined by the U.S. Copyright Royalty Board, called a statutory rate. ASCAP, BMI, and SESAC *negotiate* rates with the companies that license their music.

Digital Tracking and Reporting

With the advent of digital media, new standards were needed for efficient content and metadata exchanges between partners in the digital music supply chain. Digital Data Exchange (DDEX) is a consortium of industry content, device, and digital rights management companies who created a common standard for music-use reporting. DDEX was founded in 2006 to help streamline the way the performing rights licensing sector interacts with digital media.

Companies like Music Reports, Inc. and RightsFlow have emerged to help digital music *users* handle the complex tasks of identifying the millions of rights *owners* in order to license their work and pay royalties. The ability to track and record music usage more accurately than the old, traditional systems allows for more transparency and accountability in the growing digital music market.[18]

However, these improved accounting systems have encouraged some music users to bypass the PROs and go directly to the rights holders for 'á la carte licensing.'[19] Universal Music Group and EMI Music Publishing were among the first majors to issue bundled mechanical and underlying musical composition performance licenses directly to online services, such as Last.fm. This move toward direct licensing, which sidesteps music users' previous arrangements with underlying musical composition performing rights societies, is causing PROs to rethink their business model as they face more competition and uncertainty in the marketplace.[20]

Finally, the Answer . . . and It's Still Complicated

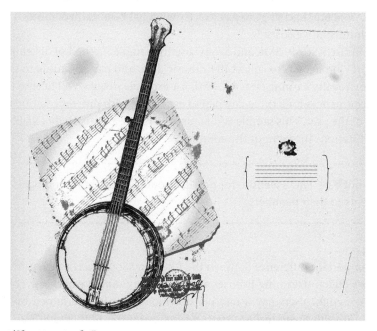

teacept/Shutterstock Images

Ken Jacobsen/Imagezoo/Getty Images

So, will Phoebe and Earl get a check for their song playing on the radio? Yes and no.

In the U.S.: If their song is played on terrestrial AM/FM radio, they will receive royalties from ASCAP for the writer's share and the publisher's share. Phoebe and Earl will not receive anything as the performers and copyright owners of the recording *unless* that radio station broadcasts simultaneously over the internet.

If Phoebe and Earl's song is streamed on non-interactive digital radio, such as cable TV music stations, Sirius XM, and Pandora, they will receive writer and publisher royalties from ASCAP *and* from Sound Exchange.

If Phoebe and Earl heard their song on a music service like Spotify, MOG, Slacker Premium Radio, and Rhapsody (called 'on-demand' services), they will receive writer and publisher royalties from ASCAP. Additionally, their record label will receive a payment from the on-demand music services, which negotiated a licensing deal with the label before being allowed to play it.

In Europe: If Phoebe and Earl's song played in Europe on terrestrial AM/FM radio, they would receive writer and publisher royalties from ASCAP, which has a reciprocal agreement with each member country of the EU. They will not receive royalties for the performance right in the sound recording.* If Phoebe or Earl were born in or were a resident of a foreign country, or if they created their sound recording in a foreign country, then they could receive payment.

Phoebe and Earl made a good business decision to sign with a songwriting PRO (ASCAP) and to register with Sound Exchange. Without those organizations, they wouldn't receive any money at all for public performances of their music.

But does the process of getting paid have to be so complicated?

Opportunities Ahead

It may be difficult to see a clear path to entrepreneurial opportunities in the large, complex, and highly regulated performing rights sector of the music industry. However, you can see that there is rapid change, uncertainty, and increasing competition in this area, which suggests that it's prime territory for entrepreneurial thinking.

Use the problem-solving techniques from Chapter 2 to get the process started. First, do some creativity warm-ups to make your thinking more fluent and flexible.

Next, make a list of the problems you see in the performing rights sector. What's working, what isn't working? Consider the songwriters, publishers, record labels, and music-using companies when trying to identify the problems. Try to resist the desire to shrug and say "That's just the way it is. We should leave the complex legal stuff to lawyers." Remember, laws can be changed.

CONCLUSION

ASCAP, BMI, SESAC, and Sound Exchange provide valuable services to music rights holders, helping them receive payment for the public performance of their works. The definition of 'performance' is very broad, which provides many opportunities for rights holders to earn money. However, the laws governing this area of the music industry are complex and vary from country to country. An entrepreneurial thinker will have to dig deeply to find opportunities that will untangle and streamline the dense web of laws and customs that govern the performing rights sector.

---

* The U.S. doesn't pay performance royalties to any domestic or foreign sound recording artists or rights holders for terrestrial broadcasts. Not surprisingly, European rights societies will not pay U.S. sound recording rights holders or artists for terrestrial broadcasts, even though EU recording artists and rights holders are paid for public performances or terrestrial broadcasts.

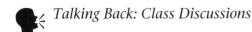
Talking Back: Class Discussions

Sound Exchange is the only PRO authorized by law to collect and distribute royalties from sound recordings that are publicly performed via non-interactive digital audio transmission. Why did Congress want to make this distinction? Wouldn't it have been easier just to add digital transmission to the list of performance licenses that ASCAP, BMI, and SESAC already administer?

PROs work on behalf of their members to license music, and to collect and distribute the licensing fees. Compare that to the function of a third-party music publisher. How are they the same, and how are they different?

Up until the 1960s, most songwriters worked as employees of publishing houses, and were paid to write songs for others to sing and record. This changed with the emergence of rock bands, which wrote most of their own songs. Tin Pan Alley and the Brill Building are important contributors to U.S. songwriting legend. Who were some of the famous songwriters who worked there? Who owned the rights to the songs that were created by songwriters who were employees of publishing houses?

Resource: Begin your research at the virtual Songwriters Hall of Fame website.

Web Links

- ASCAP, BMI and SESAC
  ASCAP.com
  BMI.com
  SESAC.com
- BMI
  BMI.com/international/entry/C2258
- The virtual Songwriters Hall of Fame
  songwritershalloffame.org/exhibits/eras/C1109

PART 3

Performing and Recording

CHAPTER 9

Concerts and Touring

CHAPTER OVERVIEW

In this chapter, entrepreneurial artists and bands tell the story of the live music industry. Hundreds of online tools help DIY bands manage their shows, book tours, and stay in touch with fans. For many bands, however, this is only a short-term strategy. The live concerts sector of the music industry is a global business, with complex travel, customs, tax, and rights issues. The chapter concludes with short entrepreneurial sound bytes featuring artists and business people in the concert business.

KEY TERMS

- Ancillary revenue
- Artist manager
- Booking agent
- Crowd funding
- Paper the house
- Primary and secondary ticket markets
- Talent buyer/Promoter
- Ticket scalper/Broker
- Venue manager

An Entrepreneur's Story: Andrew Cyr and the Metropolis Ensemble[1]

By Yifan Qin and Catherine Radbill

> Critics, musicians, and fans alike bemoan the death of classical music. But couldn't these times also be viewed as a tremendous growth opportunity for reaching new audiences and expanding the boundaries of our art form? (Andrew Cyr)

The idea for creating a chamber orchestra devoted to contemporary classical music came to Andrew Cyr in 2004. Cyr, a musician and conductor, was attending the opening night of a performance art

---

installation. He was astonished at the number of young New Yorkers who clearly had an appetite for the arts. What was it about a gallery opening that attracted such an enthusiastic crowd? Why didn't classical music attract these same young people to attend classical music concerts?[2]

When he compared the two experiences, Cyr realized that gallery openings were opportunities for casual social interaction, eating, and drinking as well as an exchange of contemporary ideas about art and society. Classical concerts, on the other hand, required respectful silence from its audiences, with very little chance for mingling and socializing, and not very much new music.

Cyr's own professional experiences pointed to a related problem: The current classical music industry did not provide a supportive environment for talented emerging composers and artists devoted to creating and performing contemporary classical music. He wondered if there was a way to connect both these challenges and satisfy an audience hungry for cutting-edge art.

For an entrepreneur, identifying unmet needs in the marketplace is the first step. While most people saw only problems for the future of classical music, Cyr saw the potential in it. "Why not upend the status quo and try something new?" he thought.

Cyr's question gave birth to the Metropolis Ensemble, a professional chamber orchestra and ensemble devoted to broadening the audience for contemporary classical music. It began with Cyr's focus on finding creative solutions to fill the needs of audiences. This in itself was a revolutionary concept, as most classical ensembles take the "if we play it they will come" approach to their audiences.

Cyr spent the following year thinking about who, what, where, and how, arriving at the vision to expand the audience base for classical music and create new entry-points for young professional musicians and composers. Cyr's idea was that classical music could encourage social interaction just as rock 'n' roll does, without the formal trappings of a traditional concert experience. He spent the next year asking advice from professionals in a diversity of fields to find collaborators who shared the same vision.

First, Cyr moved the performance stage to non-traditional venues like the nightclub Le Poisson Rouge in Manhattan. Non-traditional venues provide a more casual social environment where young audiences can enjoy eating, drinking, and watching the performance at the same time.

Next, he decided to set very affordable ticket prices in order to attract his target audience—the young arts enthusiasts.

Third, Cyr sought funding from private foundations and government arts organizations to launch the Metropolis Ensemble. For a non-profit organization, finding enough supporters is the "life-blood to survival," according to Cyr. He described the Metropolis' supporters as a gathering of people who come from different walks of life, not just other musicians or his friends. When asked how he managed to persuade people to support his innovative concept, Cyr replied: "Asking for support is not about persuading anyone. It's just framing what you are doing in a way that resonates with an individual's values and passions."

Metropolis has successfully transformed the relationship between music, artists, and audiences with its new model for classical music. Esa-Pekka Salonen, principal conductor of the London Philharmonia, described the Metropolis Ensemble as "a great addition to the U.S. music scene." John Corigliano, a Pulitzer Prize winning composer, considers Cyr and his Metropolis Ensemble "the future of what we know as classical music."[3]

Cyr possesses traits that are common among successful entrepreneurs, such as creativity, determination, and perseverance. What makes him really different from others is his deep commitment to the quality of life and education of school children in his New York City community. One of Metropolis' projects is collaboration with the TEAK Fellowship, an organization that helps talented students from low-income families succeed at top high schools and colleges. Another Metropolis project is aimed at helping young composers hone their craft and gain exposure to the public, producers, and the larger music community.

Launching and sustaining a new venture takes a lot of hard work, and sometimes it helps to know that your efforts are appreciated. Working late one night in 2011, Cyr received an e-mail from Avner Dorman, one of the composers on the Metropolis roster. Metropolis' first studio album had just been nominated for a Grammy in the 'Best Instrumental Soloist with Orchestra' category.[4]

When asked whether the nomination changed his vision for the Metropolis, Cyr said:

It changes both everything and nothing. It definitely says to the world at large that what the Metropolis Ensemble is doing is respected and recognized on a national platform. This really helps our composers and performers and amplifies the reach of our mission. It also has given our organization, which is young and emerging, instant credibility and fantastic branding, especially among those who are less familiar with classical music. Does it lead directly to new opportunities—perhaps not—but it does open many new doors and it will be forever part of our story.

Every year we see more and more people dream about founding a new business. Some of them actually start it but only a few of them survive and even fewer of them finally make it a success. For Cyr, communication is critical to success. "The places where I've failed—and there have been many—seem to have been prompted or made worse by ineffective communication. In seeking solutions, the path has been always to understand how the failure occurred, and to find a way to communicate to others that you have learned how and why you made the mistakes in the first place, and that you've found a way forward."

There are several factors that make Cyr and the Metropolis Ensemble successful: a creative environment, an accurate identification of opportunity, innovative practices to fill the unmet needs in the classical music industry, and a "why not us?" attitude that liberates them to try new things. For Andrew Cyr, a revolutionary in the world of contemporary classical music, the Metropolis Ensemble and its young, enthusiastic audiences are proof that there is a vibrant future ahead.

The classical/contemporary music world and the commercial music world have much more in common than one might think. Entrepreneurs like Andrew Cyr are using creative thinking and problem-solving techniques to keep their music fresh and accessible to many different types of audiences. There are many opportunities for collaboration and innovative projects that bridge these two distinct musical genres. As you read the pages ahead, think like an entrepreneur to find unexpected ways to bring these communities together.

INDUSTRY ESSENTIALS: CONCERTS AND TOURING

Photodisc/Digital Vision/Getty Images

Meet Ruby

Ruby, lead singer of the occasionally Christian music band Evolution, was struggling to keep their show from self-destructing. Evolution was in the middle of a concert at a national youth ministry conference, and it was definitely an off night. Their guitarist Simon was in his customary foul mood, and it had everyone in the band on edge.

Suddenly Simon struck the opening chords to their song "Don't Look Down." Ruby froze, her mic half-way to her mouth. It was a great tune, but they had agreed only to play it at non-church gigs. The lyrics would offend most of the crowd here tonight. She glared at Simon, who gave her an angelic smile and kept right on playing. The rest of the band joined him, all eyes on Ruby. What would she do? If she sang the song as written, they'd be booed off the stage. If she just stood there everybody would know something was wrong. Ruby closed her eyes, brought the mic to her face, and . . .

Sure It's Thrilling, But Where's the Innovation?

What is it that makes live events so compelling? Nothing can come close to the feeling of being in the same physical space as the performers and other fans. It's an experience that ignites all our senses. You never quite know what's going to happen at a live event, as Ruby discovered.

Think back on all the concerts you've attended and name the *one* that defined you. Describe that moment during the show when you had a flash of recognition: "*This* is who I am, *now* I get what my life is about."

At first glance the live music sector may not seem to be a rich environment for innovation. The basic idea—musicians performing for an audience—has been around for hundreds of years in one form or another. The digital revolution has impacted it, of course, but that's not what drives this sector. The essence of a live show is personal, face-to-face communication between the artist and the fans. We may be able to watch a live event in real time on a movie screen or in an online social media environment, but so far we haven't figured out how to download the three-dimensional electricity and excitement we feel at a concert.

The entrepreneurs in the live events sector are the bands and artists themselves. The best of them find innovative ways to connect with their fans, keep their ticket prices reasonable, and give unforgettable, life-changing shows. In this chapter we'll take a look at how the industry works today and meet some entrepreneurial musicians who are shaping its future.

Entrepreneur Sound Byte: Livestream

Livestream co-founders Max Haot, Phil Worthington, Dayananda Nanjundappa, and Mark Kornfilt have a different point of view about the excitement of experiencing live events on digital social media. They've raised millions of venture capital dollars since 2007 to build Livestream.com, and have some very impressive content partners.

Resource: Visit the Crunchbase website where Haot talks about how Livestream got its start.

Let's get the big myth out of the way first. It's impossible to have a sustainable life in music without putting in the time to learn the craft. The idea that a band breaks overnight, or is discovered busking in the streets and becomes a star in a month is an enduring but misleading and romantic interpretation of reality.

The rapid pace of music discovery today can be a double-edged sword for emerging bands. A global buzz can erupt around an artist in lightning speed, making him a social media darling in a matter of days. However, the internet can thrust artists into the public spotlight long before they are ready to play a full set at the local bar, much less take on all that's required to have a solid music career.

To sustain a career over time, the band will need to put in the hours honing their skills at writing great songs, developing their unique sound, and playing out. What do they have to offer a crowded marketplace where thousands of other musicians toil to get attention?

Fans play a huge role in deciding which artists make it in today's music world. In Chapter 3 we talked about the explosion and significance of social media spawning a global 24/7 surveillance culture. Fans are not only interested in the artist's music—they want to know about the artist's lifestyle, family, vacations, struggles with their weight, and dust-ups with friends or ex-spouses. Artists are brands, companies in their own right that have to keep their customers—the fans—happy, informed, and hungry for the artist's products and services.

While it may seem pretty random that some bands make it and other don't, there are compelling similarities in the story of musicians who have staying power.

Knowing the basic business structure of the live industry will free bands to focus on entrepreneurial ways to propel their careers.

Getting Started

If you're a band, you need songs to play and people who will listen to them. Every band starts out playing small gigs, often with only two or three people in the audience—their moms and friends they've bribed with free drinks. It's a humble beginning.

At some point the band will decide they need to step up the pace and join the legions of musicians who hit the road. Touring is the proving ground for bands. If they can draw a crowd, get some buzz going, and keep those crowds growing, they'll get the attention of some pretty interesting music professionals.

DIY musicians will start their touring careers by doing all the work themselves—planning a (somewhat) logical tour route, finding the right size venues with the right vibe, and contacting the people at the venues who will book them. At this point in their careers, a DIY band will get a non-negotiable deal from the venue. That could be $5 per head from anyone who comes to see their band specifically (there's a sign-in sheet at the door), 20% of the door before the band's set, or "here's 30 tickets, keep the money from any you sell."[5]

Rich Nesin, a veteran concert tour and production manager in New York City, has this story about his band: "My own little cover band has yet to play a live gig . . . we're still rehearsing every week. Yet, there are neighborhood bars and restaurants that will pay us as much as five hundred dollars, if we can (a) play the night and (b) guarantee 20–25 people who will come in to eat, drink, and clap loudly for us. That's not a formula for success as an original band, but it shows the lack of negotiating at this level."[6]

Then there are all the other arrangements, like finding a van, someplace to sleep, and money to buy food and gas. Did we mention marketing? The only reliable way for DIY bands to get an audience is to put out the word themselves.

Everybody starts off this way, and it's a ton of work. At some point most bands hope to find somebody else to do this for them.

And who would that be, exactly? Many musicians work with industry professionals like artist managers and booking agents who are highly skilled at this very thing. The tricky part is agents get paid a commission, or percentage, of what the band earns on each gig they book. And a manager gets a commission on each gig *plus* other things the band makes money from, such as product endorsements, being on a TV show, and merchandise sales.

Why would any manager or agent in their right mind want to take on a band that's getting paid in free beer? The answer—most people wouldn't. Until they're actually making enough money from their music to share with a booking agent (traditionally a 10% commission) and a manager (15–20% commission), the band is on its own. Sounds harsh, but hey, it's a business, remember?

Let's do the math.

Hypothetical #1
Band gets paid $100 for a gig
10% to booking agent = $10
20% to manager = $20
Band splits $70 four ways = $17.50 each.

Hypothetical #2
Band gets paid $1,000 for a gig
10% to booking agent = $100
20% to manager = $200
Band splits $700 four ways = $175 each.

And the numbers above don't include the cost of gas for the van, eating, sleeping, paying taxes, and buying guitar strings.

Artists who have gained modest to medium success on their own but want to make a greater impact may be ready to sign on with industry professionals. In the next sections we'll see how the key players in live music work with artist entrepreneurs.

Entrepreneur Sound Byte: RootMusic

During his six years booking bands in venues from coffeehouses to auditoriums, J. Sider, a co-founder of RootMusic, recognized that musicians needed a simple, streamlined way to represent themselves on Facebook.[7] He envisioned an application that would enable bands and musicians to build more engaging fan pages for their music, touring dates, and merch. Sider launched RootMusic's BandPage in spring 2010. One year later it was the No. 1 selling app on iTunes, with DIY artists and superstars like Taylor Swift and Selena Gomez using the product.

Resource: Learn more at the RootMusic website.

On the Road

Many bands feel the first person they need on their team is a *manager*, the professional who oversees all aspects of an artist's career. This includes brand management and artist PR, touring and sponsorship, helping the band secure a recording partner, dealing with the band's personal problems, and long-range planning for their career. Managers typically receive 15–20% of the artist's earnings on concerts, merch, sponsorships, and other revenue streams.

Touring makes up a large part of professional musicians' revenue, and most (serious) bands tour for months or even a year at a time. An artist and her manager will decide how often to play each music market, in order to keep fans' interest high and avoid playing too soon in the same place.

Some bands employ a *booking agent* to get them paying gigs. In association with the artist, her manager, and attorney, the booking agent will route the tour, find the appropriate venues, and then negotiate dates and fees. Experts in the art of the deal, they have a vast knowledge of the venues and talent buyers in the regions where the artist wants to tour.

As the show begins to take shape artistically and technically, the booking agent will begin looking for venues along the projected tour route. The ideal venue will have a vibe that matches the band's brand and image, and can accommodate the technical needs of the show. Seating/standing capacity, stage size, tech specifications, fly space, wing space, loading dock, parking for trucks, lighting and electrical—these are among the many venue variables that a booking agent considers when routing a tour.

Another member of the artist's trusted inner circle is his *lawyer*. As bands begin to seek representation by a manager or booking agent, they will be expected to sign legal agreements stating the terms of each relationship. The band will need to consult a skilled entertainment attorney before saying 'yes' to anyone. In fact, a lawyer could even be the best guide to the right manager or agent for a band, as lawyers are paid to be an advocate for their client's goals. An experienced attorney who knows the music industry will be invaluable in giving her clients an unvarnished view of the pros and cons of all situations.[8]

Marillion in concert
Credit: Peter Wafzig/Getty Images Entertainment/Getty Images

Entrepreneur Sound Byte: Marillion

The British rock band Marillion were early adopters of the internet as a funding tool. American fans raised enough money—without the band's involvement—to fund Marillion's 1997 U.S. tour. More than a decade later, Marillion turned to their more than 30,000 fans and asked them to pre-pay for a future copy of the album so the band wouldn't have to give up the rights to a record label for their twelfth studio album. Within three weeks Marillion had received enough money to cover the costs of making *Anoraknophobia*.[9]

In some states, notably New York and California, professionals such as booking agents are required to have a talent agency license in order to procure work for performers. This is very important to remember if you are doing business in those two states and any others that require such a license.

Talent Buyers and Promoters

Strictly speaking, a *talent buyer* represents a client. That client can be

- A bar or a club

- A concert promoter like Bowery Presents, which utilizes many venues of all sizes and in a variety of markets

- A giant corporation, such as Microsoft, that wants talent for large meetings or events

- A college or university, acting as the 'middle agent' between an act and the school

- A larger venue. Nowadays more and more venues are getting into self-promoting, or even co-promoting with local promoters, as the competition to bring business into a venue gets stiffer.[10]

Talent buyers have valuable knowledge of the entertainment tastes and ticket buying habits of their communities. For the highly competitive top level of artist shows, buyers in the same market often bid against one another in order to get the superstar to play in their venue. This can lead to some lopsided contractual revenue splits with the artist, as the buyer tries to outbid his competitors.

A *promoter* has one of the riskiest jobs in the industry. She must sell enough tickets to cover the costs of putting on the show, plus make a bit of profit to stay in business. Occasionally, a show will have such weak advance ticket sales that the artist, manager, and promoter decide to cancel, rather than risk losing money and causing embarrassment for the artist. Sometimes, however, it's necessary to carry on and, in order to make the house look fuller, the promoter will paper the house (give away tickets in special promotions).

There is a saying in the live concert industry that sums up the risk that promoters take: "There are no bad shows, only bad deals." The show itself could be great, but its success is all in the deal. If everyone makes money, then the promoter made the right deal. Financial success isn't always based on what the sellable capacity is of the venue, but rather what the act is worth in a specific market.[11]

A promoter/talent buyer may own the venue(s) he books, or he may just rent various spaces as needed. Owning a venue opens up a lot of possibilities for additional revenue, including parking fees, food and beverage, merch, and renting out the venue when the promoter isn't using it.

David Hinds of Steel Pulse at the 2003 New Orleans Jazz Festival
Credit: Ebet Roberts/Redferns/Getty Images

"Steel Pulse played in Austin last spring, a market we had been struggling in for years," explains Rich Nesin, the band's production manager. "Rather than go to the same room we had been doing poorly in, we took a smaller guarantee for a smaller room (one that was harder to put our show into) for a Monday night, to boot. We walked out with double the money, a packed house, and a story to rebuild on in the future."[12]

Online Tools to Help DIY Artists

Technological innovation has created a veritable online industry of platforms and business tools for DIY musicians. Artists who are savvy and persistent about marketing themselves, and have realistic expectations about what these tools can do for their career, can certainly use them to increase their chances of being discovered and build a stronger fan base. But converting page views and video hits into significant income is unlikely for most bands that are just getting started. DIY sites and services are best viewed as effective *distribution partners*, helping bands strengthen their brand and get music and merch into the hands of people who want to buy it.

Third Rail Logo. Artist: Ariel Fitterman

Your Turn: Third Rail and Evolution

Jared (Third Rail) is friends with Ruby (Evolution). After weeks of talking, Jared and Ruby manage to persuade their bands to go out on a short DIY tour together as a co-bill this summer, when they can get time off from their day jobs. They're in the process of hammering out the basics of the tour—preliminary tour route, number of days on the road, mode of travel, how to market the tour, and the estimated costs. Then they will split up the jobs between them and get to work.

Reflect and discuss:

- What bands are touring today that you think are entrepreneurial? Use their innovations as a starting point for blue-sky thinking about the Third Rail/Evolution tour.
- What specific DIY online tools do you recommend for the Third Rail/Evolution tour? Explain how you made your choices, what they will cost to use, and how the bands will benefit.

Ticketing

Ticket pricing begins with the promoter, who bundles it into her offer to the booking agent along with other parts of the deal, such as the artist's guarantee and percentage-of-ticket-sale structure (i.e., $200,000 plus 90% of ticket sales). To get to the range of individual ticket prices for the event, the promoter will prepare a mathematical model of potential expenses and revenue. The *expense* factors include the guarantee for the artist, production costs, venue rental, sound and lighting, local stage labor, catering, show specific needs (i.e., advertising and marketing, barricades, security, rentals, and piano tuner), and variables such as insurance costs. The *revenue* factors include an educated guess on what sort of business the act will do and what the promoter feels comfortable risking.[13]

The booking agent, artist, and manager evaluate the offer based on a variety of factors, such as: is it the right venue and the right promoter? How does it compare to competing offers? Is the ticket price within the acceptable range of the artist's fans?

Occasionally, an artist will set a maximum ticket price for his tour, or a flat price across the tour, and the promoter's offer must then be submitted to fit that mold. But that is the exception more than it is the rule. Young bands with a college-age fan base, metal bands, and concerned artists like Bruce Springsteen are the most likely to take that route.[14]

It is easy to see how the ticket pricing and all other parts of the deal go round in circles for a period of time before an offer gets formally confirmed. But eventually, one will arrive at numbers everyone can agree with and a show gets confirmed.[15]

The ticketing industry is made up of primary and secondary sellers. Buying a ticket from a primary seller, such as the venue itself, means the ticket came from the original ticket inventory.

The secondary ticket marketplace is made up of tickets that are being resold by someone who purchased them from the original ticket inventory. There are formal secondary sellers (StubHub.com, TicketLiquidator.com) and informal sellers (friends, people standing outside the venue on the night of the show, or ticket scalpers who try to sell their tickets for more than face value). The price of a ticket on the secondary market is set by the seller and his best guess as to what price the market will bear. If the show is sold out and demand is high, people without tickets may be willing to pay a lot more than the price on the face of the ticket in order to get into the show.

Artists try to find the sweet spot in ticket pricing so they can cover the costs of producing the show and touring, yet still keep the price affordable for their fans. Some artists and managers are disparaging about the secondary ticket market. They worry that it is driving up the cost of tickets for fans who can't find tickets on the primary market. Managers also resent the fact that the artist does not receive a penny of the money from a ticket that is sold on the secondary market.

On the other hand, some industry people argue that the secondary market is a fair way to determine ticket prices. It's like an auction: whoever is the highest bidder gets the ticket.

The secondary market is becoming much more of a grey area. Nowadays, many artists participate in it by selling VIP ticket packages which include special souvenirs, meet and greets, photo ops, and early entry into a venue. This is done through the fan club or by ticket agencies that specialize in such things. Almost all of these deals give the fan something more than they would have gotten for the same price ticket on the open market.[16]

The average price of a ticket to one of the top 100 tours was $60.68 at mid-year 2012,[17] up from $25.81 in 1996, according to Pollstar, the live music industry trade journal. This increase has far outpaced the rate of inflation. Michael Rapino, president and CEO of Live Nation, thinks that concert tickets have been underpriced for many years. He says "musicians are just benefiting from the same trends that have enriched other superstars, like athletes and actors."[18]

Entrepreneur Sound Byte: What Not *to Do as an Entrepreneur*

Most states in the U.S. permit ticket scalping. But it is illegal to use computer programs on ticketing sites intentionally to bypass the security software intended to prevent wicked non-humans from buying hundreds of the best seats the minute they go on sale. These professional ticket scalpers, called brokers, add a hefty fee to the face value of the ticket, thereby gouging and frustrating the fans who want to be in decent seats near the artist.

A (now defunct) multimillion-dollar ticket-scalping company called Wiseguys lived up to its name when its computer program hacked into a Bruce Springsteen ticket selling site in 2008 and "bought almost half of the 440 general admission tickets closest to the stage."[19] Wiseguys' high-speed computers were shut down and their owners were fined for deliberately evading the online security safeguards of several major ticket-selling companies.[20]

 Take a look at the TicketNews website to see which companies are the top primary and secondary ticket sellers this week.

The Money Comes In

Money from ticket sales is the primary source of revenue in the live sector. In recent years the contractual split of ticket revenue between the artist and the promoter/buyer has moved aggressively to favor the artist. The most common split is 85:15, where 85% of the ticket revenue goes to the artist and the remaining 15% to the talent buyer. Some super-star artists can command revenue splits of 90:10.

Sergey Goruppa/Shutterstock Images

However, revenue from ancillary sales—merchandise, food, beverages, parking, sponsorships, ticketing surcharges—has become increasingly important to the financial success of a show. Ancillary revenue is now so vital to the profit or loss of a show budget that a promoter and venue may go ahead with a weak-selling show because they know that the band's fans will spend a lot of money on food, beverages, and merchandise.

Even some of the ancillary revenue that was traditionally the promoter's is now shared with the artist, such as parking fees and ticket surcharges. An interesting fact that most people don't realize is that ticketing companies, such as TicketMaster, return some of the ticket surcharge revenue to the promoter or venue, in exchange for being the exclusive provider of ticket services.

 What information about customers does a ticketing company collect at the point of sale? How could this information be used (for good *and* evil) by (1) the ticketing company, (2) the promoter/venue, (3) the artist, and (4) others?

The details of how a band will be paid are spelled out in a performance contract, along with the technical and hospitality requirements for putting on the show. Some DIY bands are nervous about asking for a formal contract because they're afraid the talent buyer will just laugh and find somebody else to play. That does happen, of course. But it's always better to have even the simplest written agreement outlining everyone's expectations. This helps avoid misunderstandings, shouting matches, and lawsuits.

There are a few typical deal types for how bands are paid: a flat fee, known as a guarantee; a straight percentage of ticket sales; and various combinations of the two, the most common being a fee plus a percentage of ticket sales.

Bands also make money on sales of their merchandise after the venue takes its percentage cut. For early-career bands, T-shirt and CD sales often make the difference between making or losing money on a show.

Third Rail Merch. Artist: Ariel Fitterman

The U.S. Performing Rights Organizations for authors and composers (PROs) are ASCAP, BMI, and SESAC. They license venues that host live events. Chapter 6 provides detailed information on how musicians make money from this source.

Entrepreneur Sound Byte: MAC Presents

Corporate sponsorships for tours are opportunities for creative thinking and innovation. Matching a band with a corporate brand can lead to partnerships that add marketing muscle to the tour, and maybe even some cash. Entrepreneur Marcie Allen negotiates high-profile sponsorships between the world's leading brands and artists. She launched her company MAC Presents after many years as a booking agent and promoter. Allen explains how sponsorships work in a video interview with Billboard.biz:

 Watch video: a billboard interview with Marcie Allen.[21]

 Have fun with contract riders at SmokingGun.com. Discuss what you find with your colleagues. Why do you think bands put so many detailed requirements in their hospitality riders?

Jill Sobule
Credit: Jerod Harris/WireImage/Getty Images

There is a lot of data packed into a concise Pollstar Boxoffice Summary. Look closely at the columns of information. Which bands had the highest percentage of seats sold? What company was the most frequently named in the Promoter category? Did any bands sell less than 50% of the venue's capacity?

BOXOFFICE | SUMMARY

Date	Artist Facility/Promoter	Support	Tickets Sold Capacity	Gross
05/26/11	**Miley Cyrus** Foro Sol / Mexico City, MEXICO / OCESA / CIE		22,370 52,073 / 42% / 220.00 - 1,800.00	$1,775,433 Pesos (20,444,870)
05/26/11 05/27/11 / 2 shows	**Rammstein** Palacio De Los Deportes / Mexico City, MEXICO / OCESA / CIE		31,962 19,947 / 80% / 380.00 - 780.00	$1,627,364 Pesos (18,739,793)
05/14/11 05/15/11 / 2 shows	**Ricky Martin** Palacio De Los Deportes / Mexico City, MEXICO / OCESA / CIE		20,590 15,610 / 65% / 300.00 - 1,890.00	$1,395,510 Pesos (16,069,900)
05/25/11 05/26-29 / 8 shows	**"Wicked"** Orpheum Theater / Omaha, NE / (In-House Promotion)		17,338 2,509 / 86% / 39.00 - 148.00	$1,285,827
05/20/11	**Kenny Chesney** Aaron's Amphitheatre At Lakewood / Atlanta, GA / Live Nation / The Messina Group/AEG Live	Billy Currington Uncle Kracker	18,864 18,864 / 100% / 39.50 - 79.50	$956,359
04/28/11	**Lil Wayne** Rexall Place / Edmonton, AB, CANADA / Live Nation	Nicki Minaj Rick Ross / Travis Barker / Mix Master Mike	9,350 13,135 / 71% / 49.75 - 150.75	$893,562 Canadian (867,435)
05/18/11 05/19-22 / 8 shows	**Cirque du Soleil - "Alegria"** The Huntington Center / Toledo, OH / Cirque du Soleil		14,456 3,979 / 45% / 28.00 - 94.00	$831,566
05/10/11	**System Of A Down** Rexall Place / Edmonton, AB, CANADA / Live Nation	Gogol Bordello	12,366 13,585 / 91% / 25.00 - 69.50	$790,236 Canadian (747,169)
04/01/11	**The Strokes** Madison Square Garden Arena / New York, NY / The Bowery Presents	Devendra Banhart	14,485 14,485 / 100% / 54.50	$789,433
05/21/11	**Kenny Chesney** Amphitheater At The Wharf / Orange Beach, AL / Red Mountain Entertainment / The Messina Group/AEG Live	Billy Currington Uncle Kracker	9,348 9,348 / 100% / 50.00 - 120.00	$726,790
05/19/11	**Kenny Chesney** Colonial Life Arena / Columbia, SC / The Messina Group / AEG Live	Billy Currington Uncle Kracker	12,726 12,726 / 100% / 25.00 - 79.50	$723,687
05/24/11	**Bob Seger & The Silver Bullet Band** The John Labatt Centre / London, ON, CANADA / Live Nation		7,997 8,986 / 89% / 73.25 - 248.25	$631,484 Canadian (597,069)
04/02/11	**LCD Soundsystem** Madison Square Garden Arena / New York, NY / The Bowery Presents	Liquid Liquid	13,297 13,297 / 100% / 35.00 - 49.50	$627,191
05/18/11	**Ricky Martin** Arena VFG / Guadalajara, MEXICO / OCESA / CIE		7,639 10,780 / 70% / 300.00 - 1,680.00	$594,727 Pesos (6,848,540)
05/22/11 05/23-24 / 3 shows	**Elvis Costello** Beacon Theatre / New York, NY / Live Nation		8,346 2,782 / 100% / 45.00 - 85.00	$575,850
05/29/11	**Rammstein** Arena VFG / Guadalajara, MEXICO / OCESA / CIE		11,070 11,584 / 95% / 350.00 - 880.00	$572,309 Pesos (6,590,380)
05/08/11	**Ricky Martin** Valley View Casino Center / San Diego, CA / AEG Live / Goldenvoice		6,817 6,872 / 99% / 46.00 - 166.00	$523,282
05/24/11	**Mötley Crüe** Palacio De Los Deportes / Mexico City, MEXICO / OCESA / CIE	Buckcherry	8,893 16,456 / 54% / 260.00 - 1,500.00	$520,392 Pesos (5,992,538)
04/08/11 04/09-10 / 04/15-17 / 6 shows	**Barry Manilow** Paris Las Vegas / Las Vegas, NV / AEG Live		4,312 1,024 / 70% / 65.00 - 250.00	$508,051
05/11/11	**"A Night Of Broadway Stars"** Victoria Theatre / Newark, NJ / Covenant House	Neil Berg / Rita Harvey / Ron Bohmer	505 505 / 100% / 1,000.00	$505,000
05/06/11	**Jeff Foxworthy / Bill Engvall / Larry The Cable Guy** Qwest Center Omaha / Omaha, NE / Outback Concerts	Reno Collier	8,875 10,206 / 86% / 25.00 - 59.50	$488,795
05/19/11	**Ricky Martin** Poliforum Leon / Leon, MEXICO / OCESA / CIE		4,261 9,000 / 47% / 690.00 - 1,900.00	$470,082 Pesos (5,413,200)
05/21/11 2 shows	**Chelsea Handler** Beacon Theatre / New York, NY / Live Nation	Brad Wollack Josh Wolf / Heather McDonald	5,512 2,756 / 100% / 80.50 - 90.50	$459,721
05/22/11	**Kylie Minogue** Colosseum At Caesars Palace / Las Vegas, NV / Concerts West / AEG Live		4,062 4,103 / 99% / 69.50 - 225.00	$445,612
05/21/11	**Kid Rock** Rexall Place / Edmonton, AB, CANADA / Live Nation	The Trews	7,597 12,010 / 63% / 29.50 - 69.50	$443,189 Canadian (419,036)
05/22/11	**30 Seconds To Mars** Coliseo de Puerto Rico / San Juan, PR / Lincoln Road Productions		6,297 7,034 / 89% / 45.00 - 75.00	$415,033
05/14/11	**Stevie Nicks** Colosseum At Caesars Palace / Las Vegas, NV / Concerts West / AEG Live		4,073 4,075 / 99% / 49.50 - 175.00	$388,211
05/07/11	**Ricky Martin** Nokia Theatre L.A. Live / Los Angeles, CA / AEG Live / Goldenvoice		6,688 6,920 / 96% / 46.00 - 166.00	$359,094
04/22/11	**Neil Young** Providence Perf. Arts Ctr. / Providence, RI / The Bowery Presents	Bert Jansch	2,754 2,836 / 97% / 49.50 - 250.00	$326,839
05/10/11 05/11-15 / 8 shows	**Rain - A Tribute To The Beatles** Brooks Atkinson Theatre / New York, NY / MagicSpace Entertainment / Jeff Parry Promotions		3,761 829 / 56% / 35.00 - 120.00	$313,916
05/18/11 05/19-22 / 3 shows	**"Disney On Ice"** St. Pete Times Forum / Tampa, FL / Feld Entertainment		14,504 8,002 / 50% / 16.00 - 75.00	$308,927
04/29/11	**Avenged Sevenfold** Mohegan Sun Arena At Casey Plaza / Wilkes-Barre, PA / Frank Prod. / Knitting Factory Entertainment / Stan Levinstone Presents	Three Days Grace Sevendust	8,044 8,044 / 100% / 25.00 - 44.75	$307,283
04/12/11 04/13/11 / 2 shows	**Chris Cornell** Town Hall / New York, NY / The Bowery Presents	William Elliott Whitmore	5,608 2,804 / 100% / 35.00 - 65.00	$301,680
05/23/11	**Foo Fighters** Mid-America Center / Council Bluffs, IA / Jam Productions	Motorhead Biffy Clyro	6,218 5,575 / 94% / 46.50	$289,137
05/28/11	**Chelsea Handler** Colosseum At Caesars Palace / Las Vegas, NV / Concerts West / AEG Live		4,106 4,109 / 99% / 49.50 - 99.50	$287,047
04/09/11	**Arcade Fire** 1stBank Center / Broomfield, CO / (In-House Promotion)	Local Natives	6,666 6,666 / 100% / 40.00 - 45.00	$267,105
05/13/11	**Armin Van Buuren** BMO Centre / Calgary, AB, CANADA / The Union Ltd.	Blake Jarrell	4,135 4,500 / 91% / 49.95 - 99.95	$266,946 Canadian (252,398)

BILLY OCEAN, McPhillips Station Casino, Winnipeg, Manitoba, May 11

Reprinted with permission

Entrepreneur Sound Byte: Singer-Songwriter Jill Sobule

Singer-songwriter ("I Kissed A Girl") Jill Sobule decided to go the DIY route when her label, Artemis Records, shut down. In 2008 she launched a website, JillsNextRecord.com, to raise money for her next album. Sobol created a rewards structure for donors who contributed $10 to $10,000. After collecting more than $85,000 from fans who funded the project, Sobule released the album *California Years* in 2009 on her own record label, Pinko Records.[22]

And the Money Goes Out

DIY bands usually won't have much of a budget for show design. However, once a band starts to break and adds industry professionals to its team, it will try to find the money to add production value to its shows.

As they begin tour discussions, the artist and manager will have a vision of what they want the tour to look like. If they have the budget, a high priority will be hiring a variety of professionals, such as a production manager, stage and lighting designer, choreographer, and costume designer to help them put together an exciting show for the fans, consistent with the artist's brand. Shows can be very complex, with high-tech and sophisticated special effects and literally tons of equipment. The design of the show influences its cost which, in turn, is a large factor in deciding how tickets will be priced.

The technical complexity and size of a show will determine how many trucks will be needed to haul everything that is traveling on the tour. Key players on the road may include an accountant, the tour manager, production and stage managers, riggers, carpenters, sound and lighting techs, backline techs (they used to be called roadies), bus and truck drivers, and possibly security personnel, production assistants, plus dressing room and wardrobe assistants. Local crews, provided at each venue, may include stagehands, truck loaders, more riggers and electricians, audio and lighting specialists, as well as spotlight operators.[23]

From a promoter's perspective, the costs that go into putting on a show can include the artist's fee, venue rental and production costs, advertising, PRO licenses, ushers, security, insurance, catering, box office, technical crew, and equipment rental. These costs can and do fluctuate if problems arise during load-in or load-out of a show. If ticket sales fall short, the promoter may lose money on the event.

The Future of Music Coalition is a national non-profit organization specializing in education, research, and advocacy for musicians. It is an important forum for discussion about issues at the intersection of music, technology, policy and law.[24] In January 2012, Future of Music released the first results of its Artist Revenue Stream project at MIDEM, an international music industry trade show. The ground-breaking survey was undertaken to better understand how artists earn money from music. More than 5,000 U.S.-based musicians took part in the Artist Revenue Stream survey.[25] All genres of music were represented, as well as full- and part-time musicians, teachers, orchestral and session musicians, TV and film composers and songwriters.

Resource: Visit the Future of Music Coalition website for details and some surprises.

Opportunities Ahead

I. Festivals have been a mainstay of the summer music scene in Europe for many years. Over the past few years the number of U.S. and Canadian festivals has grown substantially. Are we approaching festival-market saturation? What musical niches still remain to be filled by festivals? Is summer the best time (or perhaps the only time) to hold a music festival? What do you think some of the challenges could be in staging a large outdoor festival?

Here are suggested research sources to get you started:

- Festival-outlook.consequenceofsound.net
- NME.com/festivals
- FestivalSearcher.com
- FestivalFinder.com

II. The $17 billion global musical instruments and products industry is a vibrant sector of the music industry, yet it is often ignored in music business textbooks. Explore the Appendix in this book, 'A Visit to 2012 Winter NAMM, the World's Largest Music Products Tradeshow,' to learn how deeply and widely this area of the marketplace affects the entire music industry.

CONCLUSION

Demand for live concerts has remained strong, even during the prolonged economic downturn. Artists who are entrepreneurial understand how to position themselves in the market, stay close to their fans, and give thrilling shows. Most artists whose career attains some level of success decide to build a team of supporters, which could include a booking agent, artist manager, or business manager. It is important for artists to be well matched to the venues in which they perform. The talent buyer and concert promoter play key roles in introducing new artists and supporting tours.

The ticketing area of the live concert business abounds with opportunities for the entrepreneurial thinker. The financial risks involved in touring can be daunting, but the face-to-face excitement of a live concert makes it worthwhile for both artists and fans.

Talking Back: Class Discussions

If you had been Ruby in the opening story of this chapter, what would you have done, both in the moment on stage and after the concert? Discuss the pros and cons of your ideas. Do you think what happened that night could affect the tour of Third Rail and Evolution?

Web Links

- Crunchbase
  crunchbase.com/company/livestream
- RootMusic
  RootMusic.com/
- TicketNews
  Ticketnews.com/ticket_industry_rankings
- A billboard interview with Marcie Allen
  Macpresents.com/2010/06/10/branding-sponsorship-strategies-from-mac-president-marcie-allen/
- Future of Music Coalition
  futureofmusic.org/article/research/artist-revenue-streams-resources.

CHAPTER 10

Recorded Music

CHAPTER OVERVIEW

In this chapter you will learn about the challenges and opportunities for recording companies in the digital age. You'll examine the record industry's failures and reflect upon lessons learned. Third Rail and other DIY artists are finding entrepreneurial ways to market and monetize their recorded music without a third-party record label. You will help them decide if DIY is a long-term strategy or something to pursue while they're waiting to get signed.

KEY TERMS

- Arbitron
- Big Champagne
- Cross-collateralization
- DRM
- Expanded (or 360) rights deal
- IFPI
- Independent labels
- Joint venture
- Loss leader
- Major labels
- Monetize
- Nielsen Soundscan
- Ownership vs. access
- RIAA
- TEA

An Entrepreneur's Story: Meet Pomplamoose

Pomplamoose is a quirky DIY collective of Bay Area musicians, anchored by Nataly Dawn and Jack Conte. They broke onto the scene in 2008 with irreverent music videos shot in Conte's house. Pomplamoose quickly became indie music blog darlings for their humorous covers of original pieces, Beyoncé's "Single Ladies Put A Ring On It," and Lady Gaga's "Telephone."

If you haven't met the band, take a look at Pomplamoose.com.

We don't know if Pomplamoose will have lasting success as a band, but they were working very hard at it in 2012. Pomplamoose's approach to its career shows the basic elements of entrepreneurship: opportunity, creativity, innovation, and a 'What if?' attitude. They also appear to be enjoying themselves and have consistently charted their own path, steering clear of the 'industry.'

In 2008, it was unusual to release new songs as homemade videos on your own website. Staging the production as a weekly show to playfully introduce a song was innovative and compelling. Fans tuned in, bought the homemade soap the band sold, and purchased the new song each week. The model harkens back to old-time serial radio shows, movies, and books where a new chapter or development in an ongoing plot or series was released over time.

Pomplamoose is generous with advice to other DIY bands about how to make a living without a label. Dawn and Conte focus on playing music, keeping fans engaged, and treating Pomplamoose like a business. They produce, write, market, tour (a little), and do all the paperwork involved in running the band. For the covers they record, Pomplamoose buys mechanical licenses online, which is a straightforward and simple process. "That's the thing," Dawn says. "People think that all of these things have to be done by geniuses behind huge desks or at the top of skyscrapers, but you can just go online and do it yourself."[1]

Pomplamoose has its own YouTube channel and participates in YouTube's Partner Program. Independent artists can generate ad revenue on YouTube from their videos, plus get help with rentals, concert management, and analytics.[2]

Says Dawn: "I mean, if you can't just do it all yourself, then you do need help. If, for example, you're somebody who writes songs, like Lady Gaga, and you need everything, you know, that's going to make you Lady Gaga, then you need a big, fat label. But if you're just a band, I don't think we're in an era anymore where you need that sort of major backing."[3]

Pomplamoose is forging a career as a DIY band. Thanks to changes in technology, abundant online resources, and supportive fans who want to be engaged in an artist's career, the DIY path is appealing for some artists. Reflect on the personal and professional characteristics that Nataly Dawn and Jack Conte possess. Do you think they eventually will need to sign to a big label to move to the next phase in their career? The information in the pages ahead will shed some light on Dawn and Conte's options and guide you in your thought process.

Lady Gaga
Credit: Newspix/Newspix/Getty Images

INDUSTRY ESSENTIALS: RECORDED MUSIC

Surprises Ahead

Whether your music collection is on vinyl, cassette tapes, CDs, a USB stick, or somewhere in the cloud, capturing and preserving performances for repeat playing is big business. Global recorded music revenues totaled $15.9 billion in 2010.[4]

That's a lot of money. But it's only half of what this sector of the music industry was worth in 2000. Have record labels, the once-mighty gatekeepers to the music industry, been dealt a mortal blow by the digital revolution?

You may be surprised to find a chapter in this book devoted to record labels. After all, we're focusing on the future of music as you, the next generation of entrepreneurs, will define it. Why bother exploring an industry that has been in distress for more than 10 years, and has spent a lot of effort to maintain the status quo?

You may be even more surprised to learn that three out of four independent musicians say they want to be signed to a major label deal, according to a recent ReverbNation poll.[5]

How can this be? Why would any self-respecting artist want help from The Man to make it in today's music industry?

There seems to be a disconnect in the music industry between reality and conventional wisdom. We read how the internet has leveled the playing field for musicians, and that anyone with 1,000 fans,[6] a Facebook page, and a YouTube channel can have a career. Clearly, these media-fueled beliefs are in sharp contrast to what many indie artists feel they need to be successful.

Myth Busting

The truth may be more nuanced than we think. So let's look at a few facts and do some **myth busting.**

Myth: Nobody buys music anymore.
Busted: In 2011, global physical recorded products (such as CDs and vinyl) accounted for $10.2 billion, while global digital sales brought in $5.2 billion.[7]

Myth: Traditional broadcast radio is dead.
Busted: More than 90% of all Americans aged 12 and older listen to the radio each week—a higher penetration than television, magazines, newspapers, or the internet, according to Arbitron, a media, marketing, and consumer research company that collects listener data on radio audiences.[8] Listeners tune in to AM/FM radio for more than two hours a day, according to Bridge Ratings, a company that provides audience measurement services for radio.[9] As of March 2011 there were 14,728 full power radio stations: 4,778 AM, 6,533 FM, and 3,417 educational FM. Additionally, there were 859 low power FM stations.[10]

Myth: Most musicians don't want or need a record label deal.
Busted: Who knew? In 2011, ReverbNation and Digital Music News surveyed 1,869 hip-hop, rock, pop, and alternative musicians. The results? Three out of four indie musicians want to be signed to a record label. Their top choices were all major labels: Sony Music Group, Def Jam (owned by Universal Music), Atlantic (owned by Warner Music), and Geffen (owned by Universal Music).[11]

So it looks as if record labels still matter—for now.

In 2012, the major labels were Universal Music Group (which has recently purchased EMI recorded music), Sony Music Entertainment (which has recently purchased EMI Publishing), and, Warner Music Group. They are called 'major' as opposed to 'independent' because of their size, scope, and influence in the market. They are enormous, multi-national companies. In exchange for signing artists and guiding them as they record and release their music, labels own the rights to the artists' recordings. Majors own publishing companies (Universal Music Publishing, Sony ATV, Warner Chappell Music, and EMI Music Publishing), which share control of the rights to the underlying composition with the songwriter. They own major and independent distribution companies that put physical product into retail stores. Majors have very effective marketing departments to support their artists' record releases. And, in recent years, labels have become involved in non-recording aspects of their artists' careers, including concerts, merchandise, and endorsements through expanded rights deals.

Third Rail Logo. Artist: Ariel Fitterman

DIY or Try to Get Signed: A Third Rail Story

Jared and Walter don't see eye to eye on what Third Rail should do about their recordings. They have about 30 original songs so far, and have been working on making an EP so that they have a tangible product that says to people, "Hey, this is what we sound like now." Jared thinks they should try to get signed to a label—any label. Walter doesn't agree, and wants to stay the DIY route.

The band has been really busy lately playing shows all over the region. One thing they've noticed is that whenever they play to strangers (which Walter thinks is the best litmus test for music because friends cannot be trusted for honest answers), people seem to love them. Third Rail played at a music festival last week. When they started, there were 20 people in the audience at their stage. When they were done with their first song, an additional 100 or so people had walked over to see what was going on.

Jared is convinced that this proves the band has traction and is ready to get a lawyer's help in finding them a record label.

"This DIY stuff is going nowhere," says Jared. "We need to be working with people who can advance our careers. Playing at random venues wherever we can get booked is no kind of strategy."

Walter shakes his head. "Why would a label sign us? They only take on bands that already have a career going. Besides, record labels are losing money like crazy."

"*You're* the loser," Jared says. "I met this guy who told me . . ."

"Yeah, that's right," interrupts Walter sarcastically. "You're always meeting some guy who has all the answers. I'm telling you, the DIY thing is the only reliable way these days. We've got to stay in control of our music. We don't need someone at a label telling us what to do."

Jared shoves an amp out of the way, glares at Walter and stomps out of the room, cursing. Walter shouts after him, "Don't bring this up again unless you've got solid ideas about how some Suits at a label could help us."

Frustrated and hungry, the guys call it a day, and head over to their favorite hangout for beers.

The Challenges

Even though digital music sales topped physical sales for the first time in 2011, the popularity of digital music has not come close to making up revenue lost from the growing obsolescence of CDs. Labels are working hard on many fronts to stop the financial hemorrhaging and increase their earnings from licensing and non-traditional sources. But it's an uphill battle.

Below is a playlist of the key challenges facing the industry. As you read these, look for ways to turn the negatives into positives. 'Flip' the problems to find creative solutions and unexplored income sources for the recording industry.

'Music Should Be Free': The Psychological Devaluation of Music

It's true that more people are listening to more music than ever before, but most of us aren't paying to do so. Only about 5% of people who download music have acquired it legally, according to the *International Federation of the Phonographic Industry* (IFPI), an organization that represents the recording industry worldwide, with a membership of some 1,400 record companies in 66 countries.[12]

Illegal file sharing has long been blamed as the greatest threat to the recorded music sector. But in fact, the real problem may be the psychological devaluation of music.

Has music become 'trivial?' *New York Times* music critic Jon Pareles suggests that the act of separating music from its packaging—and the rituals associated with unpacking it, placing it on a music player, and hearing it through decent-quality audio speakers—has made songs feel less valuable. Digital music is limitless, ubiquitous. It's just another folder on a computer screen that can be tossed away without much thought or difficulty, despite the effort that musicians put into making the recording.[13]

Perhaps recorded music in the form of CDs has joined printed receipts, magazines, and recipe books in the rubbish pile that the paperless-age internet has created.[14]

 What opportunities can you find in the challenge above if you flip it as you learned in Chapter 2? Try these:

- Music should not be free.
- Free should be music.
- Music should be expensive.

Music as Bait

When retail merchants deeply discount music to lure customers into their stores to spend money (known as a loss leader), it contributes to the perception that music has lost value in the eyes of the consumer.

Ownership vs. Access

With the convenience and affordability of cloud storage and streaming options, many customers are migrating to services that provide *access* to music, as they move away from *owning* music. This leaves the recording industry struggling to figure out how to monetize a significant consumer behavioral change.

Culture Clash

Record labels approach new ideas from a bottom-line, 'What's in it for us?' mentality. This is common for any business that's focused on making profits and keeping shareholders happy.

Conversely, the technology community—especially start-up tech businesses—approach things from a 'What can we make it do?' perspective, looking to find the best experience for the user.[15]

This noticeable culture gap between the tech and music industry communities is problematic for everyone, especially consumers who expect their new tech gadgets to provide easy access to music.

Many digital tech music start-ups are frustrated by the labels' unwillingness to license their music at financial rates that entrepreneurs consider reasonable for creating a "sustainable, scalable music business," states Zahavah Levine, director of content partnerships for Google's Android unit.[16]

The record labels "tend to not look at these things as opportunities, but as someone taking advantage of their business," said Fred Goldring, a former top music lawyer who invests in media and technology companies. "Until they figure out how they're going to deal new technology on their terms, they don't make a move. And when they finally do, it's usually too late."[17]

 Practice the entrepreneurial mind-set; consider the hidden opportunity in the story above.

It's a Singles Business

To complicate matters, consumer habits have changed: when people *do* buy music, they prefer to purchase single tracks and build playlists, rather than buying albums. Record labels make more money selling albums, so this change in consumer behavior is a major factor in the labels' revenue slide. It's even impacted the traditional way of counting and charting sales. Nielsen Soundscan, the company that tabulates record sales, created a new category called Track Equivalent Albums (TEA) to tabulate the number of digital tracks sold by a given artist. TEA is computed by dividing an artist's total number of digital tracks sold by 10, the average number of tracks on standard albums.[18]

The Lights Went Out

You may have noticed that nearly all the small, independent record stores, the large music outlets such as Sam Goody, Tower Records, and Virgin Megastores, and even music-friendly bookstores like Borders have gone dark. Consumers don't need to go to a bricks and mortar store to download a digital music track. Physical music distribution—putting records into retail stores—was one of the areas where record labels excelled. It's now a shadow of its former self.

Consider: Where *is* there still need for distribution? How are labels exploiting that opportunity?

Cost to Break a New Pop Act

Let's do the numbers. The IFPI gives us a major-label example of the "Typical Label Investment In A New Pop Act" in the following chart:

Artist Advance	$200,000
Recording	$200,000
3 videos	$200,000
Tour support	$100,000
Promotion and marketing	$300,000
TOTAL	$1,000,000[19]

Major labels might provide this level of support to an artist whom they believe could be the next Beyoncé or Kanye West. They'll spend close to a million dollars developing their product (an album) before it even goes on sale.

To put this in perspective, if the artist turns out to be the next mega pop-star hit, the label will recoup its investment and the artist will see a profit. But the numbers are tough—most new acts don't come anywhere near the wattage of Beyoncé or Kanye. It's a guessing game as to what will catch on. The A&R process—finding and signing new artists—is like throwing spaghetti against the wall to see how much will stick.

Even Lady Gaga wasn't an overnight sensation. American radio stations resisted her European-influenced, four-on-the-floor beat. Jimmy Iovine, the chairman of Gaga's label Interscope Geffen A&M Records, said it took six months to get her first single, "Just Dance," on the air. It rose quickly to the top of the charts. "The masses will accept something new," Mr. Iovine said. "It's the people in between who will fight you."[20]

Reading the Fine Print in Those Pesky Contracts: A Sale or a License?

Contracts signed before 2000 usually had no provision for splitting revenues from digital sales between the label and artist. This tiny problem blew up into a major concern for labels after Universal was sued by Eminem's producers over how royalties were computed for his digital sales.[21] The labels felt that sales from online retailers like iTunes should be counted as a sale. Artists and others who earn royalties from records argued that digital sales should be counted as a license, which would result in a substantially larger royalty payment. How much money are we talking about? "Recording contracts vary, but most artists get a royalty of 10 to 15 percent for the sale of a CD, minus many deductions, while licenses pay a royalty of 50 percent and may not be subject to the same deductions."[22]

Battle over Song Rights after 35 Years

There is a provision in the revised U.S. Copyright Act of 1976 that gives creators of works of art the right to reclaim ownership of their work after 35 years if they have assigned it to a third party and meet certain conditions. This 'termination right' affects recordings from 1978 and later, and could be a major revenue loss for labels. As mentioned in Chapter 7, Loretta Lynn, Tom Waits, Bob Dylan, and Charlie Daniels are among the artists who have filed to regain control of their work from the labels that own the master recording. The labels claim the artists were 'employees' when they made the records, and therefore not eligible to regain rights they never possessed in the first place. States Kenneth J. Abdo, an entertainment attorney, "This is a life-threatening change for them [the labels], the legal equivalent of internet technology."[23]

Still in Free Fall

IBIS World Reports projects that recorded music revenue will fall at an annual rate of 4.16% through 2015.[24] When will the record industry hit bottom?

Someone *Had to Dream It Up*

Using tin foil wrapped around a 4" diameter drum, the inventor and innovator Thomas Edison launched the record industry in 1877. One year later, the technology evolved to etching grooves on wax cylinders. By 1909 the industry had moved from cylinders to recording disks,[25] and the sound revolution was underway.

The Way It Used to Be

A Good Ride While It Lasted

Eric Garland, the CEO of Big Champagne, had these words of wisdom in a recent article from *Music Row* magazine:

> Nothing is everything. There is no ONE thing that is everything. That is a really profound shift in a long and established history for the recorded music industry. Everything has always been about one thing. We all bought vinyl. Then we all bought cassettes,

then CDs. There was always one monolithic product or experience that defined the business both culturally and financially. What the last 10 years are . . . remind[ing] us is that there will not be one thing. There will be many things, and perhaps all together those streams will resemble something that is a sustainable business.[26]

The traditional role of record labels was A&R (finding new artists and music for them to record), selling records, and licensing recordings for other uses. Over the years the industry moved from a collection of small independent labels started by entrepreneurs to an industry dominated by large, corporate-owned companies. Indie labels often served as a kind of farm league, where the entrepreneurs did the heavy lifting involved in discovering and nurturing new artists. After reaching a certain level of success with the indie—measured in record sales or radio airplay—many of the artists moved on to the bigger machine of the majors.

Sometimes major labels bought entire indie labels, or merged with other companies and acquired former indies. As the record business consolidated, lawyers and business people replaced the entrepreneurs who had founded smaller labels.

The majors controlled nearly all the aspects of their business, owning recording studios, publishing companies, employing their own A&R people and producers, manufacturing the records, distributing them to retail outlets, and marketing their artists through retail and other commercial partnerships. Labels had a cozy relationship with radio stations. (Remember the bad old days of payola? These were financial incentives in the form of bribes paid to radio stations to place certain songs in on-air rotation to saturate the market and boost ratings.) As long as people bought records, listened to music on the radio, and waited patiently for record labels to find and introduce new artists and songwriters, everything was great—for the recording industry, anyway.

The Key to Power in the Traditional Music Industry Is Ownership of Intellectual Property

The labels owned the rights to nearly all of their artists' master recordings. From a business perspective this made sense. Labels invested time and money into developing artists and getting their music reproduced and distributed without knowing for certain that they would be able to sell their only product: recordings. But from an artistic perspective, some artists and fans chafed at the restrictions labels placed on the music. Labels controlled nearly everything about the artist's records, including what songs would go on it, who would produce it, how the record would be marketed, and where it would be sold. In exchange for label support, artists signed multi-year contracts committing to a specific number of new album releases.

The labels also controlled how, when, and if a new album was released. It often took years for many artists and labels to complete a recording. Sometimes the artist's main supporter at the label quit or was fired before completing the album, leaving the artist and her project on the shelf, unreleased. Occasionally the public's tastes in music changed, so the label cut their losses and didn't release the album at all.

Artists were paid a percentage of the money (a royalty) that the labels received from selling the CD. Labels acted like a combination parent and loan officer, bankrolling the costs of recording, marketing, distributing, and tour support. The artist paid back the label not with real cash, but from future sales of her records.

Few people outside the recording sector knew that artists received royalty checks *only* if they'd sold enough albums to cover (recoup) the label's investment costs. When an album didn't sell well, the debts from the first release would be added to the cost of the next album release. This accounting practice is known as cross-collateralization. An artist could be in debt to his record label for years, or even forever, if his records didn't sell enough to cover the label's financial investment.

Labels used their massive marketing muscle to push artists into the mainstream media. Many of those artists became superstars. Labels were very successful at 'turning spins into purchases,' meaning that the more airplay a song received the more copies of the record were sold. It was not widely known that these very successful artists, selling millions of records, made up for the 9 out of 10 artists on the label whose record sales never covered the label's costs.

In the past there was a clear distinction between the indies and majors. The biggest differences were money (majors have more), size (majors are mammoth), marketing and distribution power (majors spend more), artistic freedom for recording artists (indies give more), and time spent to develop careers (indies win, hands down).

Today the bright line between indies and majors has disappeared. In the late 1990s major labels began investing in and doing joint ventures with indies that created cost- and profit-sharing deals. Now the three majors own independent distribution networks, including Alternative Distribution Alliance, RED, Fontana, Caroline, and IODA, which are used by indie labels to get their records into the physical retail marketplace.

The following story shows how complex and murky the distinction between indies and majors can be.

In 2007, indie label Octone Records entered into a joint venture with major label Interscope Geffen A&M (IGA) to launch a new label, A&M Octone. (Background: IGA was formed in 1999 when indies Geffen Records and A&M Records were merged into Interscope Records. Universal Music Group owns IGA.) As part of the deal, A&M Octone acquired Sony BMG Music Entertainment's interest in OctJay, a joint venture between Sony BMG and Octone. (Background: Sony and Bertelsmann Music Group merged briefly in 2004 but split up in 2008.)

Resource: To unravel these mysteries, read the Harvard Business School case study "A&M/Octone Records: All Rights or Nothing?"

What Is a Hit Song?

Traditionally, a hit song was defined by its position in charts such as Billboard, which were compiled using record sales and radio airplay data. Today, the definition of a 'hit' is more a matter of interpretation than a chart number. New voices in the marketplace, such as Next-BigSound and Big Champagne, measure a band's buzz by compiling data from social media, Twitter, and other online sources.

The process of making a hit song is complex and expensive. Take the song, "Airplanes" (Parts I and II), for example. It took a year for it to morph from a demo by two college students into a massive global success for artists B.o.B., Hayley Williams, Eminem, and Rebel Rock/Grand Hustle/Atlantic Records in 2010. "Airplanes" claimed fifth on Billboard's Top Selling Songs in 2010, selling more than 4 million digital downloads by December 2010, according to Nielsen Soundscan.[27] The song was nominated for a 2010 Grammy in the Best Pop Collaboration With Vocals category.[28]

Discussion: The making of "Airplanes" required exquisite care and handling of myriad details, including legal clearances, licenses, artistic temperaments, egos, career building, money, and the tastes of a fickle public. Do you think the size of this hit would have been possible without major label backing? Why or why not?

The Opportunities: Why Labels Still Matter—For Now

Although there have been many challenges, there are some bright spots emerging for the industry, as shown below. Each titled subsection describes a possible growth area within the music industry. Look for opportunities for Third Rail as they try to figure out their recorded music strategy.

What's in a Name?

"We don't call ourselves a record company," Warner Music Nashville president John Esposito said at the June 2011 Billboard Country Summit in Nashville. "It's entertainment companies more than it is record companies."[29]

Perhaps reconfiguring itself as something much more comprehensive than a record label is the recording industry's biggest opportunity. Whether this actually is a new approach to artist care and feeding, as the labels claim, or simply a way to reach into other industry sector pockets for money to replace lost CD sales revenue, the fact is most labels now require artists to sign expanded rights (or 360) deals.

Think about the importance of a name. Imagine you are the CEO of a grocery store chain. Try re-defining your business in terms of how you want your customers to experience shopping in your stores. Example: Starbucks defines itself as a lifestyle and ambiance business, not a coffee business. They're selling customers on the idea that they should consider Starbucks as their alternative office or living room. Now apply this thinking to an aspect of the music industry.

Rappers Kanye West (left) and Jay-Z perform during a New Year's Eve show at The Cosmopolitan of Las Vegas January 1, 2011 in Las Vegas, Nevada Credit: Ethan Miller/WireImage/Getty Images

In April 2008, entrepreneur Shawn "Jay Z" Carter partnered with Live Nation, one of the largest producers of live concert tickets in the world, to create Roc Nation, a full-service entertainment company.

Roc Nation artists are signed to expanded-rights deals, also known as 360s, which are all encompassing and include ticket sales, record sales, and endorsements. The company's services include artist, songwriter, producer and engineer management; music publishing; touring and merchandising; film and television; new business ventures; and a music label. The label is only one part of the services Roc Nation offers and, perhaps tellingly, it's listed last on its webpage.[30]

Getting Paid For 'Free'

For people who claim that no one will pay for something they can get for free, consider the bottled water industry. Americans spend approximately $11 billion a year on a product that is safe to drink and readily available without charge in homes, offices, and stores all over the country.[31]

The labels have beaten back every excuse consumers gave for not buying music. Gone is the ball and chain of Digital Rights Management (DRM). Online music stores have improved audio to near-CD quality; and the number of songs available to download keeps growing, particularly obscure back catalogue.[32] Labels have even given us easy-to-use free, legal streaming services like Spotify, Rhapsody, and eMusic.

Wired writer Paul Boutin exhorts us all to realize we've won the revolution. To every fan who still cries 'but music should be free!' Boutin replies: "It's art! Friends, a song costs a *dollar*. Every download sends [money] straight to the band. If . . . you can still rationalize not [paying], then maybe there's another reason you're still pirating music: You're cheap."[33]

Time will tell if labels can succeed at weaning customers off unauthorized downloading sites, in favor of the legal online options.

Subscription Services May Be Catching On

Subscription-based streaming models provide users with more access and features, and fewer (or no) annoying ads. Most of the free providers use the 'freemium' model, which allows consumers to select a higher level of service for a nominal monthly subscription rate. This gives labels three revenue streams: royalties from licensing their music to the provider, such as Spotify, Slacker, and Rhapsody; a share of the ad revenue; and a share of the subscription revenue.

According to U2's manager, Paul McGuinness, "Spotify could be the future model, but it will have to demonstrate that not only can it collect revenue from its users and advertisers, but that it will fairly pass on those sums to the artists, labels, and publishers."[34]

Your Parents

You knew they were handy to have around, but listen to this: one of the largest age groups in the country—people 45 years and older—is a dominant force in the industry, responsible for 33.7% of all music purchased in 2009. The re-release of obscure back catalogue music, mentioned above, is one of the reasons people over 45 are coming back into the marketplace. Also, people over 45 are less likely to seek unlicensed music online than the industry's traditional target market, 15–24 year olds.[35] Call your folks and thank them for supporting the recorded music industry.

Music-Based TV

The prime-time American television shows *Glee* and *American Idol* are money-pumping machines for record labels. Revenue to record labels from TV deals grew 15.3% in the period 2005–2010, and is expected to continue to grow.[36]

Music Publishing

For the labels that own publishing companies, the resilience of the publishing industry through troubled economic times and the digital revolution is welcome news. In 2011, the U.S.-based publishing companies owned by the majors—Universal, Sony, and Warner—produced more than half of the $4.9 billion in music publishing revenue.[37]

Yet Again, Apple Innovates and the Recording Industry Benefits

In 2011, Apple harnessed cloud storage to come up with a clever way to get people to actually pay for the music they've acquired illegally. iTunes Match allowed consumers to pay a modest annual fee for convenient digital music storage and access to their music collections, including songs that were not purchased. Apple gave the record labels more than 70 percent of the annual fee, in addition to the licensing fees Apple paid the labels. Many other cloud storage services have joined the party; perhaps labels will see a significant new revenue stream.

Help from Governments Regarding Illegal Downloads

The Edge and U2 Manager Paul McGuinness
Credit: Dave Hogan/Getty Images Entertainment/Getty Images

Many recording executives fault ISPs for allowing illegal downloading to occur. ISPs have declined to cooperate in cracking down on illegal file sharing, citing concern over potential competitive disadvantages. One of the most vocal critics of the ISPs' hands-off behavior is Paul McGuinness, U2's manager. His calls for global action may finally be producing results. France, the UK, Ireland, New Zealand, Taiwan, Chile, and other countries are considering or have passed legislation enacting a graduated response by ISPs to infringing customers. ISPs will take increasingly tough measures against customers who engage in illegal file sharing after being warned to stop.

Baidu, China's largest search engine, signed its first licensing agreement with major labels in 2011 to allow legal and free downloads. Baidu had formerly been a conduit to stolen content on other sites, known as 'deep linking,' which is a massive problem for labels in China and other countries with ineffective methods of copyright enforcement.

Mobile Music, Games, and Video

As more consumers opt for smartphones, the demand for licensed content continues to grow. Record label partnerships with mobile phone operators offer customers instant access to a wide variety of entertainment, including music, games, and video. LiveWire Mobile and RealNetworks are two mobile music providers that work with mobile operators such as Vodafone, Telecom New Zealand, and Sprint.

A Little Help from Their Friends

The record industry has strong trade organizations that support and promote the creative and financial health of the major music companies, including the IFPI and the RIAA. Independent labels join forces for more clout in the marketplace under the umbrella of the American Association of Independent Music (A2IM), which has more than 270 label members.

 ### Lessons Learned

For entrepreneurs, failure is an opportunity to learn in business and in life. How did the record labels fail in the early days of the digital revolution? How can they re-invent themselves and take advantage of those lessons learned?

Here are a few topics to include in your discussion of lessons learned from the recording industry's failures:

- Customer relations
- Product value
- Strategic planning
- Disruptive technologies
- Building a healthy musical ecosystem.

DIY Record Labels: Short- or Long-Term Strategy?

The type of artists who come out of the traditional major label system—such as superstar mainstream pop and Top 40 acts—are fine up to a point, but fans also want the pleasure of discovering artists who don't fit the big-business model. The DIY scene is where the wacky, status quo-busting, genre definition-challenging artistic action is.

As Brian McTear from Weathervane Music said in Chapter 1, a healthy music ecosystem includes all the necessary working parts to bring music to our culture. These include the people making, recording, and promoting the music, and the fans who see themselves as vital contributors to the creative process. It's up to you, the future leaders of the entertainment industry, to help create an environment where more indie musicians can support themselves through their music.

The people and ideas in the next few pages will get you started in imagining a world where DIY artists thrive.

Hip-Hop Blogs Mean Business

Hip-hop blogs and websites are fertile ground for discovering mixtapes of artists in this genre who are unlikely to be heard on radio. Blog surfing on sites like Fake Shore Drive, Cocaine Blunts, LiveMixTapes, and Digital Dripped help artists like Rick Ross find musicians from remote corners of the world, as he did for his Warner Music-released album, *Self Made*.[38] Mixtapes often circulate for years on the internet, creating opportunities for DIY musicians to get attention.

Innovation from a Major Label in India

Live from the Console is a monthly showcase of emerging bands from all over India. It's an initiative by Day 1 (Sony Music's independent label in India) and Oranjuice Entertainment, a successful Indian concert and festival producer.

The Console is actually a portable 'venue' that is built from scratch in alternative spaces for each showcase. The very first show took place in July 2011 in a long-shuttered room that had been used for large orchestras and films at Mehboob Studio in Mumbai. The venue was set up in one day and, with no advertising or publicity, the show was filled to capacity after people started Tweeting about the gig. Check out some of the DIY artists who played: Vimeo.com/26906593.

Get Signed to an Energy Drink

As we saw in Chapter 3, businesses have understood for a long time how associating their brand with music can speak effectively and directly to the consumers they want to reach. Some companies have moved beyond the traditional means of

Kristian Dowling/Getty Images Entertainment/Getty Images

support—tour sponsorship and licensing songs for ad campaigns—and created actual recording labels and studios to support indie musicians. Often the advertising and production budgets of these companies exceed the support that major labels can give their artists.[39]

Starbuck's started its own record label in 2007 in partnership with Concord Music Group.[40] The energy drink company Red Bull launched Red Bull Records in 2007 by building a recording studio in Santa Monica, California, to record indie bands for free.[41] Converse Rubber Tracks is the 5,200-square-foot space in Brooklyn that holds a sleek recording studio built by the beloved sneaker company in 2010 for indie musicians.[42]

Mountain Dew has an online label called greenlabelsound.com. Stella Polaris is both a label and the biggest annual chill-out event in Denmark. Proctor and Gamble named its label after a deodorant—Tag Records.

Toyota's Kia Soul has assembled an entire artistic collective to promote its cars. Kia Sole's website explains: "We got together with a group of really cool people to celebrate Music (Janelle Monae), Film (Jonas & François), Design (Jeff Staple), and

Entrepreneur Spirit (Jeffrey Kalmikoff). We call them The Soul Collective."[43] During the summer, fans can catch shows with bands like MGMT, Silversun Pickups, and Santigold. In a purely commercial twist, the only way to get tickets is to test-drive a new Kia Soul.

Levi's Jeans, Dr. Martens, Bacardi—they're all eager to embrace under-the-radar DIY musicians, hoping that some of the bands' hip, cool fans will become their fans, too.

What if . . . the Fans Started a Record Label?

Entrepreneur Roie Avin launched the first totally online record label run 'by fans for fans.' Pick The Band lets fans decide who gets 'signed' and which single gets released. Fans also help design the artwork, select the tour stops, and make the videos for the artists.[44]

 What unmet need did Avin identify and pursue? How does Pick The Band make money? Apart from the fact that fans are involved in making decisions, how else does Pick The Band's business model differ from that of a traditional label?

Share Your Music and Widen Your Artistic Community

Sound designer Alex Ljung and artist Eric Wahlforss created SoundCloud to address an unmet need in the music track-sharing community.

"We both came from backgrounds connected to music," said Ljung. "And it was just really, really annoying for us to collaborate with people on music—I mean simple collaboration, just sending tracks to other people in a private setting, getting some feedback from them, and having a conversation about that piece of music."[45]

An elegant and straightforward solution to an irritating problem, SoundCloud has become a full-fledged, easy-to-use, collaborative publishing tool used by indie artists and high-profile bands alike.

DIY Distribution

Jeff Price, Gary Burke, and Peter Wells launched TuneCore based on their belief that every artist should have access to distribution and receive 100% of the revenue from the sale of her music without having to give up any of her rights.[46] In 2009, TuneCore partnered with Interscope/A&M/Geffen Records, owned by Universal Music Group, to launch Interscope Digital Distribution (IDD). As a bonus for indie musicians who secretly crave a major label's attention, Interscope/A&M/Geffen's top A&R people monitor the IDD service as a way to discover new talent.[47]

Trent Reznor
Credit: Martin Philbey/Redferns/Getty Images

Get Advice from Trent Reznor of Nine Inch Nails

In case you missed this blog post on NIN's website, check out Trent Reznor's thoughts on "What To Do as a New or Unknown Artist." Here's a preview: "If you are an unknown/lesser-known artist trying to get noticed or established . . . Forget thinking you are going to make any real money from record sales. Make your record cheaply (but great) and GIVE IT AWAY. As an artist you want as many people as possible to hear your work. Word of mouth is the only true marketing that matters."[48]

Help Selling Your Stuff

DIY artists who don't agree with Mr. Reznor can use sites like Bandcamp to sell music and merchandise. Bandcamp allows artists to monitor their sales statistics live, do tie-ins and bundled offers with physical and recorded product, and even answer fans' questions. Bandcamp currently takes a 10–15% commission on sales, which is about the same as a typical label distributor's cut.[49] Check out bandcamp.com/pricing to see how artists get paid.

Third Rail Logo. Artist: Ariel Fitterman

Third Rail *Still* Can't Agree: DIY or Flirt with a Label?

Walter meets up with Sam and Cody to tell them about the blow-up he had with Jared. Walter is surprised to hear Sam say he was thinking along the same lines as Jared, and wanted to bring up this idea to the rest of the band.

"I think a label might be what we need to take us to the next level," Sam admitted. "Someone who can put us in front of more people, get our music on the radio, maybe even give us some money for touring or new equipment."

"How can some label help when they're busy going out of business themselves?" demands Walter.

"You've got a point," concedes Sam. "But I can't name another band in the state like us. We're way more commercial sounding than most rock bands and way less angry and metal than the 'rock' bands calling themselves punk, metal or indie."

"I don't see our problem as 'how do we stand out' or 'cut through the clutter' of all the other bands," says Cody. "I see it more like who is the right group to get us and know what to do to bring us into the public eye."

Walter shakes his head in disbelief. "Where is this coming from? I thought we were solid as a DIY band."[50]

 Getting all parties 'on the same page' is a challenge for any organization, company, or band. If you were a consultant or the band's manager, how would you help Third Rail work out this important issue?

Entrepreneur Sound Bytes: Ariel Publicity and Topspin Media

Ariel Hyatt founded her music PR company, Ariel Publicity, before the digital revolution began. Seven years ago she realized that pitching stories to online portals was much more effective and faster than working with traditional media—newspapers, magazines, TV, and radio. She re-vamped her business, and today Ariel Publicity is exclusively a digital PR firm and an educational experience wrapped up in one. Her bi-weekly ezine and YouTube series "Sound Advice" help musicians learn how to market themselves in the crowded music marketplace.[51]

Another example, Topspin Media was established by entrepreneurs Peter Gotcher and Shamal Ranasinghe to help indie artists connect directly with their fans. Through Topspin, bands can build a customized online store and sell media, merch, and tickets, plus receive data analysis on all the transactions to help them understand where to focus their marketing efforts for maximum results.

Reflect

How could an indie band sign with a label in some kind of relationship that feels less exploitative than a traditional label deal? What strategies could artists use when trying to maintain more artistic and financial control of their music if they sign with a label?

CONCLUSION

The recording industry faces many challenges in the digital age. Changes in consumer habits, disruptive technologies, and a slow start out of the gate to embrace digital media have lead to massive changes in how the labels do business. Having one's own label may be a good strategy at the beginning of a career, but most bands still want to have access to the power and resources of a major label. DIY bands like Third Rail need to be entrepreneurial in marketing and distributing their music. At the time of this writing, labels still exert a big influence on the marketplace even as they struggle to stabilize the crippling effects of illegal downloads and the psychological devaluation of music. The music industry is no longer about 'one thing'— records. This is the time for creative problem solving as we work toward creating a healthy musical ecosystem.

Third Rail Logo. Artist: Ariel Fitterman

Talking Back: Class Discussions

Third Rail needs some strategic advice. What's next for them? Should they start their own record label, or try to get signed? Discuss the pros and cons of all their choices involving recorded music. Create a detailed plan for achieving the goals you've set for them.

Web Links

- Harvard Business School case study
  http://cb.hbsp.harvard.edu/cb/web/search_results.
  seam?Ntt=octone&conversationId=89990

CHAPTER 11

Digital Music Services

CHAPTER OVERVIEW

In this chapter you will meet some of the entrepreneurs whose creativity and innovation are blurring the boundaries between television, radio, games, smartphones, video, and music. You'll use your creative problem-solving skills to explore new media ventures. A short history of music's old media friends—TV and radio—will conclude the chapter. Thinking like an entrepreneur, you will devise a strategy for Third Rail as they try to achieve their digital media goals for the band.

KEY TERMS

- Arbitron
- Branded social video
- Freemium model
- Interactive and non-interactive webcasting
- Media convergence
- Music ownership vs. music access
- Music supervisor
- NARIP
- Terrestrial (as in radio and TV broadcasting)

Two Entrepreneurs' Stories: Panos Panay (Sonicbids) and Perry Chen (Kickstarter)

Here are two entrepreneurs who recognized opportunities to help DIY musicians and built successful innovative digital music services.

Panos Panay got the inspiration to start Sonicbids as a direct result of his experiences as an agent. "Every week I was getting buried with press kits from many, many talented artists who wanted to get booked by us, but we just could not afford to take on. So I thought—and this was 1999 or so—'if you can trade stocks and buy books online, why can't you get a gig or book a band using the web?' I quit my job, maxed out my credit cards, and launched Sonicbids on February 25, 2001."[1] Panay saw an unmet need in the music industry, and founded one of the first companies to help artists and concert promoters find each other.

 Watch video: Panos Panay gives advice to indie artists.

Kickstarter founder Perry Chen wondered if there was a way to know whether or not anyone would buy tickets to a show *before* he went to the expense of mounting a production. He asked, "what if we flip the usual model? Let's sell tickets *first*, and stage a show only if there's enough of a market." From this creative problem-solving approach, Chen launched the online crowdfunding site, Kickstarter in 2009.[2] Users define a specific project, set up rewards for contributors, and announce a dollar target with a deadline for raising the money. If they don't meet their target, no money changes hands.[3]

 Watch video: Perry Chen talks about Kickstarter on TechCrunch's Founder Stories.

Both Sonicbids and Kickstarter are veteran companies in the online digital music world. Many ventures rise and fall in record time, owing to this now-crowded marketplace. As you read the pages ahead, compare these two companies to the newer ventures in digital music services. Can you predict which ventures will still be around in a year or two?

INDUSTRY ESSENTIALS: DIGITAL MUSIC SERVICES

Convergence: The Media Buzzword

One of the most exciting areas for entrepreneurial innovation in the digital revolution is the convergence of media—TV, video radio, smartphones, games, social media, advertising, and apps. The internet is not only revolutionizing the business of media; it has upended the way we think about and interact with it, as well.

Our digital life is being emancipated from devices and moved into the cloud. Remote storage has changed the way entertainment products are delivered and consumed, freeing up space on personal gadgets so we can stream music and video without worrying if we'll have enough capacity.

The convergence of media services has blurred the distinction between them, giving customers multiple entry points to information, entertainment, music, lifestyle, news, and social sharing.

Almost every day another new and exciting tech gadget or service hits the market. The breathtaking pace of newer, faster, sleeker devices, game-changing technologies like the smartphone, and the fleeting popularity of internet media startups only add to the chaos.

Traditional media may still control a lot of the money, but today innovation is occurring in the digital media space. A roiling mixture of creativity, culture, and technology is driving this area, and music plays an important role. Creating content for cross-platform media is a large global industry and a huge opportunity for entrepreneurs.

The Economics of Digital Music, or How Does the Money Flow?

The public's enthusiasm for digital music services represents the ongoing transition from music ownership to music access. The economic impact is significant. *Purchases* (ownership) return a small but noticeable chunk of money. *Streams* (access) result in much less money, with revenues measured in parts of pennies.

David Harrell, guitarist for the Chicago indie rock band The Layaways writes a blog called Digital Audio Insider. In his July 2011 posting, Harrell explained on his blog that the band's average payout from Spotify (a service that offers music *access*, not ownership) from August 2009 to March 2011 was 0.2865 cents per stream.[4] Compare that to the roughly 70 cents the band would receive for each 99-cent download (a music *purchase*) on a service like iTunes. In this model, it would take 244 streams to earn the same amount of money for the band as one download.[5]

Even within the digital webcasting world, the rates vary. Spotify is an interactive music service, and pays more to license its music from rights holders than non-interactive webcasters do. If The Layaways' music had played on a non-interactive webcaster like Pandora during that time, they would have received only 0.01 cents per stream, compared to the .02865 cents per stream from Spotify.[6]

The lesson here? Bands make more money selling their music than streaming it, but fans often choose streaming over ownership.

So what *is* the secret of making money from digital distribution of music? Some feel it might be advertising. Robert Pittman, Clear Channel's Chairman of Media and Entertainment Platforms, explained that advertising dollars come slowly to new media and services, based on his experience at MTV and AOL.[7]

"The good news is that we [Clear Channel] have billions of dollars in advertising revenue from our terrestrial radio business," stated Mr. Pittman. "So even though it's not big business now, we can afford to invest and grow our online audience. We have the deep pockets to wait it out."[8]

Great for Clear Channel, but not such welcome news for entrepreneurs starting new digital media ventures.

Billboard's Glenn Peoples sums up the new economics of the digital music era this way: "We're increasingly living in a streaming world but we want download royalties. When the download market was growing, people wanted to return to the boom years of the CD. But in ten years, streaming revenues will be the norm. Just as today's young musicians grew up without CD revenues, musicians of the future will know little else than streaming royalty rates."[9]

McMillan Digital Art/Photodisc/Getty Images

Are We Suffering from Digital Media Overload?

Some weeks it feels as if a new digital media service is launched every hour. While it's exciting to be among the first to try out a new app or online product, the sheer volume of these new businesses can be overwhelming. Has the digital music media sector reached a saturation point, with too many choices for the plugged-in? Is the relentless pressure to be active on the newest networks causing social media burnout?

As many as 95% of new products introduced each year fail, according to Cincinnati research agency AcuPoll. That's true even when these new products or services are rolled out by big, deep-pocketed companies and attached to well-known brands.[10]

Why do they fail? Some products are fussy or complicated to use. Many are too similar to others in the marketplace. Often it's bad timing of the new product launch, or the product doesn't live up to the marketing hype. Some new companies run out of money trying to compete with category leaders. And then there are just plain confusing ideas—Coors bottled *water*? Who wants to drink water from a *beer* company?

The Digital Media Hotness Rating Scale

Imagine that you've just read about the launch of a new digital entertainment product. Spend three minutes answering these eight questions to decide if the product has merit and utility.

1. Can you describe the business in 10 words or fewer?
2. What need is it addressing, what problem is it solving, and for whom?
3. Who's the target customer?
4. Is the product or service fun, easy to use, and interactive?
5. How does it make money?
6. What opportunities does it open up for partnerships with other companies, media, or markets?
7. What's the coolest thing about this new product or service?
8. Do you think it's going to become a must-have product or service? Why or why not?

Reflect

Use the Digital Media Hotness Rating Scale on two new companies you've heard about recently. Compare your scores with those of your colleagues. Predict which companies will survive, and which will fail due to lack of customer attention.

Today's Music Tastemakers

For Third Rail (and the rest of us) cutting through the digital noise of new companies and helping bands and fans find each other is a major entrepreneurial opportunity. With millions of people discovering new music and artists in television shows, films, games, and ads, it's easy to see why so many musicians work hard to get the attention of music placement experts.

These experts, known as music supervisors, are responsible for bringing Feist, M.I.A., Yael Naim, Ingrid Michaelson, Moby, and many others to public attention via music placement in non-traditional formats.[11] Supervisors have become today's talent scouts and tastemakers, replacing radio station DJs, record label A&R departments, and record stores.[12]

Three of the best-known music supervisors are Jon Ernst for *The City* (MTV), Kier Lehman for *Entourage* (HBO), and Alexandra Patsavas for *Gossip Girl* (CW).[13]

 Watch video: Alexandra Patsavas discusses her job as a music supervisor on Beta TV.

The technologists who find, tag, and 'fingerprint' the songs that go into recognition databases like Shazam are a less visible but equally important group of music tastemakers. These music spotters seek out artists from all kinds of sources, hunting down albums in dusty record shop bins and touring the clubs listening for popular songs being played by DIY artists. Toiling in relative obscurity, music technologists are the engines behind recommendation services such as Pandora, iTunes Genius, and Last.fm.

Blogs and ezines also serve as curators of the new music scene, wielding influence in the business of music discovery, news, and reviews. These include Consequence of Sound, Idolator, Brooklyn Vegan, Pitchfork, Gorilla vs. Bear, Spinner, and Stereogum—just a few of the most influential in 2011. If the blog scene is too overwhelming, check in with HypeMachine, a music blog aggregator that selects the 'best' of the bunch.

Time for a Strategy: A Third Rail Story

Third Rail Logo. Artist: Ariel Fitterman

The members of Third Rail are trying to work out a strategy for promoting the band using digital media. For once, all four members agree that something has to change, and that they're the ones to do it.

"I think we should make a music video," says Cody. "I can check into how to do that."

"I've been working on an idea for an app that is killer," says Jared, "but I have no idea how to make money with it. I'll do some research."

Walter offers to take the lead on figuring out how to get the band's music into video games.

Sam says he thinks better when he's in a group, so he's taking Phoebe and Earl out for coffee to get their advice.

"Let's meet back here at 5 to compare notes," says Sam. "And while you're at it, see if you can think of ways to find the money to pay for all these great ideas."

Creative Problem Solving for New Media Ventures

Every new venture is the result of an entrepreneur looking at a problem or unmet need and coming up with a solution. In the next section we'll flip the usual problem-solving process by starting with the *solution* and working backwards to imagine the problem-solving process used by entrepreneurs whose new companies solved some very thorny problems.

Will the Internet Kill the TV Star?

The problem: It's spring 2011 and controversial commentator Glenn Beck has a problem. His polarizing, often inflammatory yet highly rated TV show on Fox News is coming to an end after two and a half tumultuous years. Beck is a cultural icon, has a massive following, and a strong brand. Yet his show has cost Fox 400 advertisers who were skittish of Beck's style and political views.[14]

His solution: Launched in fall 2011, Beck is betting that his fans will migrate with him when he turns his popular TV show into its own internet subscription enterprise, GBTV. Richard Greenfield, media analyst for BTIG Research, believes that Beck is trading the near-term financial rewards available in the traditional media ecosystem for full ownership of his show in the new medium of subscription internet TV. Beck will no longer be at the mercy of "the content gatekeepers at the major media companies; [he will gain] complete creative control to exploit content across all platforms globally, which could create far more value over time."[15]

Hypothetical problem-solving techniques: Beck looks at the elements of his problem and sees:

- Highly emotional and often abrasive personal style
- No-holds-barred political comments
- Millions of fervent fans
- Controversial content that frightens away some advertisers
- New options for distribution of his show
- A recognizable brand.

He then asks, "How can I keep my fans engaged, have control of my own creative content, find ways to cover my costs besides advertising, and take advantage of the new media options available?" His solution: GBTV.

Tomorrow's Television

The problem: It is 2007, and the broadcast television industry is watching in horror as the music industry is ravaged by changing technology and consumer habits. TV execs know they're only a bigger bandwidth away from the same fate as their smaller music-file brothers, who are hemorrhaging content to illegal downloading.

Their solution: Hulu, billed as tomorrow's television, launched for public access in March 2008. It is a joint venture by three of the majors in broadcasting: NBC Universal (Comcast), Fox Entertainment (News Corp), and ABC (Disney). While Hulu's parentage may sound similar to iTunes' relationship with the major record labels, iTunes is different in two significant ways: Apple is neither a music company nor is it owned by music companies, and Apple uses music to sell more of its core product, electronic devices.[16]

Hypothetical problem-solving techniques: The TV industry execs sat around a big table and asked "What did consumers want from the music industry that they didn't get?" They came up with flexibility, pricing, control, and portability.

Then they asked themselves: How can we give television consumers

- More flexibility in how they watch our shows?

- Expanded pricing options, including how can we make it *feel* free?

- More control over their television experience in general?

And their final, million-dollar question was: What other technologies are out there for airing our shows?

Epilogue: Hulu has helped free television from the tyranny of the TV set. However, its creators put it up for sale in 2011. What seemed like a great idea dissolved into the predictable executive suspicion of new technology, control of creative property, and fear of jeopardizing lucrative content deals with cable companies.[17]

Your Turn: Finding Common Ground

The problem: It's 2009. How can we combine two seemingly unrelated companies and launch an innovative and useful product or service? The two companies are:

- Intel, a computer processing-chip manufacturer.

- Vice, an irreverent and provocative music-TV-magazine-merch conglomerate.

Their solution: The Creators Project, founded in 2010, is a global Petri dish of content creation that supports collaborations between artists in music, art, film, and design. The new works are available through a variety of media including television, mobile, and print.[18] In 2011, The Creators Project became Coachella's first-ever creative partner, collaborating with the festival and headlining acts to create visual pyrotechnics using state-of-the-art technology.[19]

Hypothetical problem-solving techniques: Write down your best possible scenarios.

Just Call This TV Station 'The Future of All Media'

VBS.TV is an online broadcast network that streams free original content 24 hours a day. They cover a mix of domestic and international news, music, and pop and underground culture. VBS promises viewers that it will "fulfill every utopian vision the Internet has failed to live up to so far."[20]

Exploring New Media Partners

Third Rail Logo. Artist: Ariel Fitterman

Music Gaming

Walter is pushing hard for licensing Third Rail's music in video games. His friend Morey gave him some tips on how to get music placed in games from a workshop he attended by the National Association of Recording Industry Professionals (NARIP). After his conversation with Morey, Walter writes down some ideas to pitch to the band.

- Learn everything we can about the video game industry. Check out Gamasutra.com and GameIndustry.biz.

- Find the developers who are making the kind of games that would be a good fit for our music. Focus on how we can help the developers solve their problems, not why the developers should license our music.

- Try to get our music placed first with smaller developers. The big companies won't be interested in us until we've got a track record.

- Make it easy for music supervisors and licensors. Clean up our website and put up with music that they can stream, not download. Clear all music samples and get the paperwork ready so we can send out a license fast.

- Stay humble: The music is secondary to what's happening between the game user and the art on the screen.[21]

Walter found information on the ASCAP website about licensing video games. He discovered that most licenses provide for a one-time buy-out fee per composition regardless of the number of games actually sold or how many times the game is played. Buyouts range from $2,500 to more than $20,000, depending on the value of the music, budget for game development, and the bargaining power of the two parties.[22] Armed with this information, Walter is sure he can convince the band to get moving on licensing their music for games.

Pixie Lott launches Guitar Hero 5
Credit: Neil Mockford/Getty Images Entertainment/Getty Images

Music-related video games make up 12% of the U.S. video game software market, which was valued at $40.7 billion in 2011.[23] Sony, Nintendo, and GameStop dominate the field, together making up 39% of market share, while Microsoft, Activision Blizzard, and Electronic Arts are in fourth, fifth, and sixth place, respectively. But these 'majors' are feeling the squeeze of competition from innovative new players that are redefining the industry. The tens of thousands of simple, downloadable, inexpensive, and free games available on social media sites, smartphones, and tablets are giving the majors a run for their money.[24]

Your Turn: Create Your Own Game

With a few of your colleagues, think up a new, music-related video game that combines at least three of the following: social networking, sunglasses, artist/fan interaction, bowling, concerts, smells, TV, and the Colbert Report. You could begin by brainstorming plot ideas for the action, or start with the music and work back from there. Try sketching out your ideas on paper, like a film or ad storyboard.

Digital Radio

Third Rail Logo. Artist: Ariel Fitterman

Sam thinks Third Rail might have some luck getting their music played on internet radio. Over coffee with Phoebe and Earl he asks how they figured out the radio scene for their bluegrass duo. The minute he asks he regrets it, because Earl immediately moves into his professor mode and starts to lecture. Sam is bored to death, but pretends to listen. What he really wants to know is which stations would be good for Third Rail's music, and how to get them to play Third Rail's music.

According to media and marketing research firm Arbitron, about 43 million people listened to online radio in a given week during 2010. That's about 17% of the population, an impressive increase since 2007, when only about 11% tuned in online.[25]

Streaming internet, customizable online radio stations, and portable music devices are making inroads into terrestrial stations' traditional turf. Consumers enjoy listening to music tailored to their moods and tastes, and many want to avoid listening to broadcasters' annoying ads. New cars with built-in MP3 adapters and satellite radio are another headache to traditional broadcasters, as the majority of radio listening occurs in cars.[26]

What is radio, anyway? How do we define it in this age of convergence? For example, some feel that Pandora is not actually radio because it's not curated by someone other than the listener, doesn't give local information, or have local personalities. On the other hand, services like DAR.fm, the self-proclaimed 'free TiVo for radio,' is a website that makes available free streaming of every radio show on 1,800 AM and FM stations in the United States. Rdio, MOG, Napster, and Rhapsody are subscription services that have huge music catalogues that can be transferred to portable devices, but disappear if the customer discontinues the subscription. Spotify offers an equally huge amount of on-demand music using the freemium model—it's free if you don't mind the ads. And if you do, just purchase a premium subscription.

Digital radio is a crowded and risky marketplace for entrepreneurs, and it's contributing to the overload and demise of some online music services. Here's how Evolver.fm sums up the music licensing challenges for start-ups using music: "For super neat music technologies like [Turntable.fm], the usual progression goes something like this:

Big splash ▶ Performance issues ▶ Get sued ▶ Go under/get bought ▶ Be lame."[27]

Advertising dollars account for roughly 90% of the budgets of streaming radio, podcasts, and portable music players. New media are competing with traditional broadcast media for advertisers, whose fortunes are tied to the general health of the economy, and fluctuate accordingly. Satellite radio companies have dual revenue streams of subscription fees and advertising on non-music channels.[28]

Radio stations attract advertisers by playing music that appeals to the specific segments of the population the advertisers are trying to reach. Radio personalities and the level of interaction with listeners also play a large role in keeping people tuned in to a specific station over time.[29]

In addition to competing for advertising dollars, digital radio ventures can encounter 'performance issues' as shown in Turntable.fm's technology lifespan progression above. This refers to music licensing regulations, whose requirements and costs vary considerably. At issue is whether or not the webcast is considered interactive or non-interactive, according to the provision in the U.S. Digital Millennium Copyright Act (DMCA). Rights holders worry that interactive webcasts like Spotify, MOG, and Rdio could *substitute* for music purchases, whereas non-interactive radio services, like Pandora and simulcast terrestrial broadcasts, are considered *drivers* of music purchases.[30]

Interactive 'on-demand' webcasts allow listeners to choose the actual songs they hear. Interactive services require a negotiated license agreement with the rights holders. Non-interactive 'lean back' (passive listening) webcasts don't allow individual song choice. Non-interactive webcasts require a much less expensive 'compulsory license' from Sound Exchange, to whom webcasters pay a per-stream royalty.

 Your Turn: Give Sam a hand in figuring out the 10 best digital radio stations to target. What strategy do you recommend for getting Third Rail's music played on these stations?

Reflect

Log onto to Turntable.fm and wander into the Listening Room. How effective is it as a source for listener-recommended music? Do you feel Turntable.fm is truly a non-interactive webcast? Why or why not?

Music Videos

Third Rail Logo. Artist: Ariel Fitterman

Beyond radio and games, Third Rail is thinking about using video of their rehearsals and performances to connect with fans. While looking into this, Cody finds out how things have changed due to the digital revolution.

New Approaches

Record labels have routinely approved music video budgets in the millions of dollars for their biggest stars (check out Michael Jackson and Janet Jackson's 1996 video for their single, "Scream," and Madonna's 2002 "Die Another Day"). Many of these bigger-than-life videos were aimed for MTV's *Total Request Live*, a popular show that ran from 1998 to 2008. The labels enthusiastically gave MTV free content in exchange for its massive audience reach.[31]

However, changing consumer tastes, technology advances like YouTube, shrinking record sales, and smaller record label budgets have unleashed a desire in some of the most innovative directors, companies, and musicians to upend the definition of the entire music video genre.[32]

Tossing out the over-the-top props, dancers, lip-synching, and soft-porn gauze, companies such as Google have stepped forward to propel the genre in new directions. Entrepreneurs like Chris Milk, a video creative director, are combining complex computer graphics, digital art tools, and a 'What if . . .' attitude to make fresh, compelling music videos and short films.[33]

One of Milk's earliest projects was an interactive film entitled *The Wilderness Downtown* that used the Arcade Fire song "We Used to Wait." Showcasing Google's new-at-the-time Chrome browser, viewers could zoom in on their childhood neighborhoods via Google maps and street views. Check out thewildernessdowntown.com.

In a 'commerce leads art' twist, a relatively new form of advertising known as branded social video is upending the status quo. Deliberately avoiding the old-school sales-pitch format, online video advertising aims to create entertaining content that is a soft sell or no-sell approach to brand awareness.[34] Marketers understand that if their message feels like entertainment instead of advertising, it's more likely to be watched and forwarded to friends.

For example, Dove's 2011 "Fresh Spin" ad campaign used a video series, social media, and websites to provide behind-the-scenes looks into the lives of three young female DJs—Jessica Who, Chelsea Leyland, and Diamond Kuts. Dove teamed up with MTV and New York's Fashion Week in a multi-platform effort to blend the potent touch points of youth, lifestyle, fashion, and music. All three of these companies were targeting females aged 12 to 34, a top demographic for their products and services. Says Joe Maceda, an advertising executive involved in the campaign, "As a brand, Dove does not want to focus on celebrities. The DJs are real girls who are culturally relevant."[35]

Budgets for music videos can go in two directions. One is the 'event' video, such as "I Need a Doctor" by Dr. Dré and Eminem, in which they crashed (on purpose) a $75,000 Ferrari. Lady Gaga, never one to let money stand in the way of an artistic statement, used approximately 150 dancers and extras in her video, "Judas."[36]

Then there's the other, quirkier direction—videos with tiny budgets designed for the web by professionals. These are often deliberately understated and non-sleek. The entrepreneurs working in this genre, including Chris Milk, are leading a creative surge as the 1980s, big label video re-imagines itself.[37]

Back to the Third Rail

Third Rail Logo. Artist: Ariel Fitterman

After about an hour of searching, Cody found the blog Yours Truly. The guys there make cool videos, but it was the name of their studio—Different Fur—that really got Cody's attention.

If Third Rail made a video, how would they use it? Cody heard that the band Pomplemoose made some money from the YouTube Partners Program, which pays artists for views. And what about Vevo? Cody checked—it only accepts postings from their media partners, some of the biggest names out there. Nobody he knows has a connection to any of them. Check it out: YoursTru.ly/, VEVO.com.

How much money are we talking about for online videos? According to the *Wall Street Journal*, 10 million streams of a video on Vevo could produce around $70,000 for the video rights holders.[38] But that's a *lot* of streams. Unless you're a superstar, how do you get 10 million people to care about your video?

Reflect

If a start-up is founded by major corporations is it still considered entrepreneurship? Vevo was created in partnership with Universal Music Group, Sony Music Entertainment, and the Abu Dhabi Media Company—some very major players. Do you think this qualifies as an entrepreneurial venture? Why or why not?

Smartphones

Jared wants to create an app that will make the band some money plus catapult him to fame. He met Dave Machinist at the CMJ Music Marathon last fall and saw a demo of his app, Shinobi Ninja. Jared thinks of himself as a creative genius, and knows he could design something just as exciting. He's getting ready to make his pitch to the band.

Apps rule the smartphone entrepreneurial world. Those little programs serve as portals to information, games, music, and entire virtual worlds. In 2011 Apple iPhone lead the app world, with its competitors Android, Palm, Blackberry, Palm/HP, and Windows trailing behind.[39]

Entrepreneurs who want an app design approved by Apple have to fight through a lot of competition. Apple receives 8,500–10,000 submissions each week.[40] Even if the app does finally make it into the Apple store, it's up to the entrepreneur to create the buzz that will drive people to buy his app.

Social Media

As you're well aware, social media are web 2.0-based technologies that allow for interactive communication between users and user-generated content. Wikipedia, Twitter, YouTube, Facebook, Second Life, and World of Warcraft are examples of the different types of social media: collaborative projects, blogs and microblogs, content communities, social networking sites, virtual social worlds, and virtual game worlds.[41]

Some of the most intriguing new ventures in the music industry blend social media with something else, such as internet radio, casual gaming, and education. Entrepreneurs Seth Goldstein and Billy Chasen have founded two companies using the 'What if we combine this plus that?' approach to innovation:

Company 1

App + bar codes + treasure hunt + reward points = StickyBits (check it out, Stickybits. com)

Company 2

The answer is Turntable.fm. Can you figure out what they combined?

_____ + _____ + _____ + _____ = Turntable.fm

In 2012, Facebook was one of the most powerful social media platforms, accounting for 90% of time spent on all social networking sites in the U.S. Roughly three out of four internet users had a Facebook account, and the majority of them visited the site daily.[42] However, as we saw with MySpace, social sites can wax and wane in popularity.

Every company on the planet is trying to figure out how to use its advertising dollars effectively in social media. There is vast opportunity for entrepreneurs who help marketers reach their customers in creative ways. Word of mouth has always been the most effective form of advertising, and social networking is word of mouth on steroids. Products, services, and artists live or die by opinions that are shared virally.

Who knows which internet platform will be the biggest news six months or a year from now? Use the Digital Media Hotness Rating Scale to evaluate a few new social media sites. Compare your scores to your colleagues' and see if you can predict the next Facebook.

Music's Old Media Friends

3d brained/Shutterstock Images

Vladir09/Shutterstock Images

The digital revolution has shaken up traditional media, but by no means has it vanquished this important sector. The power and money are still concentrated in the hands of a few large corporations, much as it is in the music industry. This is another example of powerful mass media influencing consumer demand, which we identified in Chapter 3 as the 'culture industry.'

The top four U.S. television broadcast companies earned 43.9% of the entire industry's revenue in 2011. That percentage has remained constant over the past six years. The major players, in order of market share from largest to smallest, are Walt Disney (owned by ABC TV), News Corporation (owned by Fox Television Stations), CBS (largely owned by Viacom), and NBC (co-owned by Comcast and GE).[43]

The major players in traditional broadcast radio are Clear Channel (owned by CC Media Holdings), Sirius XM satellite radio, CBS, and Cumulus/Citadel. These companies each operate several dozen radio stations in multiple markets across the country, thanks to relaxed media ownership regulations that came in the form of the 1996 Telecommunications Act. The majors' wide reach enables traditional broadcast media to offer advertisers more coverage than smaller, independently owned stations.[44] And advertising is the economic engine of traditional broadcasting companies.

Both traditional TV and radio broadcasting receive approximately 90% of their revenue from advertising. Advertisers want viewers to watch or listen to their ads, so stations are tempted to focus on content that appeals to the widest possible audience. This often leads to conservative programming and a reliance on hits, as stations fight to retain listenership and viewership, and keep their advertisers happy.[45]

The U.S. is the only developed country that does not require terrestrial TV and radio broadcasters to pay a performance royalty to the rights holder of sound recordings (usually record labels) and the recording artist who performs on a sound recording. For decades, U.S. terrestrial broadcasters have successfully lobbied Congress to continue their exemption from compensating artists and labels for using their recordings on the air. This means that the rights holder of an *underlying composition* gets paid by the terrestrial broadcaster when her song airs, but the rights holder and recording artist of the song *recording* do not.

Radio

Broadcast radio has been a powerful music partner for decades. Major labels still use it to great effect to break artists and promote new releases. Many people in the industry still believe that success on traditional radio is necessary for an artist to achieve star status.

More than 90% of all Americans above the age of 12 listen to the radio each week,[46] a percentage that is expected to increase as unemployment rates fall and Americans spend more time in their cars and at work, the two places where most radio listening takes place.[47]

Traditionally, listeners selected a radio station whose music they liked and whose broadcast strength allowed them to hear it clearly. If they moved too far out

badahos/Shutterstock Images

of the station's signal, they would lose it. DJs or station managers chose the music. Advertisers used jingles to sell their products and services to anyone who tuned into that station. Since advertising paid the bills, stations worked hard to keep listeners from changing to another station. 'Don't touch that dial!' became the DJ's mantra.

More recently, large, traditional companies have purchased innovative start-ups to accelerate development and growth in specific areas of their business. This was the case in 2011 when Clear Channel, the broadcast giant, purchased Thumbplay, a cloud-based digital music subscription service. Thumbplay was founded in 2004 by Are Traas-dahl and Evan Schwartz, and at the time of acquisition had more than 8 million songs under license from the major record labels and more than 25,000 indie labels.[48]

Television

Egyptian man in café watching TV
© Ingetje Tadros/The Image Bank/Getty Images

Although the four largest players' hold on the market has declined in recent years, they still command an enormous audience of viewers and listeners. According to Nielsen, most Americans watch approximately 153 hours of TV every month at home.[49] It's not hard to see that the sheer penetration of traditional television remains a huge draw for advertising dollars.

One area that has boosted broadcast revenue in recent years is music-based TV shows. The TV production and broadcasting industries earned 5.5% of their 2010 revenue from music-related content, including channels like MTV and CMT, and shows like *American Idol* and *Glee*.[50]

Glee in particular has been a goldmine,[51] producing more than 75 hit singles on the Billboard Hot 100 chart. The show pays a sync fee to record the song and then must pay royalties every time that recording of the song is aired, downloaded, or sold in a CD. (See Chapter 7 for a specific example of *Glee*'s licensing fees.)

Table 11.1 shows how music television revenues contributed to various music-related industries in 2010, with projections for 2015, based on data provided by IBISWorld Reports.

TABLE 11.1 *Contribution of music television revenues to music-related industries*

Industry	Total Revenue from Music Television ($ millions)			Description
	2010	2015	5-year CAGR*	
Live Music, Sports and Event Promotion	$215	$457	16.3%	Concert promotion for current TV shows (e.g. *American Idol, Glee*) as well as alumni (e.g. Adam Lambert, Carrie Underwood)
Major Label Music Production	$120	$245	15.3%	Current TV singles, soundtracks and recording contracts with TV stars (e.g. Kelly Clarkson, Susan Boyle)
Music Publishing	$467	$744	9.7%	All music featured on TV
Television Broadcasting	$1,913	$2,594	6.3%	Music-specific channels and shows featuring music
Television Production	$1,696	$2,244	5.8%	Music-specific channels and shows featuring music
Beauty, Cosmetics and Fragrance Stores	$223	$259	3.1%	Celebrity-sponsored perfumes
* Compound annual growth rate				

Reprinted with permission

Telecommunications Act of 1996: Still Controversial After All These Years

"Those who advocated the Telecommunications Act of 1996 promised more competition and diversity, but the opposite happened," said Common Cause President Chellie Pingree."[52] The following is an excerpt from a research report entitled *The Fallout from the Telecommunications Act of 1996: Unintended Consequences and Lessons Learned*, prepared by the Common Cause Education Fund in May 2005. The report shows how the Act's legislation drastically redrew the media landscape, often to the detriment of the public.

The Telecommunications Act of 1996:

- Lifted the limit on how many radio stations one company could own. The cap had been set at 40 stations. It made possible the creation of radio giants like Clear Channel, with more than 1,200 stations, and led to a substantial drop in the number of minority station owners, homogenization of play lists, and less local news.
- Lifted from 12 the number of local TV stations any one corporation could own, and expanded the limit on audience reach. One company had been allowed to own stations that reached up to a quarter of U.S. TV households. The Act raised that national cap to 35 percent. These changes spurred huge media mergers and greatly increased media concentration. Together, just five companies—Viacom, Disney, News Corp, NBC and AOL, now control 75 percent of all prime-time viewing.
- The Act deregulated cable rates. Between 1996 and 2003, those rates have skyrocketed, increasing by nearly 50 percent.
- The Act permitted the FCC to ease cable-broadcast cross-ownership rules. As cable systems increased the number of channels, the broadcast networks aggressively expanded their ownership of cable networks with the largest audiences. Ninety percent of the top 50 cable stations are owned by the same parent companies that own the broadcast networks, challenging the notion that cable is any real source of competition.
- The Act gave broadcasters, for free, valuable digital TV licenses that could have brought in up to $70 billion to the federal treasury if they had been auctioned off. Broadcasters, who claimed they deserved these free licenses because they serve the public, have largely ignored their public interest obligations, failing to provide substantive local news and public affairs reporting and coverage of congressional, local and state elections.
- The Act reduced broadcasters' accountability to the public by extending the term of a broadcast license from five to eight years, and made it more difficult for citizens to challenge those license renewals. Citizens, excluded from the process when the Act was negotiated in Congress, must have a seat at the table as Congress proposes to revisit this law.

Resource: Read the complete report on the Common Cause website.

The Federal Communications Commission (FCC) regulates interstate and international communications by radio, television, wire, satellite, and cable in all 50 states, the District of Columbia, and U.S. territories.[53]

Opportunities Ahead

Think back to the music industry problems you identified in Chapter 2. Combine two or three in a sort of 'opportunity mash-up' exercise. Use your creative problem-solving skills to imagine a single digital media solution to the combined problems. Answer the following questions about your new venture concept:

- Who are your customers?
- What problem(s) are you solving for them with your new venture?
- Do you think they'll be willing to pay for your service or product?
- If not, how will you make money?
- How can you give your venture a brand identity to distinguish it from the competition?
- Rate your venture on the Digital Media Hotness scale. What are your chances of making it to your second year?

CONCLUSION

Cloud storage, advances in digital technology, and media convergence has encouraged an outpouring of entrepreneurial products and services in the music industry. These new media entrepreneurs are challenging the traditional ways in which we discover, enjoy, and share music today. Like most artists, Third Rail wants to connect with its fans in as many ways as possible. Have we reached the social media saturation point, or is this the landscape of the future? How can DIY artists and bands leverage the digital opportunities while remaining focused on their music?

 Talking Back: Class Discussions

Third Rail Logo. Artist: Ariel Fitterman

And now for that strategy . . .

Cody, Sam, Jared, and Walter meet up later that day to compare notes. Sam has brought Phoebe along as a peacekeeper in case things get rowdy. Look at Third Rail's options, discuss them with your colleagues, and create a detailed action plan in the areas of radio, TV, video, social media, apps, games—and whatever else you think is relevant.

Web Links

- Panos Panay gives advice to indie artists
  youtube.com/watch?v=7yvaP_lzQaE

- TechCrunch's Founder Stories
  Techcrunch.com/2011/01/10/startup-sherpa-kickstarter/

- Alexandra Patsavas discusses her job as a music supervisor on Beta TV
  Youtube.com/watch?v=YEsrm3gfJGE

- The complete report on the Common Cause
  commoncause.org/site/pp.asp?c=dkLNK1MQIwG&b=4773601#Media_and_
  Democracy

PART 4

You as Entrepreneur

HOW TO USE CASE STUDIES TO CREATE AN INTERACTIVE CLASSROOM

I conceived of and wrote the case studies in Chapters 12 and 13 so that you, the student, could practice your entrepreneurial thinking in actual business settings.

The case study method is a very effective pedagogical tool for creating interactive classrooms. Active participation in case discussions helps you learn how to make convincing arguments based on solid evidence, astute analysis, and good communication skills.

In addition, the case study method helps you acquire analytical and diagnostic thinking skills, which you will put to use in an environment where circumstances are always changing. The classroom becomes the lab for comparative reflection on and lively discussion of your findings and conclusions.

Case studies are not designed to provide up-to-the-minute information on a particular company. That information is readily available from other sources. Rather, the overarching purpose of the case study method allows you to be the CEO of a company which finds itself at a crossroads. Events have conspired to create a moment in the company's trajectory which forces the CEO to make a potentially game-changing decision. Using the information found in the case, you will decide on a course of action and discuss your reasoning in class.

Your study of a case promotes detailed contextual analysis of specific events and conditions. In preparing for class, you will examine a problem from many perspectives using deep analysis, logic, and reasoning. The classroom-as-lab supports you as you work with your peers to reach a decision about an appropriate course of action.

Using the case method in entrepreneurial studies has four key benefits. First, case studies can deepen your understanding of many areas of entrepreneurship, including finance, law, marketing, balancing risk and reward, and growth. You will learn to identify the constant and the variable parameters of a problem, an important tool for future industry leaders.

Second, active participation in case discussions assists you in developing strong persuasive skills. To become a leader and manage tough situations, you need to be able to make a convincing argument based on solid evidence, astute analysis, and good communication skills.

Third, the classroom discussion of the case allows you to understand that there can be many different solutions to a problem. There is no right or wrong conclusion in a case study. It doesn't matter if you and your colleagues come to the same decision as the actual CEO of the company. The pedagogical benefit is the work you do to prepare your analysis of the case, and the active participation in the ensuing class discussions. The most effective case study discussions come from you listening to your peers and being open to divergent ways of thinking about an issue.

Lastly, using the case study method will help you learn how to make decisions under conditions of uncertainty. You must envision yourself as a leader of a company. You will have limited information, as leaders often do, and must use your best strategic analysis and creative problem-solving skills to find viable solutions to the problem at hand. This calculated risk-taking compels you to make decisions and take action even with a limited amount of knowledge.

I have provided some study questions to help you prepare for each case. I recommend that you read the case twice, taking time in between each reading to reflect on the study questions. I have found that my own students participate much more confidently in the class discussions when they write up their answers to the study questions and use them as a reference during class.

One last point: it's important to remember that your professor is there simply as a moderator. He or she does not guide the discussion toward a specific conclusion. In my classes at NYU, students arrange their chairs so that they are facing each other, rather than facing the front of the room. You may want to suggest this to your professor. A case study discussion usually lasts about 45 minutes. It concludes with a class vote on the course of action you feel the case's CEO should take on the issues identified at the beginning of class.

The following cases put you in the driver's seat as an entrepreneur. I hope you enjoy the journey.

CHAPTER 12

Case Study: Falcon Music & Art—A Jazz Haven on the Hudson

By Professsor Catherine Fitterman Radbill,
New York University, 2011

It's a warm May night, 2010, in the tiny hamlet of Marlboro, New York, 70 miles north of New York City in the scenic Hudson Valley. Inside Falcon Music & Art, on Route 9W, jazz musician Julian Lage is winding down his set.

As the last note fades, the audience leaps to its feet, clapping and shouting. Lage acknowledges the ovation with grace and gratitude, the sweat showing on his beaming face. He holds up his hands to quiet the crowd of 150 and says "There's a person who's not up on this stage who deserves your applause more than I do, and that's Tony Falco. Tony, come on up here!" The crowd roars its approval as the man with the curly graying hair makes his way through the packed room.

Everyone recognizes him as Tony Falco, the owner of Falcon Music & Art, and the local resident who has turned Marlboro into a rural Mecca for jazz, folk, blues, indie, world, and contemporary chamber music. He's the man who, before introducing each artist, reminds the audience to respect the music by not talking, and to support living artists by making a donation in the blue box near the door. Lage says to the crowd, "The Falcon spoils its artists. The last time I played here I slept over at Tony's house and ate dinner with his family."

The crowd stomps and whistles for its most famous music entrepreneur and his family, all of whom are working at the Falcon this evening. As Tony leaves the stage, the band begins an encore. He sits down for a minute to listen to the music before moving over to a table to clear away the dishes. As he disappears into the kitchen, Tony relishes the moment: Great music, an appreciative and respectful audience, a busy kitchen and bar, and his family working close by.

At home later that night, after the Falcon is locked and dark, Tony find he cannot get to sleep. "How can I get more people to come to the shows?" he wonders. "We need full houses in this new building, and we're only half-way there. If we build out the middle floor to expand our events business, will we be able to compete? Will weddings and private parties dilute The Falcon's brand, which I've worked for nine years to build? Can I afford to keep paying Rosie, who's been here two weeks and is my first business-trained employee? Should we add Thursday nights to our Friday–Saturday concert lineup?"[1] (See Exhibit 1.)

THE LIVE CONCERT INDUSTRY

According to Nielsen SoundScan's first quarter reports for 2010, recorded music continued its decade-long downward spiral, with U.S. album sales falling 8% over the same quarter of 2009. And, for the first time since 2003, when Nielsen began tracking digital downloads, digital music sales fell 1%.[2]

As the music industry continues its long period of contraction and mergers, and overall album sales decline quarter after quarter, frequent touring has become a financial necessity for most artists. As more and more artists take to the road to earn a living, the live music marketplace has become very crowded, particularly in the peak touring season of May through October.

Although 2010 began on a strong note, with global concert ticket sales surpassing $1 billion in the first three months (up 6.2% over the same quarter of 2009[3]), the early months of the summer season have been plagued with cancelations and tour postponements by major artists. The Eagles, Maxwell, John Mayer, Rihanna, Lilith Fair, U2, Simon and Garfunkel, Christina Aguilera, and Limp Bizkit have all backed away from summer concert commitments.[4] Some of the changes were due to illness, but the number of cancelations has people in the industry worried that most were due to poor ticket sales and the sluggish economic recovery.

"Everybody thought 2009 was the recession summer and 2010 was the recovery year," says Glenn Peoples, a senior editorial analyst at Billboard. "Well, just because economists say that there's a recovery doesn't mean that people feel there's a recovery."[5]

"We in this business really gauge what is happening by our advance ticket sales," says Troy Blakely, a booking agent at the APA Agency who works with rock band Rise Against and the latest incarnation of Sublime. "Sometimes it looks so horrendous, you have to pull back and say, 'We can't go through with this.'"[6]

To further complicate the landscape, the traditional boundaries within the music industry have become blurred, if not erased altogether. Record labels, promoters, booking agencies, and management companies are all evolving into multilevel entertainment companies, as each struggles to capture new revenue streams. The major booking agencies are moving into the recording business and other areas of the content world beyond live performance. And the ticketing industry discovered years ago that all the data they were capturing was marketing gold.

Major labels began their highly publicized, high-stakes multi-right deals, called 360s, in the early 2000s. Robbie Williams and EMI were one of the first, in 2002, followed by Korn and others. Not to be outdone, the behemoth concert promoter Live Nation signed a multi-million dollar 360 deal with Madonna in 2007, followed by deals with Jay-Z, U2, and the Jonas Brothers. These rights deals include access to the artists' touring, merchandising, licensing, recording, and fan club management.[7]

The live concert industry is still reeling from the January 2010 merger of the world's largest ticketing company and the world's largest concert promoter, Ticketmaster and Live Nation. Live Nation Entertainment is now the largest live entertainment company in the world, consisting of five businesses: concert promotion and venue operations, sponsorship, ticketing solutions, e-commerce, and artist management. In 2009, Live Nation sold 140 million tickets, promoted 21,000 concerts, partnered with 850 sponsors and averaged 25 million unique monthly users of its e-commerce sites.[8] Billboard estimates the combined company will sell about 200 million tickets this year.[9]

In order to foster competition within the industry, the Department of Justice approved the merger with certain conditions. Live Nation had to lease its ticketing system to the second largest concert promoter, Anschutz Entertainment Group (AEG) for five years, with an option to buy Ticketmaster's source code. Ticketmaster had to sell its subsidiary Paciolan, a ticketing software company used primarily by college athletics and performing arts centers, to Comcast-Spectacor. And Live Nation's ticketing side was barred from sharing data with its promotion side.[10]

One of the pressing issues for concert promoters in this shifting landscape is getting help from the artists' labels and managers in promoting their shows. Industry cuts have led to less effective promotion of artists, Bruce Houghton, president of the Skyline Agency believes. "Who is left to market the shows in more than a cookie-cutter fashion?" he asks before answering his own question. "No one—promoters, managers or agents—has been willing to fill that void."[11]

Brian Jones, VP at the Bobby Roberts Talent Agency, sees today's market as "too many artists looking for work and not enough ticket buyers who will pay the amount for a ticket it takes to cover promoting the show," he says. "Like many products in today's economy, it's a buyer's market. The fans are in control."[12]

Still, Jones says he's not overly concerned about the long-term viability of live entertainment. "People will always go to live shows; it's just finding the right formula to make it affordable for the promoter, artist and the ticket buyer," he says. "We've all adjusted, and we will adjust some more."[13]

THE EARLY YEARS

Tony Falco was born and raised in West Brighton, Staten Island, NY.[14] His father was a clerk for the A&P grocery and a singer in a wedding band called the Keynotes. Tony was the third son in a family of seven children. His mother stayed home to care for her family.

Family finances were a bit tight, so Tony began working at a young age. His earliest jobs were collecting old newspapers, rags and batteries and selling them at the junkyard. After he got his working papers at 12, he got jobs delivering the local newspaper and pumping gas.

Tony tagged along with his father on quite a few wedding gigs over the years. He became fascinated with live performance after seeing Taj Mahal play at a local park when he was 12 or 13. "Staten Island had only a couple of good music venues in the early 70s. I was really fond of one of them, the Ritz Theatre, and went to shows there as often as I could scrape together the money to buy a ticket."

"I was always drawn toward music," Tony says. "I spent a lot of time singing and playing guitar but never excelled as a performer."

Tony left Staten Island in 1974 to attend college at the State University of New York in New Paltz, deep in the Hudson Valley. "I was a mediocre student, and felt guilty that my family was scrimping and saving to send me to college. So I let my parents off the hook and dropped out as a full-time student after one semester. I'm very independent by nature, so it was no big deal to work at various jobs and put myself slowly through college."

Tony showed his entrepreneurial inclinations early on. He paid for his tuition by driving a truck down to the Hunts Point Market in the Bronx and buying produce for Windsor Farms in New Windsor, New York. The owner of Windsor Farms allowed him to use the extra room on the truck to start his own produce purveying business. "I had a small route of restaurants, markets, and delis that I would supply. I almost dropped out of school to do it full time, but decided to stick with college."

Tony changed majors at New Paltz from Biology to Music to Chemistry over an eight-year period before graduating with a Bachelor of Science degree in Chemistry. While at New Paltz he got a work study job in the school's Water Analysis laboratory and taught Water and Wastewater adult education courses. He liked water studies and business but was floundering through many of the other chemistry requirements. He saw in the school handbook that you could design your own major so he used his connections and work experience and called himself a Water Resource Management major. "I believe that I am the only one ever to graduate from New Paltz with that degree," Tony states.

He worked as an assistant engineer on construction of water and sewer systems during his college years. After graduation in 1983, Tony got licenses to run these systems and started a company called Water Quality Management, Inc. running municipal and commercial systems. He added another, related company called Water Quality Management Laboratories shortly after that.

Tony hired his first employee, Sarah Cole, in 1988 to help him in the lab. Sarah was exceptionally organized and hardworking. Equally important, she was supportive of Tony's outside projects and kept the lab busy and growing. "I'm a very independent person, but I realized how important it was to keep Sarah involved in the lab. So, in 1990, I offered her 50% of the business. I've never regretted that move." They renamed the company Environmental Labworks, Inc.

This business, housed in the basement of the building, is the economic generator that helps keep Falcon Music & Art running. Environmental Labworks,Inc., a water quality analysis lab, is certified by the New York State Department of Health for testing non-potable and potable water quality. It now employs four full-time and three part-time people.

THE HUDSON VALLEY

The Falcon is located in Marlboro (Ulster County) NY, an active Hudson Valley farming community 70 miles north of Manhattan. Surrounded by rolling hills and glacial carved knolls, the Hudson Valley has long been known for its agricultural bounty. Grape vines and apple trees thrive in the well-drained soils of the Hudson Valley's hillsides and bluffs. Local wineries, farms and orchards dot the countryside.[15]

In 1996, Congress designated the Hudson River Valley as a National Heritage Area, describing it as the "landscape that defined America."[16]

This is the region that spawned the Hudson River School of Painting, a 19th-century art movement that includes Thomas Cole, Asher Durand, Frederic Edwin Church, and Albert Bierstadt, among others. It is also home to Sleepy Hollow, the village that inspired Washington Irving's famous supernatural short story featuring the headless horseman and the unlucky Ichabod Crane.

The rural beauty and slower pace of life bring visitors year-round to the Hudson Valley. An abundance of New York State parks and land preserves offer scenic views on thousands of acres of natural forest. For the more adventuresome, there is hiking, boating, skiing, and snow shoeing. Shopping, antiquing, dining, music, history, art galleries, and quaint inns lure tourists to this region.

Some of America's great families chose the Hudson Valley as home, and their estates are now open to the public. Hyde Park (the Roosevelts), Kykuit (the Rockefellers), Van Cortlandt Manor, and the Vanderbilt Mansion are a few of the historic manor homes in the Valley.[17]

Many people who live in the Hudson Valley travel into New York City for shopping, concerts, and museums. In fact, those are the very people whom Tony considers his primary market for shows at Falcon. "I choose artists for our shows that I would travel to see. I think people in the Hudson Valley appreciate having that caliber of artist right here, without having to drive far to enjoy a show." (See Exhibit 3.)

THE FALCON GETS ITS START

In 1984, Tony and his wife, Julie, bought a home in Marlboro and began renovating it. "It was a $45,000 handyman special, the worst house on the block," says Tony. In addition to running Environmental Labworks, starting a family, and creating a free summer concert series at a local park, Tony played guitar and sang in a band called The Wild Animals of North America.

In a gig that was to prove fateful for the direction of Tony's career, the band was hired to play at a beautiful but decaying former church in Marlboro. Tony saw magic in the space, and thought he could make it into a community center. So he bought the building and renovated it. He rented half to a local day care, and began developing the other half as a space for music. He put on only a few private concerts, but never finished it enough to open it to the public.

"I lost money," states Tony. "It was fun, and the space was beautiful, but we couldn't make a financial go of it."

Salvation arrived in the form of the U.S. Postal Service, who wanted to buy the land to expand their facilities. Tony sold it to them, but not before carefully dismantling the old church and storing the pieces for re-use.

Still bitten by the live performance bug, Tony began construction of a performance space for private concerts in the backyard of his Marlboro home. He used the stained glass, wood, and other architectural details from the church, creating a two-story wooden structure with an acoustically excellent listening room for live shows. Outfitted with a grand piano, stage lighting, a back line, and sound equipment, the space seated about 80 people.

From the beginning, Tony wanted the Falcon to be a place where his friends in the community could enjoy great music in a respectful and home-like environment. He and Julie cooked dinner for everybody in the kitchen of their home, and served it in the Falcon. Eating together at the Falcon's large tables allowed the artists and audience to mingle before the music began.

Tony explains: "I began by booking musicians I knew, and they turned me on to other great musicians. Eventually, I started having artists contact me to play, instead of the other way around."

Slowly, the word got out and the private Falcon started filling up for the two or three Saturday night concerts a month. In 2001 Tony formed his fourth company, Falcon Music & Art Production, Inc.

Within a year, the artist-friendly facility was attracting top artists who were willing to play for donations. The Falcon was packed with music enthusiasts from the community and beyond. The early Falcon didn't have a kitchen or bar. Some of Tony's friends started bringing hot casseroles and other food to share. The "Pay What You Wish" admission policy and the pot-luck meal added to the feeling that this was a private house concert with friends.

Concerts at the Falcon have been free of charge since Day One. Tony encourages the audience to support the musicians by buying their CDs and contributing what they can in the blue wooden donation box by the front door.

"The box was my daughter's elementary school project," Tony explains. He put a sign on it that says Support Living Artists. One hundred percent of the money collected in the box went to the musicians, who were not paid a guarantee. The performers also keep 100% of the revenue from CD sales at their shows.

Tony and Julie often invited the artists to sleep over at their home after the show, and eat meals with their family. There's good reason that many artists refer to the Falcon as their home away from home, and loyalties to Tony and his family run deep.

However, over the years the Falcon slowly became a victim of its own success. Understandably, not all of Tony's neighbors were thrilled to have the crowds, parking, and noise that came with the sell-out shows. And Tony wanted to have more room to accommodate the growing audience.

In 2005, Tony purchased a former button factory on Dock Road in the center of Marlboro, adjacent to Marlboro Falls. He painstakingly set about renovating the building, which fronts onto Highway 9W, the main road through this part of the Hudson Valley. Falcon Music & Art, Inc. officially opened in its new home in December 2009.[18]

The main floor of the restored three-story building has 3,500 square feet of finished space, complete with hardwood floors, wood walls and high-beamed ceilings. Tony supports local artists by giving them space to exhibit free of charge on the walls. The art exhibits change every two months, and the artist keeps 100% of all proceeds from any sales.

The main floor includes an entrance foyer, the blue wooden donation box, a small bar (created entirely with recycled materials—a shuffleboard table is the actual bar), bathrooms, seating for 120 at tables, 50 chairs in five rows of chairs facing the stage, a 24' × 16' stage, and a commercial kitchen. The kitchen is large enough to provide a full menu of food and beverages to the audience. (See Exhibit 2.)

Behind the stage and above the kitchen is a loft area that can sleep up to five artists who need a place to crash overnight. A large deck wraps around the front and side of the building. The deck overlooks a large ground-level flagstone patio beside the creek, which can seat up to 100. Chairs and tables on the upper deck can comfortably seat up to 60.

Tony designed the entire space and oversaw the renovation. He actually did a lot of the work himself. "This was built out of the heart. I'm not a good capitalist. I see money as a necessary evil that will allow me to do good things."

Tony admits that he's not a great businessperson, and didn't have a traditional business plan when founding the Falcon. "I have trouble balancing my own checkbook. My goal is to create a good scene with the right musicians and environment. If I get that right—if the business thrives artistically—the money will follow."

And the business *is* thriving artistically. Literally hundreds of the world's top musicians have played at the Falcon. "Quality music is my thing," explains Tony. "I'm trying for a small room sound and vibe. I don't book bands that need a lot of space."

The Falcon's interior performance space has been approved for several different capacities, depending upon the room's configuration:

Standing only	375 people
Tables and chairs	130 people
Chairs only	275 people

The audience can order food and drinks from any spot in the room or bar. The staff consists of a chef, wait staff, and a bartender. Tony, Julie, and their four children, aged 13–18, all work at the Falcon in some capacity. Lee, their 15-year-old son and a talented performer in his own right, is the Falcon's technical engineer. He learned how to operate sound and lights by setting up his own equipment at gigs, which began at the tender age of five.

ROSIE JOINS THE TEAM

The newest person to join the Falcon is Rosie Rion, a friend of the family and a cellist who performed with her band at the old Falcon location. Rosie graduated from Syracuse University in May 2010, with a degree in cello and a minor in business and entrepreneurship. "I'm the only person in my entire music graduating class who has a real job in music. I'm thrilled with this opportunity," she says. Rosie is drawing on her business studies and experience to advise Tony.

"Tony is a visionary," Rosie continues. "He respects the musicians and visual artists he showcases at The Falcon, and does not take a nickel of their art or merchandise sales. He is the only person in the industry who could make this work because he refuses to compromise his ideals."

Hiring Rosie was a leap of faith for Tony, who admits he needs the input of someone with Rosie's talents and energy. Yet it's a big change for Tony. "He has a strong personality and is used to working on his own. But he's getting better at listening to my ideas for change and improvements at The Falcon," Rose states.

One of the first things Rosie changed was the bar menu. She simplified the types of drinks that were served, which makes ordering and inventory management much less complicated.

"Another idea I have is to move to a three-day performance schedule, adding Thursdays. But only if we can pack the house," Rosie explains.

Indeed, Tony has begun booking some Thursday night shows. He will feature less well-known but artistically excellent artists, and offer a smaller menu to cut down on his staffing expenses. Like the Friday and Saturday concerts, the doors will open at 6p.m., the opening act goes on at 7p.m., and the headliner begins at 8p.m.

One new idea that did not succeed was a weekly outdoor Saturday afternoon reggae concert featuring a local band called the Young Lions. It began well, but after six weeks Tony pulled the plug. "We got fewer and fewer people attending, and it was a financial drain." The shows took place outside on the patio next to the creek, and when the weather was hot and humid it was miserable.

Rosie is working to help Tony get a handle on all the costs associated with running The Falcon. He estimates his break-even on shows at $1,800–2,000. "This is a very rough estimate," states Rosie. "It only covers the variable costs of buying food and beverages, and paying servers. Tony is trying to keep the fixed and variable costs separate for now as we grow into this new facility."

Without ticket sales, parking charges, or food and drink minimums, the Falcon flies in the face of the traditional economic model for small music venues. Relying solely on revenue from food and beverage sales during shows, there is enormous pressure on Tony to book artists who will fill the house for each event. He must juggle his impeccable artistic taste and the financial realities of running a business. In this labor of love, Tony is trying to create a new economic model for small music venues, which rely heavily on alcohol to keep the doors open.

PRIVATE PARTIES: ANOTHER REVENUE SOURCE

The Falcon occasionally rents out the indoor performance space for private parties and special events. Tony has averaged one private event per month since the new space opened in January. "We have the space, we have a kitchen and servers. The problem is the events customers want Friday and Saturday nights, when we've got the live music."

At the moment, the Falcon is only available for private events on nights when there is no concert. Typical events include engagement, birthday, and college graduation parties. The West Point Music Department rented the space for rehearsals and a competition. In keeping with Tony's desire to support living artists, no DJs or recorded music is permitted. The events must use live music, and Tony happily provides a list of local bands for hire. The Falcon can provide food at a per-head cost ($35–80 per person), or the renter may hire their own caterer. The room rental fee is $1,500.

On the middle level of the building, below the Falcon's performance space, is an unfinished area about the same size as the main floor, with wooden floors and high ceilings stripped back to the beams. Tony has two bathrooms framed out and has sketched some designs for how he wants the space to look. He is thinking about finishing it in order to expand the event and catering part of his business, which at the moment represents only a tiny portion of his revenue. He's concerned, however, about how he could handle noise from a party in the space below the music venue. "I work hard to create a laid-back but respectful environment for the artists. I certainly can't allow noise coming from a party downstairs to interfere with the show, even if I do make money on it."

Fully soundproofing the middle level is cost-prohibitive. If Tony were to finish the middle level in order to book private events on nights when there was a concert in the performance space, the renter would not be permitted to have any live. Audio speakers will be installed in the middle level so the private function can hear the concert going on upstairs.

One idea Tony has to solve the potential noise issue is to build an interior staircase between the performance space and the middle level, and then construct a new bar on the middle level. He would close the upstairs bar to the public, allowing only his servers to use it. This construction project would cost $60,000–70,000, but it would solve two problems: it would remove the usual but annoying bar noise in the back of the performance space, and it would make catering much easier for private events.

There is free parking for 40 cars on a paved asphalt lot behind the Falcon. In early spring, Tony used local materials to create the flagstone patio and landscape the creek bank next to it (he owns the land on both sides of the creek). The paving, patio construction, and landscaping cost more than $60,000.

There are spaces for 50 more cars in a second parking lot that Tony recently created across the street from the Falcon. Tony leases this lot, which he just finished paving with shale and landscaping at a cost of $20,000. The lot is lit by solar lights and Tiki torches. A sign on the road by the Falcon's front door advertises the location of the off-site lot to passers-by.

An additional 30 legal spaces on Dock Road, the small road adjacent to the Falcon, are available for patrons to use for parking. Tony owns a plow to clear the lots in snowy weather.

Tony is constantly investing in the property to upgrade and improve its functionality and appeal. He has plans to create a sturdy, secure walkway and deck along the creek to the Marlboro Falls overlook point. "That will be great for wedding pictures," he says.

Despite the larger and more comfortable location for The Falcon, Tony confesses that he misses the personal side of the business. "My kids grew up hanging out with artists in our home, and they've become close family friends over the years. I try to make the new space feel as much like our home as possible."

MARKETING THE FALCON

The Falcon's marketing efforts are overseen by Fern Franke, one of Tony's friends in the community, and Tony's son Lee, who manages the website, LiveAtTheFalcon. com. The main methods of getting the word out about the shows are (1) free listings in local weekly and monthly publications, (2) updates on the Falcon's website, (3) weekly posts to their email list of 750 names, (4) printing and posting flyers, and (5) sending press releases to local radio stations. There is no budget for paid advertisements.

"There are a couple of really good jazz stations that give on-air mentions about the Falcon, including 94.7 FM WDSD, Woodstock and 91.3 FM WVKR, Vassar College Radio," says Tony. "I can only afford to pay Fern to work a couple of hours a week. I could use a lot more help getting the word out, especially to colleges in the area. I think we could draw from them if we could get awareness."

"Our marketing efforts need to reach the right people for our shows. We're looking for a sophisticated audience. This is a rural area, it's not New York City," Tony explains. To underscore that message, every chair in The Falcon faces the stage, even chairs at the tables, to show respect for the artists and encourage the audience to really listen to the music.

A *New York Times* story in the Sunday, March 5, 2010 Travel Section boosted awareness of the Falcon to a global readership.

THE COMPETITION: MUSIC AND SPECIAL EVENTS

What else can people in Marlboro do on a Friday or Saturday night besides catch a show at the Falcon? Aside from the usual options of watching television or going to the movies, there are a handful of small, high-quality live music venues that seat around 100 people and serve food. "I welcome the competition because it brings more music to the area," states Tony.

The Falcon's main competitors in the live music marketplace in all in the Hudson Valley within a 45 mile radius of Marlboro.[19] They include:

- Bean Runner Cafe, located in the Artists District in Peekskill

- Bearsville Theatre in Woodstock

- Club Helsinki in Hudson

- Howland Cultural Center in Beacon

- Rosendale Cafe in Rosendal

- Towne Crier Cafe in Beekmanville

- Unison Arts Center in New Paltz.[20]

In the area of special events, the Falcon has lots of competition. The Hudson Valley has hundreds of hotels, inns, vineyards, and other venues that are available to rent for special occasions. Without renovating the middle level, the Falcon could host one or two events per month on non-concert days. Tony estimates that it will cost close to $60,000 to renovate the middle level, but he's not sure that he will have the business he needs to make up for the construction costs, advertising, and extra staffing expenses he'll incur to be competitive.

FINANCIALS

Tony's goal is to fill the house for two out of three shows per week, and rent out the performance space twice a month for private events. He doesn't plan to slow down his bookings in winter. "I only had one cancellation due to weather this year," he states, "and it was a long, cold, snowy winter."[21]

The Falcon takes in approximately $20,000 per month from three sources: $16,000 from sales of food and beverages (two concerts per week); $2,000 rent from Environmental Labworks; and $2,000 from private parties.

The Falcon has a monthly debt load of $5,600 from construction loans and mortgages to build the new space. Taxes, insurance, payroll, equipment, food, and drink expenses amount to approximately $14,630 per month.

"From a restaurant standpoint, we have not found a way to make money because the tables don't turn over," Tony explains. People usually arrive at 6:00, grab a table, and stay there through the end of the night. So far, the kitchen has not been able to sustain itself on food sales. Labor costs are the biggest drain. The kitchen needs at least two cooks, a dishwasher, and a bus boy in addition to the four wait staff to service the food."

One hundred percent of the proceeds from the donation box go to the headline performers. The box takes in anywhere from $300 to $1,400 a night. "There are many nights when I have to put in some of my own money to give the artists enough to cover their travel and time," states Tony. "And we always provide all of the performers with food and drink."

"We're breaking even, but I need to be in a more stable financial position," explains Tony. "I just don't know which direction I should take. I know I couldn't fill the room if we sold tickets. The Hudson Valley just wouldn't support us. There's no shortage of outstanding artists who are willing to play for donations. When I ask people to pay what they can, I suggest $5, $10, $20. Sometimes we even get a $50 bill in the donation box." (See Exhibit 4.)

MAKING THE DECISIONS

As sleep continues to elude him, Tony wrestles with the pressing decisions he has to make. "I have to get more people to come to the shows," he mutters. "Can I find the money for an ad budget, and would that help? Should I take out another loan and build out the middle floor to expand our events business? Can Rosie take on more of the marketing and budgeting? Will adding a Thursday night to our Friday–Saturday concert lineup help us or hurt us? How can I get the food service to bring in more revenue?" With dawn approaching, and a busy day ahead of him, Tony decides to forget about trying to sleep. He goes into the kitchen, makes a cup of coffee, and begins to tackle the email that has piled up since yesterday.

FALCON MUSIC & ART STUDY QUESTIONS

Careful and focused preparation is the key to a meaningful case study discussion. Please prepare for the Falcon Music & Art case by reading it twice and *typing* your answers to these study questions. Bring your typed responses to class.

1. Give a thorough description of the issues that need to be solved in the case.

2. List the main factors influencing the decisions to be made.

3. State how you would resolve the issues if you were Tony Falco.

4. Here are some of the questions posed in the case. Please be sure your answers to questions 1–3 touch on each of them:

   • Is Tony's viewpoint about artists and live shows a refreshing change from most clubs or a liability for Falcon's economic success?

   • Should Tony think about holding some weekend time for lucrative private events, instead of money-losing shows? Would the extra money help or hinder his goals for the Falcon's music events?

   • How could Tony make better use of social media and advertising?

   • What colleges and schools in the area might be good partners for the Falcon?

   • Do you think Tony should move ahead with the renovation? Why or why not?

EXHIBIT 1: PARTIAL LIST OF ARTISTS WHO HAVE PERFORMED AT THE FALCON IN RECENT YEARS

Marcus Strickland Trio

Marta Topferova

Akie Bermiss

Lucky Peterson

Jim Campilongo

Tigran Hamasyan

KJ Denhert

Gustafer Yellowgold

Rachel Loshak

Marta Topferova

John Raymond

John Abercrombie

CKS

Jeremy Baum

Rosetta Trio

Project Percolator

Stryker/Slagle

Kristen Diable

Cyro Baptista

St. Patrick's Blast

Club d'Elf w/Medeski

Funk Junkies

Simone Felice

Saints' Swing Dance

Adam Cruz

Parkington Sisters

Spottiswoode

Billy Hart

Sheila Jordan Duo

Ben Van Gelder

Pedro Giraudo

Adam Levy & The Mint Imperials

Adam Arcuragi's 'Lupine Chorale Society'

The Bethany & Rufus Roots Quartet

World View

Edmar Castaneda

Kevin Hays, Joe Lovano & friends—A Benefit Concert for Haiti . . .

The Pedro Giraudo Jazz Orchestra

KJ Denhert

Glenn Zaleski Modern Jazz Quintet/Neil Alexander & Nail
Parkington Sisters
Bethany Yarrow
Hersch & Gori Duo
Milk & Jade
Jonah Smith Band
Arturo O'Farrill
Chris Bergson
Brad Mehldau
Marc Ribot
Roswell Rudd
Dominick Farinacci
Tom Freund
Anne McCue
Jamie Saft Trio
Lovano & Silvano
Bjorkestra
Sofía Rei Koutsovitis
Scofield/DeJohnette
John Escreet
Julian Lage Group
Vic Juris Trio
Stephan Crump
Cyro Baptista
Knights of Jazz
Four For
Sharrard & Charette
Jay Collins
Hugh Brodie
Edmar Castaneda
John Stetch
Nadav Snir Zelnike
Marc Black & Joe Fitz

EXHIBIT 2: THE FALCON'S FOOD AND DRINK MENU

The Falcon's restaurant is open at 6p.m. every day there is a music event.

We accept reservations, to make one please call (845) 236–7970 (leave your name, phone number, show you will attend, and the time you will be there before 7PM). We accept all major credit cards.

Appetizers

Local Tomato Bisque w/ Gruyere & Provolone Mini Grilled Cheese $8

Chilled Pea Soup with Crab Salad $8

Homemade Hummus w/ Fresh Focaccia, Carrot & Cucumber Chips (v) $6

Crispy Calamari tossed with Shaved Cabbage & Cilantro over a Bed of Spicy Roasted Tomato Chipotle Ragout $12

House-Smoked Chipotle-Glazed St. Louis Ribs over Local Veggie Slaw $9 | $17

Salads

Best-Dressed Caesar w/ Homemade Dressing, Grated Parmesan, Anchovies & Croutons $7 | $9

House Salad w/ Organic Field Greens and Fresh Seasonal Veggies tossed in House Balsamic (v) $7 | $9

Local Summer Salad Local, Organic, Seasonal Veggies Lightly Tossed w/ Lemon, Mint, Extra-Virgin Olive Oil & Sprinkled w/ Feta (v) $8

Panzanella Local Tomatoes, Onions, Basil, Fresh Mozzarella & Toasted Bread Lightly Marinated w/ Extra Virgin Olive Oil (v) $11

Sandwiches

Grilled Tuna Niçoise Sandwich w/ Olives, Chopped Egg, Roasted Red Pepper Relish, Sprouts, Sunflower Seeds & Olive Dressing $15

Grilled Chicken Panini w/ Pesto Mayo, Roasted Red Peppers & Fresh Mozzarella (f/s) $14

Local Tomato & Fresh Mozzarella Served on Focaccia with Arugula, Basil Pesto & Local Green Salad (v) $13

Add Prosciutto $2

Grassfed Hudson Valley Burger All Natural Beef—w/ Gruyere, American, Cheddar or Provolone (f/s) $15 (f/s) Served with Fresh Cut Fries or a Salad

Entrées

Sun-Dried Tomato Ravioli (p) w/ Local Summer Squash, Eggplant, Cherry Tomato, Goat Cheese & Basil Pesto (v) $18

Handmade Tagliatelle (p) w/ Local Corn, Prawn, Chili, Basil & Baby Tomato Ragout $21

Fish of the Day Check with your Server—MARKET

Pan Roasted Organic Tofu w/ Corn & Black Bean Succotash, Lime & Chili Oil (v) $17

Grassfed Hudson Valley Hangar Steak Pan Seared & Served w/ Tobacco Onions, Hearty Local Greens & Brandy Peppercorn Sauce $25

. . . .
(v) Vegetarian (Or Could Be—Check with Your Server)
(p) Pastas by La Bella Pasta—Kingston, NY
8% NY STATE TAX IS INCLUDED ON ALL CASH SALES—PLEASE TIP YOUR
    WAITSTAFF
Please Notify Your Server of Food Allergies or Special Dietary Needs
WE PROUDLY SUPPORT FARMS THAT PRACTICE SUSTAINABLE AGRICULTURE

EXHIBIT 3: A SAMPLING OF ACTIVITIES IN THE HUDSON VALLEY

- Benmarl Winery

- Shawngunk Wine Trail (showcases 11 wineries)

- Meet Me In Marlboro is a group of Milton & Marlboro, farmers & businesspeople working together to promote local agriculture and tourism to a regional market

- Minnewaska State Park

- Walkway over the Hudson—the longest pedestrian walkway in the country

- Franny Reese Scenic Hudson Preserve

- Black Creek Scenic Hudson Preserve

- Shopping & Antiquing

- Woodbury Commons Premium Outlets

- Historic villages of New Paltz, Beacon, and Rhinebeck

- DIA Beacon—a world-renowned modern art gallery

- FDR Presidential Library

- Vanderbilt Mansion

- Mills Mansion

- Culinary Institute of America

- DIA Beacon

- West Point

- Bannerman's Island

EXHIBIT 4: STATISTICS ON MARLBORO, NY

Read more: http://www.city-data.com/city/Marlboro-New-York.html#ixzz0qJg5Nn1k

Population in July 2007: 2,387.
Males: 1,155   (48.4%)
Females: 1,232   (51.6%)

Median resident age: 36.9 years
New York median age: 35.9 years
Zip code: 12542.

Estimated median household income in 2008: $55,527 (it was $43,073 in 2000)
Marlboro: $55,527
New York: $56,033

Estimated per capita income in 2008: $27,401

Marlboro CDP income, earnings, and wages data

Estimated median house or condo value in 2008: $292,833 (it was $134,200 in 2000)
Marlboro: $292,833
New York: $318,900

Mean prices in 2008: All housing units: $299,370; Detached houses: $295,974; In 2-unit structures: $275,019; In 3-to-4-unit structures: $452,691; In 5-or-more-unit structures: $749,987; Mobile homes: $151,136

Races in Marlboro:

- White Non-Hispanic (92.0%)

- Hispanic (5.0%)

- Black (1.8%)

- Two or more races (1.1%)

- American Indian (0.9%)

- Other race (0.8%)

Dec. 2009 cost of living index in Marlboro: 97.2 (near average, U.S. average is 100).

CHAPTER 13

Case Study: TicketLeap—Social Media Integration in the Cloud

By Professor Catherine Fitterman Radbill, Gregory Allis, Pedro Avillez Costa, Katonah Coster, Jillian Ennis, and Cristine Mayer, New York University, 2011

On a bitterly cold January 2010 afternoon, Chris Stanchak listened intently as his four senior TicketLeap engineers demonstrated a prototype of the new ticketing platform they had built. Just three weeks ago they had given him the news: TicketLeap's existing ticketing platform was too old and cumbersome to handle the crucial upgrades the company needed to make. Built and maintained by an offshore developer since 2003, the system had been patched together and upgraded many times. TicketLeap, an online ticketing platform used by thousands of small to mid-sized event organizers across the U.S. and Canada, had grown to 17 employees and tens of millions of dollars in ticket sales just two years after raising its first outside capital. Its services were deeply integrated with social networking sites. Stanchak knew they were poised for exponential growth if they could upgrade their ticketing platform.

In August, Stanchak had given his engineers the express mission of moving TicketLeap's ticketing platform in-house in order to have more control over its redesign. As part of his expansion plan, Stanchak was exploring the idea of migrating the operation to cloud computing. Still a relatively new concept, cloud computing would allow him to have access to multiple servers that could quickly scale up or down to handle the sudden surges in activity of online ticket purchasers.

Stanchak had hoped that his engineers could simply bring the offshore platform in house and make the necessary upgrades. But now he realized there was no amount of tech wizardry and cyber duct tape that could turn this sow's ear of a ticketing platform into a silk purse. It had to be scrapped and rebuilt from the ground up.

Working late into the night, Stanchak and his engineers determined that it would take eight months to build the first working prototype of the new platform and a year in total to migrate users completely onto it. It was exciting to think that the platform would move TicketLeap "from oil tanker to speed boat."[1] But it also meant that Stanchak's four senior (and most expensive) engineers would be dedicated to a year-long project that wasn't bringing in any revenue and, as in all new software projects, wasn't 100% guaranteed to work.

Stanchak estimated he would have to raise several million dollars in a financing round to cover the costs of such a major undertaking. Unless he shut the company down while the new system was being created, he would need two parallel ticketing systems running simultaneously for nearly a year—the old, legacy system and the alpha test of the new one.

To further complicate matters, Stanchak had been preparing to speak to his investors about scaling back the in-venue hardware side of its business. Providing laptops, touch-screen kiosks, and scanners to thousands of customers was a labor-intensive headache. Investors loved it for its top-line growth potential, but so far it hadn't shown profitability. Stanchak felt the in-venue hardware pulled the company away from its core mission of leveraging the efficiencies of the internet to sell tickets. However, he needed his investors' support before moving ahead on this major change.

As midnight approached and the meeting drew to a close, Stanchak saw that TicketLeap was at a critical juncture. Could he pursue all of these goals at the same time—a new ticketing platform, raising the money, and letting go of the in-venue hardware aspect of the business? He remembered their 2008 attempt to create a new platform, which had looked promising but had not lived up to its potential. Would the next attempt be successful? How would his investors react?

A STRONG INTEREST IN TECHNOLOGY AND MUSIC

Stanchak's independent spirit and business savvy began to develop in his teenage years. Regularly taking on various odd jobs, he began assembling computers for a Taiwanese man in his basement at the age of 14. The experience honed Stanchak's technical skills and provided him with invaluable experience working hands-on with early technology that would later fuel his career.

By the time he graduated from high school, Stanchak was already an active participant in the explosion of internet culture that defined the late 1990s. At the insistence of his parents, he began college at the University of Pittsburgh, but spent most of his time developing his technological skills and acumen outside the classroom. Within a few semesters he decided that college wasn't for him and left the University of Pittsburgh in 1997 to pursue a career in technology. Stanchak explains, "I was watching guys making tons of money off these new ventures in technology, and I decided I didn't want to wait around and miss my chance to get a piece of it."[2]

Utilizing his technical expertise, Stanchak went to work building information management systems and intranet interfaces for clients at S.I. Services, Inc, a systems integration company. In 1999, he was hired as a freelance computer technician by the University of Pennsylvania to prepare the university's computer systems for Y2K.[3] This entailed migrating all of the school's data to one centralized back-up server and preserving the integrity of their information architecture. Stanchak did such a good job that the university invited him to join the staff full time as a senior media specialist, a position he accepted.

Taking full advantage of the tuition benefits offered to University of Pennsylvania employees, Stanchak enrolled in courses at the Wharton School to complete a bachelors degree in business administration. In his free time, he pursued his passion for music as a local DJ. Stanchak wanted to use the internet to find and share music, but this was 1999 and he couldn't find an existing website to meet his needs. So he built his own site, opening it up to other DJs and musicians in order to drive traffic. He called his website Skoolhouse.com. It was the first to enable streaming capabilities for unknown and emerging artists. Despite a steady increase in traffic, Stanchak had difficulty turning a profit from running Skoolhouse.com. It was out of this dilemma that TicketLeap was born.

THE BIRTH OF TICKETLEAP

In August 2001, a friend approached Stanchak with a problem. He was planning a huge Halloween party at a popular New York City club, but he had no way to sell tickets online. Existing ticketing companies would not work with him because it was a one-off event, so he was forced to find an alternative means to make tickets available. Thinking this could be a way to make money to run Skoolhouse.com, Stanchak took on the challenge of developing a ticketing platform for the event.

While the event was canceled due to the events of 9/11, the experience showed Stanchak that event organizers were a customer base whose needs were not being met by existing ticketing services. Again taking advantage of the resources offered by the university, he submitted a business plan to the 2001 Wharton Venture Initiative Program for an online ticketing business he called TicketLeap.

"The quality of Chris' undergraduate business plan was higher than that of many graduate students' plans," states Wharton professor James Thompson who, at that time, was head of the Venture Initiative Program. "Chris was driven, had the Skoolhouse site up and running, and had vision. He wanted to be in the internet space using social media. This was well before the big hit of Facebook and MySpace."[4]

The social networking scene was still in its infancy in 2001. Emerging from the early internet world of online bulletin boards and chat rooms, sites such as GeoCities and theglobe.com paved the way for people with similar interests to meet and gather on the web. Classmates.com and SixDegrees.com were the precursors to modern social networking sites, following Friendster, which launched in 2002.[5] MySpace and Facebook followed in 2003 and 2004, respectively.

Although it did not win, Stanchak's business plan made it through several rounds of the competition and provided him with invaluable mentoring to help get his idea off the ground. He spent the next year working to develop the project, searching for software developers who could bring his idea to fruition. Ultimately forced to use developers off-shore due to his budgetary constraints, the project dragged on far longer than he'd planned, and the software was not ready for public use until August 2003.

The year 2003 proved to be a monumental for Stanchak and TicketLeap. He had saved enough money to launch his company, which he did just after graduating from Wharton in August. Next, Stanchak invited fellow Wharton classmate Christian Mayer to be his business partner. The two worked jointly on TicketLeap to develop and refine the software while building relationships with investors and clients.

October brought another milestone: a paying customer from Anchorage, Alaska. "We were new, we had a pretty good idea what we were doing, but we still didn't have all the kinks worked out," Stanchak said. "But they came in, gave us a chance, let us mess up a few times, but really believed in our product. It was a huge moment for the company as a whole, and for me, personally."[6]

Then, one month later, Stanchak's mother, Connie Stanchak, came on board as TicketLeap's first employee, working for free as head of sales and customer service. "We were able to sustain a pretty balanced work–life relationship," Stanchak said. "We knew when it was work time, and then when we would go to dinner with family afterwards, it was back to mother and son."[7]

GROWING PAINS

For the next year Stanchak, Mayer, and Mrs. Stanchak worked part-time at TicketLeap, signing up and servicing customers, and looking for investors to help grow the company. Setting out with an ambitious capital goal of $1.5 million, Stanchak and Mayer received commitments for nearly half but, in a typical chicken-and-egg dilemma, the money would only be given when the rest was secured. The funding round stalled out, and no money was raised.

"I had no idea how to raise money," says Stanchak. "I realized much later that we had aimed way too high with our $1.5 million goal." With a $38,000 school loan due immediately, $15,000 in credit card debt, and $11,000 owed to his father, Stanchak was broke. In February 2005, he moved back in with his parents. He took jobs working in e-commerce at GSI Commerce and Spencer Gifts to support himself and keep TicketLeap going. Christian Mayer moved back to Germany and left his role with the company at this time.

Refusing to give up his company, Stanchak worked on TicketLeap every night from 8p.m. until 2a.m., slept for four hours, and then went off to his day job. Mrs. Stanchak began working full-time at TicketLeap.

During this period, Stanchak focused on upgrading TicketLeap's software platform so he could offer expanded services to his clients and remain competitive. By 2007, TicketLeap had hundreds of clients and had grown to more than $200,000 in revenue.

Stanchak was convinced that there was a viable business here, and continued to look for capital to fund its growth. His mentor, James Thompson, put him in touch with a venture capitalist. After Stanchak's pitch to the VC, Thompson followed up to see how it had gone. The friend was very enthusiastic about the company, but said "Chris needs to commit full-time to TicketLeap in order to be taken seriously and attract investors."[8]

In March 2007, Stanchak quit his day job and returned full time to TicketLeap. Continuing his search for working capital, he began making the rounds of banks, looking for $200,000 in loans. It was a tough spring, as Stanchak received a string of rejections. Then one day, after turning him down for a bank loan, the loan officer told Stanchak that he was so impressed with the company that he would like to become a private angel investor. The tide had turned. By August, Stanchak had raised enough angel money to open his first office in Philadelphia.

"I rented a 2,800 square foot office on the advice of a colleague," says Stanchak. "It was insane. My Mom and I were the only people in there at the time. But my colleague was right. As soon as we began hiring other employees the space filled up quickly."[9]

This was an exhilarating but scary time for Stanchak. His dream was really happening. Finally, investors agreed with him that the business was viable, and had put down serious money to show him. He had bootstrapped the company for four years, and now he actually had money to spend. He wanted to be sure he spent it in the right ways.

BUILDING THE TEAM

One of the first things Stanchak did was expand the team, which grew to seven within a few months. "After spending years running the company on my own, I finally had a team of dedicated people who could help me. It's absolutely crucial to find the right people. They can make or break your new venture." (See Exhibit 1 for first TicketLeap employees.)

The next thing he did was form a board of investors and advisors. "Having a board is important to investors in a startup," states Thompson. "They need to know there's someone looking over their money."[10]

THE EARLY YEARS

TicketLeap had provided online ticketing services for small to mid-size events since its inception. They concentrated heavily on festivals, performing arts, and cultural and sporting events, and worked closely with schools that needed a quick and efficient way to sell tickets to their events. The company's focus was on the customer, not the event venue. "Our years of experience in this market have taught us that selling tickets and providing great services are the two most important issues for clients," states Stanchak. "Ticketing is the biggest part of our clients' revenue. They are tossing TicketLeap the keys to their business because they trust us. We value that trust and work hard to earn it."[11]

In addition to online services, TicketLeap supplied ticketing equipment to their clients for use at their events. Part of TicketLeap's new team was an implementation group who managed the inventory of basic laptops, scanners, and touch-screen kiosks. They mailed the equipment to the client a few days before each event, went to the event site to set it up, and trained the client on how to use it. After the event, the client would mail the equipment back to TicketLeap.

The on-site equipment system was cumbersome to maintain, and the legacy ticketing platform was part of the problem. There were often glitches in the interface between the software and hardware, and the implementation group constantly worried about the quality of service they could provide. "Today people expect things to work the way they want them to work," states Keith Fitzgerald, TicketLeap's Chief Engineer. "Chris wanted a more streamlined experience for the client: get access to the internet, use a USB scanner, and start scanning people into the event. But we couldn't do that because of our legacy ticketing platform."[12]

FIRST ATTEMPT TO REPLATFORM

By fall 2007, Stanchak was looking for a way to replatform TicketLeap's ticketing and stop using the off-shore developers. The existing platform, launched in 2003, had been upgraded and relaunched many times, but TicketLeap's sales were beginning to outreach the technology, particularly in the area of social media integration. Stanchak felt they were close to hitting the ceiling on scalability, given the constraints of the legacy platform.

In October, Stanchak met Iqram Magdon-Ismail, a fellow University of Pennsylvania alumnus, who had a degree in computer science. While at Penn, Iqram created a tool to analyze web traffic and user trends to assist management with online marketing decisions. Like Stanchak, Iqram was interested in music and had founded WeMusicStore.com as a project at Penn. The site allowed musicians to quickly and easily sell music to their fans. Iqram specialized in user interfaces and was well versed in building platforms that could sustain exponential user growth.[13] When he met Stanchak, Iqram was lead developer at a highly acclaimed social flirting site, ImInLikeWithYou.com, which had been featured in a "What's Hot" article by *Wired Magazine* in October, 2007.[14]

Iqram seemed the perfect person to take on the daunting task of building a new ticketing platform. He joined the TicketLeap team and by February 2008 had a new platform designed and ready to implement. However, the actual launch caused the servers to crash. Iqram quickly fixed the problems and calmed the angry customers, but the new platform just wasn't robust enough to let them get out from under their legacy off-shore system. Iqram remained with TicketLeap for another year, leaving in 2009 to found Venmo, another successful startup.

Despite this distraction, TicketLeap's annual gross ticket sales nearly doubled between the third and fourth quarters of 2007. And by July 2008, Stanchak had raised more than $2 million in a Series A round of financing.

TICKETLEAP'S BUSINESS MODEL

TicketLeap's business model is straightforward. Organizers can create an event that is ready for sale in a matter of minutes. The only fees are transactional, which can be passed on to the customer at the time of purchase.

TicketLeap's event pages are linked with Facebook and Twitter, allowing patrons to post comments, see which of their friends are also attending, and "Like" the event on Facebook. Event organizers can see what patrons are chatting about on their event pages, and even interact with the event-goers.

Ticket sales information is available in detail immediately after a sale is completed. Event organizers also can view net revenue, average order total, and total tickets sold over the lifespan of their events, even if they've already taken place. They can collect ticketing revenue in real time directly via a PayPal or Merchant Account, or have TicketLeap process their ticket sales.

TicketLeap reduces risk for event organizers and eliminates unnecessary hurdles in customer acquisition. Features such as event surveys and event page customization are hallmarks of TicketLeap's service. The ticket purchase process can even be embedded inside an event organizer's webpage, enabling them to maintain their branding.[15]

TicketLeap's biggest differentiating factor is that it is breaking out of the "walled garden" approach that competitors have historically followed. Sites like TicketMaster and Tickets.com strive to be content destinations as much as they are ticketing platforms. However, rich content already resides on the websites of event organizations, local media groups, aggregators, social networks and blogs. So why not have the ticketing transaction happen in the same place? This is the vision of TicketLeap—the platform is a utility to power the process. TicketLeap is agnostic about where the purchase takes place. This is radical thinking in the ticketing space, but it is exactly what made PayPal successful.[16]

Social network marketing and participants sharing information about TicketLeap-affiliated events are the marketing drivers for further expansion. The primary idea is to connect with all the parties involved in the event process and get them talking. This large network can include the event organizer, participants and ticket purchasers, the customers who attend the event, and the networks to which all these participants belong.

"The most profitable business comes from organic signups. These are organizers who find us through the web or word of mouth. It's very profitable because there is zero cost of acquisition and very low account management costs," states Stanchak.[17]

Stanchak explains that business development accounts—the first-time clients TicketLeap seeks out and tries to win—take a lot of time and money, but there is a significant volume of business there.

The Ticketing Industry

The ticketing industry has seen immense growth in recent years, particularly in the number of companies involved in ticketing solutions. Although Ticketleap offers a unique service to its clientele, the company is essentially in the business of providing ticketing solutions to promoters and events. The primary competitors in this market are Ticketmaster, Tickets.com, Ticketfly, Ticketweb, Front Gate, Amiando, and Eventbrite.

Ticketmaster is one of the oldest, largest, best-known, and most profitable ticketing companies in the world. Additionally, it is the only publicly traded company on this list. Their global footprint stretches across both oceans to 18 different international markets.

Founded in 1976, Ticketmaster has focused on acquiring high-profile clients with sports franchises and venues. They also have consolidated the ticket market with strategic purchases, such as the 1991 acquisition of their main stateside competitor Ticketron.

Acquisitions of other key competitors throughout the 1990s and early 2000s, in addition to a merger with Live Nation to form Live Nation Entertainment, is proof that Ticketmaster continues to be the leader of the pack in the ticketing industry.

Originally formed by the consolidation of nine separate ticketing entities, Tickets.com is a privately held company that has built an international presence by providing online ticketing resources for performing arts centers, professional sports organizations, and various stadiums and arenas in the USA, Canada, Europe, Australia and Latin America.

Other competitors include Ticketfly, Ticketweb, Amiando, and Eventbrite.

REACHING FOR THE CLOUDS

By December 2008, TicketLeap had Stanchak had raised several million dollars from investors, and the company had grown to 17 employees. Stanchak was preparing to launch a significant Series B round of funding. TicketLeap's investors and advisors had grown to include, among others, Colin Evans, co-founder of StubHub, which had sold to eBay for $310 million; Guy Kawasaki, member of the founding team of Macintosh, venture capitalist, and author (*Art of the Start*, and eight other books); and John Legend, five-time Grammy Award winning artist and record label owner (HomeSchool Records).

Despite these successes, Stanchak had become increasingly frustrated with the legacy ticketing system. The business was growing, but not at the rate he needed. "Twenty-five percent growth in a year is terrible for a startup. We needed to grow 100–400% per year," he explained.[18] Stanchak knew that his current ticketing system "wasn't going to win the race,"[19] and began to investigate a new concept that was cropping up in tech conversations: cloud computing.

At that time, the players in cloud computing were few and far between. Amazon was breaking ground in establishing itself as the front-runner, but the term was too new and largely undefined.[20] Dr. Werner Vogels, Vice President & Chief Technology Officer at Amazon.com, gave a keynote entitled *Ahead in the Cloud—The Power of Infrastructure as a Service* at Cloud Slam in April, 2009, the 1st Annual Virtual

Conference on Cloud Computing. In his talk, Dr. Vogel explained that it is essential in today's internet business landscape to build an infrastructure that can expand or contract at a moment's notice to manage the unpredictable behaviors of online consumers.[21]

Cloud computing is a reliable, flexible architecture that allows users to have access to multiple servers for the precise time they are needed, such as a spike in traffic to a company's website when a high-demand event is announced. When a company's own servers are taxed to their limit, cloud computing kicks in to handle the surge in demand. This allows the company to meet the needs of its customers without having to invest in the number of servers in might need to handle infrequent or unpredictable surges in internet traffic.

Stanchak and his chief engineer, Keith Fitzgerald, realized that cloud computing could revolutionize TicketLeap's business model and help it expand quickly and efficiently. But they had to move their platform in-house and make major upgrades before they could even begin to explore it. In September, the TicketLeap engineers took this on as their top priority.

However, after more than three months of focused effort, Fitzgerald knew it just wasn't possible. If Stanchak wanted to make any significant changes to grow the company, they would need to build a new platform from the ground up.

This was unwelcome but not entirely unexpected news. Stanchak had been wrestling with the drawbacks and limitations of the off-shore ticketing platform for years. He knew that eventually something major would have to change, and now it was time to face the issue. He gave Fitzgerald the OK to build a working model and show him what it could do.

Three weeks later, Fitzgerald and the other engineers had a prototype ready to demonstrate. Stanchak was impressed, and thought that the new platform could work. Now he needed to talk to his investors and see if they agreed with him.

"The question for investors wasn't about the project itself," states Thompson, who by then was a board member. "The investors needed to understand the business profitability pre- and post- the proposed new platform." The questions to be answered were 'How much money would it make, and how long would it take to get there?'[22]

Stanchak knew it would not be an easy sell. He predicted that some of his investors would be against both the new platform and the move away from the in-venue hardware side of TicketLeap. As in all ventures, investors are focused on making their numbers and exiting with their profits. Stanchak felt reasonably sure that some of his investors would see the potential in the proposed changes, but could he persuade all of them to back his ideas?

CONCLUSION

As he put on his coat to leave the office, Chris Stanchak remembered the talk he had given recently to a class of student entrepreneurs:

- This is one of the best times to be alive—ever.

- "I skate to where the puck is going to be, not to where it has been." (Wayne Gretzky)

- "Life moves pretty fast. If you don't stop and look around once in a while, you could miss it." (Ferris Bueller)

Thinking about the challenging days ahead, Stanchak hoped he would still believe the advice he had given the students when this was all over.

TICKETLEAP STUDY QUESTIONS

Careful and focused preparation is the key to a meaningful case study discussion. Please prepare for the TicketLeap case by reading it twice and *typing* your answers to these study questions. Bring your typed responses to class.

1. Give a thorough description of the issues that need to be solved in the case.

2. List the main factors influencing the decisions to be made.

3. State how you would resolve the issues if you were Chris Stanchak.

4. Here are the questions posed in the case. Please be sure your answers to question 1–3 touch on each of them:

   - Could Stanchak pursue all of these goals at the same time—a new ticketing platform, raising several million dollars, and letting go of the in-venue hardware aspect of the business?

   - What could Stanchak do to ensure that the next attempt at replatforming will be successful?

   - Was the profitability potential worth the risk and the financial investment?

   - How do you think TicketLeap's investors will react to the changes?

   - What specific strategy could Stanchak use to raise the money he needs?

EXHIBIT 1: FIRST EMPLOYEES OF TICKETLEAP

Carolyn Joe Daniel—Office Manager
Iqram Magdon-Ismail—VP of Technology
Connie Stanchak—Sales Director
Chris Stanchak—CEO
Two sales people and a marketing person

EXHIBIT 2: PARTIAL LIST OF TICKETLEAP CLIENTS

TEDx Phoenix
Susan G. Komen for the Cure
Wharton, University of Pennsylvania
Business Insider Ignition
Wizard World Comic Con
San Diego Comic Con International
Sierra Nevada Brewing Co.
Ronald McDonald House Charities
Yale
DeerFest
Hauntcon
American Red Cross
Seth Godin Live
Night Rocker Live

EXHIBIT 3: TICKETLEAP ADVISORS

Guy Kawasaki, Advisor on Product Evangelism
Co-founder of Truemors, Managing Director of Garage Technology Ventures

Guy Kawasaki is the co-founder of Truemors and a managing director of Garage Technology Ventures. He is also a columnist for *Entrepreneur Magazine*. Previously, he was an Apple Fellow at Apple Computer, Inc. Guy is the author of eight books including *The Art of the Start: Rules for Revolutionaries*, *How to Drive Your Competition Crazy*, *Selling the Dream*, and *The Macintosh Way*. He has a BA from Stanford University and an MBA from UCLA as well as an honorary doctorate from Babson College.

Mark Goldstein, Advisor on Customer Loyalty
CEO of Loyalty Labs

Mark Goldstein, a recognized expert in consumer loyalty services and best customer management systems, is the co-founder and CEO of Loyalty Lab Inc. A five-time serial entrepreneur, he co-founded BlueLight.com and served as its president and CEO. During his tenure at BlueLight, he launched its successful e-commerce shopping site, built its private label internet service to almost seven million members and installed 3,600 kiosks in Kmart stores. Prior to his experience with the national retailer, Mark served as VP of Shopping at Inktomi (now a part of Yahoo), a software company that acquired Impulse! Buy Network, a web merchandising specialist that he founded in 1997 as its CEO. Earlier, Mark founded NetAngels, a web profiling firm (now a part of Microsoft), and before that he founded online gaming and trading firm Reality Online (now part of Reuters) where he served as president for over seven years. Mark has served as Entrepreneur-in-Residence at both New Enterprise Associates and SOFTBANK Venture Capital. He is a graduate of the University of Pennsylvania where he attended the Wharton School and today serves on the Penn Library Board of Overseers.

Steven Davis, Advisor on eCommerce and International Operations
President of GSI Commerce Europe

Steven Davis is president of GSI Commerce Europe the International arm of GSI Commerce, the global leader in eCommerce solutions and services for the world's most respected brands. Steven was senior vice-president, partner services at GSI, from December 2004 to March 2007. Before GSI, he held a number of management positions at Just for Feet Inc., a specialty sporting goods retailer based in Birmingham, Ala., where his last served as vice president of marketing.

EXHIBIT 4: TICKETLEAP BOARD OF DIRECTORS

Pete Albert, Managing Partner of Seneca Advisors

A leader in the mortgage and commercial banking industry for more than four decades, Pete Albert has financed commercial and industrial projects and single-family homes both locally and nationally. He was a pioneer in the mortgage-backed security market through his early involvement with GNMA. Pete began his career at Fidelity Bond & Mortgage Company, eventually becoming Chairman & CEO. Later, he was CEO at Meridian Mortgage Corporation, which became one of the nation's leading mortgage bankers. Following this, he became vice-president of Jefferson Bank, vice-chairman of Bancorp Bank and then executive vice-president of Sovereign Bank.

Michael Aronson, Co-founder and Managing Partner of MentorTech Ventures

Michael Aronson is a Co-founder and Managing Partner of MentorTech Ventures and is an internationally recognized business educator, venture investor and serial entrepreneur with substantial breadth of experience and expertise in advising and assisting early stage software and related services companies. He serves on the Board and Finance and Investment Committees of the Ben Franklin Technology Fund of the Commonwealth of Pennsylvania, which successfully invests in early stage software, biotech and manufacturing technology companies. Michael was a senior lecturer and faculty member at the Wharton School for more than 20 years. He began his teaching career at the Wharton School as a teaching assistant, became a senior lecturer and moved to teaching in the Undergraduate, Graduate and Executive MBA programs. Afterwards Michael was a faculty member for numerous Senior Executive Education courses, including the Wharton Executive Development program which was based upon a simulation model of a global high technology ecosystem that he developed. Michael was also involved in the Wharton ebusiness Fellows program, teaching simulation models of internet ecommerce.

Colin Evans, Founder and Managing Partner of Sandwith Ventures, LLC

Colin M. Evans is the Founder and Managing Partner of Sandwith Ventures, LLC, a San Francisco and Philadelphia based investment firm focusing on angel and early stage investments founded in January, 2007. Sandwith Ventures, LLC focuses investment in three main sectors: (1) retail and consumer oriented e-commerce, (2) internet marketplaces, and (3) online marketing and advertising services. Investments are concentrated in the Bay Area and Philadelphia, but SV will also look at deals on the East Coast as far south as Washington, D.C. and as far north as New York City. Previous to launching Sandwith Ventures, Colin was a Co-founder, member of the Executive Team and vice-president of Sales and Business Development at StubHub.com, a successful online ticket exchange founded in 2000 and sold to eBay in early 2007. Colin oversaw four main functions while at StubHub including all sports and music sponsorships, business development partnerships, corporate sales and the LargeSeller program, which aggregated and serviced all the inventory providers on StubHub.

Chris Stanchak, Founder and CEO of TicketLeap

As Founder and CEO of TicketLeap.com, Chris Stanchak is responsible for the company's overall leadership, strategy and direction. He is well-versed in the design and management of large-scale eCommerce operations. Previously, he worked at GSI Commerce, a global eCommerce leader, where he managed the National Hockey League's online operations. Prior to his eCommerce experience, Chris worked as an IBM systems integration consultant. He managed the migration of banks, hospitals and schools from Mainframe to Client/Server architectures. Chris is an honors graduate of the Wharton School of the University of Pennsylvania, with dual concentrations in management and marketing. He lives in Center City Philadelphia with his wife Jenny. Chris is an active member of the tech entrepreneurship community in Philadelphia.

James Thompson, Director of Wharton Societal Wealth Program

James Thompson is co-founder and director of the Wharton Societal Wealth Program (WSWP). He teaches innovation, corporate growth and dynamic strategy in

Wharton Executive Education programs. Prior to joining the academic world he was divisional director of a public South African company. James holds a BCom from the University of South Africa and an MBA from the University of Cape Town Graduate School of Business. He concluded a research fellowship in the commercialization of technology at the Wharton School of the University of Pennsylvania and is a PhD candidate in the management of technology at Ecole Polytechnique Federale de Lausanne, Switzerland working on field research in the application of WSWP programs.

EXHIBIT 5: TICKETLEAP INVESTORS

Ben Franklin Technology Partners

Ben Franklin Technology Partners of Southeastern Pennsylvania is the Philadelphia region's catalyst for Stimulating Entrepreneurial Potential. Ben Franklin invests in innovative enterprises and creates commercialization pathways that generate wealth through science and technology. Part of a statewide network in Pennsylvania, BFTP/SEP provides entrepreneurs and established businesses with the Capital, Knowledge and Networks to compete in the global marketplace. BFTP/SEP has provided more than $130 million to grow more than 1,600 regional enterprises.

MentorTech Ventures

MentorTech Ventures is an early-stage venture capital fund that invests in information technology, marketing technology and medical device companies with a primary focus on those companies originating at the University of Pennsylvania. MentorTech Ventures plays an active role with its investments from start-up to exit. Their team has been helping technology companies reach their growth potential for over 25 years.

NextStage Capital

Headquartered just outside of Philadelphia, NextStage Capital focuses on finding undiscovered early stage investment opportunities in the Mid-Atlantic region. With an emphasis on technology software, hardware and services, their goal is to find talented entrepreneurs with a compelling and validated technology offering and help them build company value. The NextStage Capital team draws on years of experience as entrepreneurs and venture capitalists. The partners have invested over $175M of early stage capital and helped build some of the most lucrative venture-backed companies in the area.

Seneca Advisors, LLC

Seneca Advisors, LLC was formed in 2007 by Pete Albert, a leader in the mortgage and commercial banking industry for more than four decades. He formed the company to continue his interest in helping to fund and develop private companies. Some of those companies include Product Partners, the nation's largest fitness and exercise direct marketing company, E-Brilliance, Smart Stick, Golf.com and E Force Compliance. Pete Albert has financed commercial and industrial projects and single family homes both locally and nationally. He was a pioneer in the mortgage-backed security market through his early involvement with GNMA. He began his career at Fidelity Bond & Mortgage Company, eventually becoming Chairman & CEO. Later, he was CEO at Meridian Mortgage Corporation, which became one of the nation's leading mortgage bankers. Following this, he became vice-president of Jefferson Bank, vice-chairman of Bancorp Bank and then executive vice-president of Sovereign Bank.

A Visit to 2012 Winter NAMM, the World's Largest Music Products Tradeshow

David Livingston/Getty Images Entertainment/Getty Images

The $17 billion global musical instruments and products industry is a vibrant sector of the music industry, one that is full of opportunities for entrepreneurs. The retail products marketplace gathers each January in Anaheim, California for the extravaganza known as the NAMM Show. NAMM stands for the National Association of Music Merchandisers.

In 2012, a record 95,700 music industry people registered and attended the four-day trade show, and I was one of them. NAMM is a cacophonous celebration of musical equipment and accessories, new-product unveilings, educational seminars, performances and autograph signings, and spirited deal-making between manufacturers and retailers.[1]

With much of the music industry still feeling the pain of a prolonged economic recession, the NAMM show felt like a trip back in time to better days. The Anaheim Convention Center and the surrounding hotel conference spaces pulsed with energy and excitement. NAMM reported a 6% increase in registered attendees from 2011, a new record for this 110-year old institution. International registration was up 15%, to 11,981. There were 1,441 exhibitors, 236 of whom were new to the NAMM show.[2]

NAMM and the NAMM Foundation's activities and programs are designed to promote music making to people of all ages. In addition to the annual trade show, NAMM has ongoing educational outreach programs for its members (through NAMM U and NAMM U Online), and for students who are preparing for their careers. The NAMM Foundation provides ongoing representation in Washington, D.C. on issues that impact the music products industry, including:

- Music education and education reform legislation and funding

- Small business health insurance legislation

- Estate tax reform

- Import/export laws

- E-commerce tax reform.

Advancing Music: Public Policy, Music Education and Music Making is the informative blog by NAMM's Director of Public Affairs & Government Relations, Mary Luehrsen. At the 2012 show, the Lacey Act was a much-discussed topic. It is a conservation law that is having an impact on trade and commerce for instrument makers.

As if seeing thousands of guitars, hundreds of drums, football-field-size exhibit rooms of pianos and keyboards, string, brass and woodwind instruments weren't enough, there were booth performances by many of the top names in the business at NAMM. Here's a partial list:

- Iron Maiden drummer Nicko McBrain at the Paiste booth

- Alice Cooper at the Shure and Fender booths

- Alex Skolnick at the Agile Partners booth

- Stevie Wonder in the Yamaha keyboard area

- Kenny Wayne Shepherd promoting AmpKit from Agile Partners

- KISS lead singer Gene Simmons showcasing his GS-AXE-2 bass guitar

- Signings and demonstrations by John Mayer, Slash, Tommy Lee, Sheila E, Joe Satriani and many others.

- Steve Vai received the Les Paul award, and jammed later with Billy Sheehan, Orianthi and others

- Brian Wilson was awarded the Music for Life award.[3]

Nicko McBrain
Credit: Larry Marano/Getty Images Entertainment/Getty Images

Kenny Wayne Shepherd
Credit: David Livingston/Getty Images Entertainment/Getty Images

Steve Vai and Joe Satriani
Credit: John Livzey/Redferns/Getty Images

Gene Simmons and GS-AXE-2
Credit: David Livingston/Getty Images Entertainment/Getty Images

In addition to instruments, musicians, and gear there were many established technology-based companies at NAMM, such as Avid, Sweetwater, and Sony, as well as just-launched ventures like ArtistGrowth, a Nashville-based start-up that offers a sophisticated set of cloud-based business management tools for artists. NAMM's Virtual Press Room provides access to Show Exhibitor news, company profiles, product launches, photos and other information: namm.org/thenammshow/2012/press-room.

Creativity, innovation, and a love of music were the common denominators for all of us at the 2012 NAMM show. See for yourself at namm.org/thenammshow/2012.

NOTES

CHAPTER 1 FUNDAMENTALS OF ENTREPRENEURIAL THINKING

1 Information for this profile is based on interviews with Brian McTear, Peter English, and Catherine Radbill, March 4 and May 16, 2011 at Miner Street Studios and Weathervane Music offices, Philadelphia, PA, as well as subsequent email communications.
2 McTear/English interviews and emails.
3 Ibid.
4 Ibid.
5 Shaking Through, "FAQ's," shakingthrough.com//faq (accessed March 1, 2011).
6 Ibid.
7 McTear/English interviews and emails.
8 Ibid.
9 Press Release from Weathervane Music and WXPN. *WXPN and Weathervane Music Organization Announce Collaborative Project to Showcase Independent Musicians*, Philadelphia, PA, January 26, 2010.
10 Grayson Currin, "Sharon Van Etten: "Love More," Pitchfork, February 11, 2010, pitchfork.com/reviews/tracks/11768-love-more/ (accessed February 11, 2011).
11 Shaking Through, "Sharon Van Etten," shakingthrough.com/sharonvanetten (accessed February 11, 2011).
12 McTear/English interviews and emails.
13 Shaking Through, "Sharon Van Etten."
14 Consequence of Sound, "Sharon Van Etten Taps The National To Help With New Album," consequenceofsound.net/2011/01/sharon-van-etten-plots-massive-tour-taps-the-national-to-help-with-new-album/ (accessed May 15, 2011).
15 Sharon Van Etten, sharonvanetten.com/ (accessed May 15, 2011).
16 Shaking Through, "Dreamers of the Ghetto," shakingthrough.com/dreamersofthe-ghetto (accessed May 15, 2011).
17 Ibid.
18 Ibid.
19 Ibid.
20 Shaking Through, "Big Troubles," shakingthrough.com/bigtroubles (accessed May 15, 2011).
21 Ibid.
22 shakingthrough.com/bigtroubles.
23 Grayson Currin, "Watch Shaking Through, One of the Very Best Online Music Series," *IFC.com*, June 23, 2011, ifc.com/news/2011/06/dreamers-of-the-ghetto.php (accessed July 11, 2011).
24 Carl J. Schramm, "The Positive Impact of Entrepreneurship in the American Economy," ecorner.stanford.edu/authorMaterialInfo.html?mid=1760 (accessed July 4, 2011).
25 Carol S. Dweck, *Mindset: The New Psychology of Success* (New York: Ballantine Books, 2006), 6–7.
26 Ibid., 61.
27 Daniel H. Pink, *A Whole New Mind* (New York: Riverhead Books, 2006), 51–52.

28 Ibid., 138.
29 P.J.H. Schoemaker and R.E. Gunther, "The Wisdom of Deliberate Mistakes," *Harvard Business Review,* June 2006.
30 Leigh Buchanan, "How The Creative Stay Creative," *Inc.* Magazine, June 2008: 102.
31 Daniel J. Levitin, *This Is Your Brain On Music* (New York: Plume, 2006), 191.
32 Addiction Science Research and Education Center, College of Pharmacy, The University of Texas, Austin, "Dopamine—A Sample Neurotransmitter," utexas.edu/research/asrec/dopamine.html (accessed April 24, 2011).
33 Ibid.
34 Levitin, *Brain On Music,* 191.
35 Ibid., 232.
36 Ibid., 231.
37 International Federation of the Phonographic Industry, The Broader Music Industry, ifpi.org/content/library/the-broader-music-industry.pdf, May 1, 2011.

CHAPTER 2 CREATIVE PROBLEM SOLVING

1 South by Southwest, "Top of the Charts in 2015," schedule.sxsw.com/events/event_MP5594, (accessed April 24, 2011).
2 Joel Warner, "Fueled By Venture-Capital Funding and a Love for Unknown Bands, Can Boulder's Next Big Sound Predict the Next Rock Star?" Westword, October 7, 2010, westword.com/2010-10-07/music/fueled-by-venture-capital-funding-and-a-love-for-unknown-bands-can-boulder-s-next-big-sound-predict-the-next-rock-star/4/ (accessed April 23, 2011).
3 Ibid.
4 "Next Big Sound," nextbigsound.com/about (accessed April 24, 2011).
5 Herb Meyers and Richard Gerstman. *Creativity—Unconventional Wisdom from 20 Accomplished Minds* (New York: Palgrave MacMillan, 2007), 122.
6 "About TED," TED.com (accessed February 10, 2012).
7 Home page, WhyNot.net (accessed February 10, 2012).
8 Michael Michalko. *Thinkertoys* (Berkeley: 10 Speed Press, 2006), 19–20.
9 Barry Nalebuff and Ian Ayers, *Why Not?* (Boston: Harvard Business School Press, 2003), 17.
10 James Diener, CEO-President of A&M/Octone Records, quoted in Anita Elberse and Elie Ofek, "Octone Records," Harvard Business School Case #N9-507-082, July 13, 2007, 3.
11 Adapted from an article by Marcus Carab, "How Turntable.fm Could Be Even More Awesome," techdirt.com/articles/20110627/19352614877/how-turntablefm-could-be-even-more-awesome-make-everyone-money.shtml (accessed June 28, 2011).
12 Joey Reiman Blog, "The Five Last Bastions for Thinking," joeyreiman.com/?p=173 (accessed July 4, 2011).
13 "What is Linux? An Overview of the Linux Operating System," Linux Foundation, linux.com/learn/resource-center/376-linux-is-everywhere-an-overview-of-the-linux-operating-system (accessed February 11, 2012).
14 Jeff Howe, *Crowdsourcing: Why the power of the crowd is driving the future of business* (New York: Three Rivers Press, 2009) 8, 14.
15 Ibid.
16 This profile is based on a telephone conversation between Kimberley Locke and Catherine Radbill on July 28, 2011.
17 Kimberley Locke Official, "Bio," kimberleylockeofficial.com/bio.shtml (accessed July 27, 2011).
18 Pulse Music Board, "Billboard's Top 50 Dance Songs Of The Decade," pulsemusic.proboards.com/index.cgi?action=display&board=dance&thread=91887&page=1#2553464 (accessed July 27, 2011).

CHAPTER 3 BRAND YOU

1 Information for this profile is based on an interview between John Janick and Catherine Fitterman Radbill at Fueled By Ramen offices, New York, March 23, 2011.
2 *Atlantic Records: The House That Ahmet Built.* Film by director Susan Steinberg. 2007.
3 Gary Graham et al., "The Transformation of the Music Industry Supply Chain," *International Journal of Operations & Production Management*, 2004, 24(11): 1087–1103.
4 T. Lathrop and J. Pettigrew, Jr, *The Business of Music Marketing & Promotion* (New York: Billboard: 2001), 44–45.
5 Ibid.
6 Graham et al., "Transformation."
7 Tom Peters, "The Brand Called You," *Fast Company*, August 31, 1997, 10: 83.
8 Chris Anderson, *The Long Tail: How Endless Choice is Creating Unlimited Demand* (London: Random House Group, 2007).
9 A. M. Muniz and T. C. O'Guinn, "Brand Community," *Journal of Consumer Research*, 2001, 27: 412–432.
10 Everett Rogers, *Diffusion of Innovations* (New York: Free Press, 1983).
11 Seth Godin, *Purple Cow; Transform Your Business by Being Remarkable* (London: Penguin Business, 2005).

CHAPTER 4 COPYRIGHT LAW AND THE MUSIC INDUSTRY

1 Ed Christman, "RightsFlow Builds A Business Around Clearing Song Rights," *Billboard*, March 18, 2011.
2 "What we do," RightsFlow, rightsflow.com/what-we-do/mechanical-licensing-and-royalty-services/ (February 13, 2012).
3 Ibid.
4 Ibid.
5 "YouTube acquires RightsFlow," *Los Angeles Times*, December 9, 2011, latimesblogs. latimes.com/entertainmentnewsbuzz/2011/12/youtube-acquires-rightsflow.html (February 13, 2012).
6 World Intellectual Property Organization (WIPO), "World Intellectual Property Handbook: Policy, Law and Use," WIPO Publication No. 489, 2004, 3.
7 WIPO, "Copyright and Related Rights," wipo.int/about-ip/en/copyright.html (accessed January 16, 2012).
8 Copyright.gov.
9 U.S. Copyright Office, "Copyright in General."
10 Randall D. Wixen, *The Plain and Simple Guide to Music Publishing* (Milwaukee, WI: Hal Leonard, 2005), Editor's Identification Page.
11 Ian Hargreaves, "Digital Opportunity: A Review of Intellectual Property and Growth," Independent Report, May 2011, 1, ipo.gov.uk/ipreview-finalreport.pdf (accessed May 14, 2012).
12 Ibid.
13 U.S. Copyright Office "Form TX"
14 U.S. Copyright Office, "Copyright in General," copyright.gov/help/faq/faq-general. html (accessed January 14, 2012).
15 U.S. Copyright Office, "Copyright in General."
16 U.S. Copyright Office, "Copyright Basics," copyright.gov/circs/circ1.pdf.
17 U.S. Copyright Office, "Registering a work," copyright.gov/help/faq/faq-register. html.
18 Ibid.
19 Ibid.
20 Ibid.
21 Ibid.

22   U.S. Copyright Office, "Copyright in General."
23   Ibid.
24   U.S. Copyright Office, "How Long Does Copyright Protection Last," copyright.gov/help/faq/faq-duration.html (accessed January 14, 2012).
25   U.S. Copyright Office, "FAQ: How Long Does Copyright Last?", copyright.gov/help/faq/faq-duration.html#duration (accessed January 18, 2012).
26   See 17 U.S.C. § 109(a) (2000).
27   U.S. Copyright Office, "A Brief Introduction and History," copyright.gov/circs/circ1a.html (accessed January 14, 2012).
28   Ibid.
29   U.S. Copyright Office, "DART," copyright.gov/carp/dartfact.html (accessed January 11, 2012).
30   "Material on David LaMacchia Case," groups.csail.mit.edu/mac/classes/6.805/articles/dml/lamacchia.html (accessed January 15, 2012).
31   Ibid.
32   U.S. Copyright Office, "Statement of Marybeth Peters, The Register of Copyrights, before the Subcommittee on Courts and Intellectual Property, Committee on the Judiciary, United States House of Representatives, 105th Congress, 1st Session, September 11, 1997, No Electronic Theft (NET) Act of 1997 (H.R. 2265)" copyright.gov/docs/2265_stat.html.
33   U.S. Copyright Office, "Online Service Providers," =copyright.gov/onlinesp/ (accessed January 15, 2012).
34   "Life Expectancy at Birth by Race and Sex, 1930–2007," infoplease.com/ipa/A0005148.html (accessed January 14, 2012).
35   Movie Licensing USA, "Understanding Copyright," movlic.com/k12/copyright.html (accessed January 18, 2012)
36   Ibid.
37   Dan DeLuca, "Girl Talk A Master of Musical Mixes," *Philadelphia Inquirer,* February 4, 2011.
38   Ibid.
39   Harry Fox, "What is a Sample?" harryfox.com/public/FAQ.jsp#11 (accessed October 4, 2011).
40   Ian Hargreaves, "Digital Opportunity," 1.
41   Duke University Law Center for the Study of the Public Domain, law.duke.edu/cspd/about.html (accessed May 20, 2011).
42   Creative Commons, "About," creativecommons.org/about (accessed May 21, 2011).
43   Shane Richmond, "Can Creative Commons solve the digital rights problem?" *The Telegraph*, February 11, 2012, telegraph.co.uk/technology/news/8608996/Can-Creative-Commons-solve-the-digital-rights-problem.html (accessed January 18, 2012).
44   Ibid.
45   Fox News.com, "Wikipedia goes dark for 24 hours to protest web piracy bills," January 18, 2012, foxnews.com/scitech/2012/01/18/wikipedia-goes-dark-for-24-hours-to-protest-us-web-piracy-bills/ (accessed January 18, 2012).

CHAPTER 5 INTERNATIONAL COPYRIGHT AND TRADE AGREEMENTS

1   WIPO (World Intellectual Property Organization), "Roundtable on Intellectual Property and Indigenous Peoples," WIPO/INDIR/RT/98/2 Add. Geneva, July 23–24, 1998, 4, 5.
2   U.S. Copyright Office, "Copyright in General," copyright.gov/help/faq/faq-general.html#protect, (accessed 5/20/11).
3   Association of Research Librarians, "Copyright Timeline."

4 About WIPO, "WIPO Treaties—General Information," wipo.int/treaties/en/general/ (accessed January 14, 2012).

5 Ibid.

6 U.S. Copyright Office, "International Copyright," copyright.gov/fls/fl100.html (accessed January 14, 2012).

7 Ibid.

8 David J. Moser and Cheryl L. Slay, *Music Copyright Law* (Boston: Course Technology, 2012), 238.

9 Conversation with Professor Shirley A. Washington, February 13, 2012.

10 World Trade Organization, "Intellectual property: protection and enforcement—The Agreement on Trade-Related Aspects of Intellectual Property Rights (TRIPS)," wto.org/english/thewto_e/whatis_e/tif_e/agrm7_e.htm (accessed January 16, 2012).

11 Audio Engineering Society, "An Audio Timeline," aes.org/aeshc/docs/audio.history.timeline.html (accessed January 16, 2012).

12 WIPO, "Summary of Rome Convention for the Protection of Performers, Producers of Phonograms, and Broadcasting Organizations (1961)," wipo.int/treaties/en/ip/rome/summary_rome.html (accessed January 16, 2012).

13 "Summaries of Conventions, Treaties and Agreements Administered By WIPO, 2011," 44, *www.wipo.int/freepublications/en/intproperty/.../wipo_pub_442.pdf*.

14 WIPO, "About," wipo.int/about-wipo/en/ (accessed January 16, 2012).

15 IFPI, "The WIPO Treaties: Top Priority for Copyright Owners," ifpi.org/content/section_views/wipo_treaties.html (accessed January 16, 2012).

16 IFPI, "The WIPO Treaties: Top Priority for Copyright Owners," ifpi.org/content/section_views/wipo_treaties.html (accessed January 14, 2012).

17 World Trade Organization, wto.org/english/thewto_e/whatis_e/tif_e/agrm7_e.htm (accessed January 15, 2012).

18 Moser and Slay, *Music Copyright Law*, 241.

19 World Trade Organization, "Who we are," wto.org/english/thewto_e/whatis_e/who_we_are_e.htm (accessed January 16, 2012).

20 Ibid.

21 World Trade Organization, "Overview: the TRIPS agreement," wto.org/english/tratop_e/trips_e/intel2_e.htm.

22 Ibid.

23 Ibld.

24 Katia Gomez, "Inside the TRIPS Agreement," *Prospect: Journal of International Affairs at the University of California San Diego*, October 2009, prospectjournal.ucsd.edu/index.php/2009/10/inside-the-trips-agreement/ (accessed January 15, 2012).

25 Joseph E. Stiglitz, "Trade agreements and health in developing countries," *The Lancet*, January 31, 2009, 373: 363 (accessed at thelancet.com on January 15, 2012).

26 Richard Smirke, "U.K. Announces Massive Copyright Reform: Scraps Website Blocking, Allows CD Copying, Music Parodies," *Billboard*, August 3, 2011, billboard.biz/bbbiz/industry/publishing/u-k-announces-massive-copyright-reform-scraps-1005301582.story (accessed January 11, 2012).

27 Quote by Creative Industries Minister Ed Vaizey, News Distribution Services for [U.K.] Government and the Public Sector, Department for Business Innovation & Skills, "Sweeping intellectual property reforms to boost growth and add billions to the economy," August 3, 2011, nds.coi.gov.uk/content/detail.aspx?NewsAreaId=2&ReleaseID=420683&SubjectId=2 (accessed January 11, 2012).

28 Ian Hargreaves, "Digital Opportunity: A Review of Intellectual Property and Growth," Independent Report, May 2011, 7, ipo.gov.uk/ipreview-finalreport.pdf (accessed May 14, 2012).

29 Nam Pham, "The Impact of Innovation and the Role of Intellectual Property Rights on U.S. Productivity, Competitiveness, Jobs, Wages and Exports," NDP Consulting, April 2010, Global Intellectual Property Center, thecacp.com/ (accessed February 14, 2012).

30 Thank you to Professor Shirley A. Washington for inspiring these two scenarios.
31 sandefur.typepad.com/freespace/2004/08/selfplagiarism.html (accessed February 11, 2011).

CHAPTER 6 THE ROLE OF THE MUSIC PUBLISHER

1   JDub Records, jdubrecords.org/ (accessed August 29, 2011).
2   Gil Shefler, "Tough Economy Crushes Jewish Music Label's Vision," *The Jerusalem Post*, July 31, 2011, jpost.com/ArtsAndCulture/Music/Article.aspx?ID=231704&R=R1 (accessed August 29, 2011).
3   Ibid.
4   Phone conversation with Aaron Bisman, August 22, 2011.
5   Joshua Venture Group, joshuaventuregroup.org/ (accessed August 28, 2011).
6   Gil Shefler, "Tough Economy Crushes Jewish Music Label's Vision."
7   Ibid.
8   Kathleen Ripley, "Music Publishing in the U.S.," *IBISWorld Industry Report 51223*, July 2011, 4.
9   Universal Music Publishing Group, Home Page, umusicpub.com/ (accessed January 7, 2012).
10 Ripley, "Music Publishing."
11 Conversation with Heather Trussell, Vice President, Memory Lane Music Group, February 13, 2012.
12 Ripley, "Music Publishing."
13 Statement of Mary Beth Peters, The Register of Copyrights before the Subcommittee on Courts, The Internet and Intellectual Property of the House Committee on the Judiciary, United States House of Representatives, 108th Congress, 2d Session, March 11, 2004, Section 115 Compulsory License, copyright.gov/docs/regstat031104.html (accessed October 4, 2011).
14 Howard B. Abrams, "Copyright's First Compulsory License," *Santa Clara Computer and High Tech Law Journal*, 2010, 26(2): 215.
15 Peter Alhadeff and Caz McChrystal, "Inflation and U.S. Music Mechanicals, 1976–2010," *Global Business and Economic Review*, 2011, 13(1).
16 "HFA Royalty Rate," harryfox.com/public/userfiles/file/Licensee/HFARoyaltyRatePR10-2-08.pdf (accessed February 14, 2012).
17 Trussell conversation.
18 Ed Christman, Billboard, May 31, 2011.
19 Trussell conversation.
20 WIPO International, wipo.int/wipo_magazine/en/2009/06/article_0007.html (accessed August 16, 2011).

CHAPTER 7 SONGWRITERS AND MUSIC PUBLISHERS

1   Larry Rohter, *Record Industry Braces for Artists' Battles Over Song Rights*, August 15, 2011, *New York Times*.
2   Stanford University Libraries, "Copyright and Fair Use," fairuse.stanford.edu/Copyright_and_Fair_Use_Overview/chapter9/9-c.html (accessed February 9, 2012).
3   Ibid.
4   Trussell conversation.
5   MEIEA Annual Conference, Hollywood, California, April 23, 2011. Panel discussion on Music Publishing.
6   Barry Nalbuff and Ian Ayers, *Why Not?* (Boston: Harvard Business School Press, 2003), 16–35.
7   Ibid.
8   Ibid.
9   Ibid.

CHAPTER 8 PERFORMING RIGHTS SOCIETIES

1 Information for this profile is based on a phone interview with Marni Wandner, August, 9, 2011.
2 U.S. Copyright Office, "Copyright Law of the United States," copyright.gov/title17/92chap1.html (accessed August 23, 2011).
3 ASCAP, ASCAP.com (accessed August 22, 2011).
4 Ibid.
5 ASCAP Press Release, "ASCAP Announces U.S. Licensing Agreement With Spotify," ascap.com/press/2011/0714_LicensingAgreement-Spotify.aspx (accessed August 3, 2011).
6 CISAC, "CISAC and Author's Rights," cisac.org/CisacPortal/afficherArticles.do?menu=main&item=tab2&store=true (accessed September 9, 2011).
7 CISAC, "Annual Report 2011/2012," cisac.org/CisacPortal/initConsultDoc.do?idDoc=23787 (accessed July 8, 2012).
8 EurActive, "EU Pushes for Single Online Music Licensing," January 8, 2010, euractiv.com/en/infosociety/eu-pushes-single-online-music-licensing/article-188665 (accessed September 9, 2011).
9 Ed Christman, "@MIDEM: Collection Societies Bemoan Contradictory Mandate," *Billboard*, January 25, 2010 (accessed September 9, 2011).
10 ASCAP, "ASCAP Payment System," ascap.com/members/payment/ (accessed August 24, 2011).
11 Ed Christman, "BMI's 2011 Revenues At All-Time High," Billboard.biz, billboard.biz/bbbiz/industry/publishing/bmi-s-2011-revenues-at-all-time-high-1005359842.story (accessed July 8, 2012).
12 ASCAP.com, "ASCAP Reports Increased Revenues in 2011," ascap.com/Press/2012/0308_ascap-reports.aspx (accessed July 8, 2012).
13 BMI.com, 8/24/11
14 Sound Exchange, "FAQ's for Artists and Labels," qa.americanbar.org/content/dam/aba/migrated/2011_build/entertainment_sports/faqforartistslabels.authcheckdam.pdf (accessed September 3, 2011).
15 Sound Exchange, soundexchange.com (accessed September 3, 2011).
16 Sound Exchange, "What Royalties Does Sound Exchange Administer?" soundexchange.com/category/faq/#question-434 (accessed August 24, 2011).
17 BMI, "US Radio Royalties," bmi.com/creators/royalty/us_radio_royalties/detail (accessed September 9, 2011).
18 Ed Christman, "Evolution of PROs in Digital Revolution," *Billboard,* June 3, 2011.
19 Ibid.
20 Ibid.

CHAPTER 9 CONCERTS AND TOURING

1 Information for this profile is based on interviews between Andrew Cyr and Yifan Qin in March and April 2011.
2 Bob Keyes, "Andrew Cyr is Having a Classical Gas in NYC," *The Portland Press Herald/Maine Sunday Telegram*, April 18, 2010, pressherald.com/life/classical-gas_2010-04-18.html (accessed March 19, 2011).
3 Metropolis Ensemble, "About," metropolisensemble.org/about/ (accessed March 20, 2011).
4 Colaneri, Katie, "Andrew Cyr, Who Serves Hoboken's Our Lady of Grace Church as Music Director, is up for a Grammy Award for Recording of Avner Dorman Concerto Made with His Metropolis Ensemble," *NJ.com*, December 4, 2010, nj.com/news/jjournal/hoboken/index.ssf?/base/news-2/1291447546263310.xml (accessed April 3, 2011).
5 Telephone conversation between Rich Nesin and Catherine Radbill, September 3, 2011.

6   Ibid.
7   Michael Brandvold Marketing, "J. Sider, CEO and Founder of RootMusic, Discusses BandPage and Facebook Marketing on *The Music Biz Weekly Podcast*," michaelbrandvold.com/blog/2011/05/j-sider-ceo-and-founder-of-rootmusic-discusses-bandpage-and-facebook-marketing-on-the-music-biz-weekly-podcast/ (accessed August 19, 2011).
8   Nesin, telephone conversation.
9   MarillionOnline, "News," marillion.com/press/anorak.htm (accessed August 21, 2011).
10 Ibid.
11 Ibid.
12 Ibid.
13 Nesin, telephone conversation.
14 Ibid.
15 Ibid.
16 Ibid.
17 "2012 Mid-Year Features," Pollstar, July 16, 2012.
18 David Segal, "They're Calling Almost Everyone's Tune," *New York Times*, April 25, 2010.
19 Ben Sisario, "Probation, Not Prison, for Scalpers," *New York Times*, June 9, 2011.
20 NJ.com, "Wiseguy Tickets Operators Admit Online Ticket Hacking Scheme," nj.com/news/index.ssf/2010/11/wiseguy_tickets_operators_plea.html (accessed August 21, 2011).
21 Mac Presents—Music and Companies, "Billboard Interview: Marcie Allen," macpresents.com/2010/06/10/branding-sponsorship-strategies-from-mac-president-marcie-allen/ (accessed August 20, 2011).
22 Jill Sobule, "About Jill," jillsobule.com/about/, (accessed August 20, 2011).
23 Nesin, telephone conversation.
24 "About," Future of Music Coalition, futureofmusic.org/about (accessed February 13, 2012).
25 Glenn Peoples, "Future of Music Coalition's Artist Revenue Study @MIDEM: Fan-Funding, Grants Outweigh Merch, Sponsorship," Billboard, January 31, 2012, billboard.biz/bbbiz/industry/legal-and-management/future-of-music-coalition-s-artist-revenue-1006049352.story (accessed February 13, 2012).

CHAPTER 10 RECORDED MUSIC

1   NPR—All Things Considered, "Pomplemoose: Making A Living On YouTube," April 11, 2010, npr.org/templates/story/story.php?storyId=12578327, npr.org/templates/story/story.php?storyId=125783271 (accessed July 30, 2011).
2   YouTube, "Partners Program," youtube.com/partners (accessed July 30, 2011).
3   Hypebot, "Pomplemoose Actually Has Terrible Internet" [Video], hypebot.com/hypebot/2011/01/pomplamoose.html (accessed July 30, 2011).
4   IFPI, "Recording Industry in Numbers Annual Report, 2010," ifpi.org/content/section_news/20100428.html (accessed July 30, 2011).
5   Glenn Peoples, "Yes, Artists Still Want Label Deals," *Billboard*, March 28, 2011.
6   The Technium, "1000 TrueFans," kk.org/thetechnium/archives/2008/03/1000_true_fans.php (accessed August 28, 2011).
7   BBC News, "Global music sales slump slowing," bbc.co.uk/news/entertainment-arts-17524458 (accessed July 10, 2012).
8   Arbitron, "Radio Today: How Americans Listen to Radio—2009 Edition," *Arbitron, Inc.*, arbitron.com/radio_stations/home.htm (accessed August 1, 2011).
9   Jeffrey Goldfarb and Wayne Arnold, "Listen Carefully for the Sour Notes," *Reuters Breaking Views*, New York Times, June 6, 2011.

10 "News," Federal Communications Commission, May 16, 2011, hraunfoss.fcc.gov/edocs_public/attachmatch/DOC-306575A1.pdf (accessed August 2, 2012).

11 Reverb Nation, "Survey Results: 75% of Indie Artists Seeks A Label Deal—Sony Top Label of Choice," reverbnation.com/2011/03/29/survey-results-75-of-indie-artists-seek-a-label-deal-sony-top-label-of-choice/ (accessed June 20, 2011).

12 IFPI, "Digital Music Report," January 2010, *www.ifpi.org/content/library/DMR2011.pdf (accessed June 21, 2011).*

13 Jon Pareles, "The Cloud That Ate Your Music," *New York Times*, June 22, 2011.

14 Stephanie Clifford, "Shopper Receipts Join Paperless Age," *New York Times*, August 8, 2011.

15 Antony Bruno, "Google's Music Beta Launch Points Out Huge Gap Between Music and Tech Communities," *Billboard*, May 11, 2011.

16 Ben Sisario, "Google's Digital Music Service Falls Short of Ambition," *New York Times*, May 10, 2011.

17 Ibid.

18 LA Times Music Blog Pop and Hiss, "Nielsen SoundScan 2011 Mid-Year Report: Music Sales Up For A Change," July 1, 2011, latimesblogs.latimes.com/music_blog/2011/07/nielsen-soundscan-midyear-report-music-sales-retail-albums.html (accessed August 9, 2011).

19 IFPI, "Recording Industry in Numbers Annual Report, 2010."

20 Jon Pareles, "The Queen Pop Needs Her to Be," *New York Times*, May 22, 2011.

21 Ben Sisario, "More Artists Sue Universal Music, Claiming It Owes Millions in Royalties," *New York Times*, May 20, 2011.

22 Ibid.

23 Larry Rohter, "Record Industry Braces for Artists' Battles Over Song Rights," *New York Times*, August 15, 2011, nytimes.com/2011/08/16/arts/music/springsteen-and-others-soon-eligible-to-recover-song-rights.html?pagewanted=all (accessed August 15, 2011).

24 Kathleen Ripley, "Low Fidelity: Consumers' Devaluation of Music has Big Four Scrambling for Revenue Sources," IBISWorld Industry Report, October 2010.

25 Tinfoil, "Early Recorded Sounds and Wax Cylinders," tinfoil.com/ (accessed July 30, 2011).

26 David M. Ross, "Facing Forward with Scott Borchetta, Jay Frank, and Eric Garland . . .", *Music Row*, February/March 2011, 15.

27 Ed Christman, "Eminem's 'Recovery' is 2010's Best Selling Album," *Billboard*, billboard.com/#/news/eminem-s-recovery-is-2010%E2%80%99s-best-1004137895.story (accessed July 29, 2011).

28 Grammy.com, "Nominees and Winners," grammy.com/nominees (accessed July 29, 2011).

29 Tom Roland, "Record Company or 'Entertainment Company'? Labels Grapple with the Future at Billboard Country Summit," *Billboard*, June 8, 2011, billboard.biz/bbbiz/industry/record-labels/record-company-or-entertainment-company-1005220832.story (accessed July 29, 2011).

30 Roc Nation, RocNation.com/about (accessed July 29, 2011).

31 Jennifer Alsever, "Bottled Water Sales Dry Up; Industry Asks 'Why?'" msnbc.msn.com/id/34451973/ns/business-going_green/t/bottled-water-sales-dry-industry-asks-why/ (accessed August 15, 2011).

32 Paul Boutin, "No Free 'Freebird,'" *Wired*, December 2010, wired.com/magazine/2010/11/st_essay_nofreebird/ (accessed September 17, 2011).

33 Ibid.

34 Paul McGuinness, "How To Save the Music Industry," gq-magazine.co.uk/entertainment/articles/2010-08/13/gq-music-paul-mcguinness-on-music-piracy/file-sharing-on-spotify-and-piracy (accessed July 29, 2011).

35 Kathleen Ripley, "Major Label Music Production in the U.S.," *IBISWorld Industry Report 51222*, October 2010, 19.

36 Agata Kaczanowska and Kathleen Ripley, "The Sound of Success—Glee, American

Idol and Other Music-based TV Shows Boost Industry Sales," *IBISWorld Special Report*, October 2010.

37 Kathleen Ripley, "Music Publishing in the US," *IBISWorld Industry Report 51223*, November, 2010, 27.

38 Jon Caramanica, "In the Hip-Hop World Blogs Mean Business," *New York Times*, May 27, 2011.

39 Ben Sisario, "Looking To a Sneaker For a Band's Big Break," *New York Times*, October 6, 2010.

40 Curt Woodward, "Starbucks Launches Record Label," usatoday.com/life/music/news/2007-03-13-starbucks-label_N.htm (accessed July 7, 2011).

41 Peter Lauria, "Pump the Music: Red Bull Eyes Starting Branded Music Label," nypost.com/p/news/business/item_SY9XQMYwCgtsf6cCoINAOO (accessed July 8, 2011).

42 Converse, converse.com/ (accessed July 8, 2011).

43 Kia Soul Collective, "The Soul Collective," Kiasoulcollective.com (accessed July 14, 2011).

44 Hypebot, "Pick The Band," hypebot.com/hypebot/2011/04/pick-the-band-draft.html (accessed July 7, 2011).

45 Eliot Van Buskirk, "SoundCloud Threatens MySpace as Music Destination for Twitter Era," *Wired*, July 6, 2009, wired.com/epicenter/2009/07/soundcloud-threatens-myspace-as-music-destination-for-twitter-era/ (accessed July 12, 2011).

46 Tunecore, "Bios," tunecore.com/index/bios (accessed August 12, 2011).

47 Interscope Digital Distribution, interscopedigitaldistribution.com/ (accessed August 12, 2011).

48 Nine Inch Nails, "Forums," forum.nin.com/bb/read.php?30,767183 (accessed August 15, 2011).

49 Glenn Peoples, "Amanda Palmer Sells $15K Worth of Music, Merch in Three Minutes," *Billboard*, July 22, 2010 (accessed August 15, 2011).

50 Story based on email discussions with musician Chris Lane, July–August, 2011.

51 Ariel Publicity, "About," arielpublicity.com/about/ (accessed August 15, 2011).

CHAPTER 11 DIGITAL MUSIC SERVICES

1 SonicBids, "Our Story," about.sonicbids.com/about-sonicbids/our-story, (accessed August 19, 2011).

2 Kickstarter, "A New Way to Fund & Follow Creativity," kickstarter.com/ (accessed August 20, 2011).

3 Rob Walker, "The Trivialities and Transcendence of Kickstarter," *New York Times*, August 5, 2011.

4 David Harrell's blog, "Digital Audio Insider," digitalaudioinsider .blogspot.com/.

5 Glenn Peoples, "Business Matters: Did you know 48 streams equals one download?" Billboard, July 19, 2011.

6 Ibid.

7 Alex Pham, "Company Town: Facetime; Exec Tunes in to Listeners," *Los Angeles Times*, May 5, 2011.

8 Ibid.

9 Peoples, "Business Matters."

10 Forbes.com on MSNBC.com, "New, improved . . . and failed," msnbc.msn.com/id/36005036/ns/business-forbes_com/t/new-improved-failed/ (accessed August 15, 2011).

11 Music Supervisor Guide.com, "Music Placement on TV—From Background Music to Breakthrough Music," musicsupervisorguide.com/article/music-place ment-on-tv-from-background-music-to-breakthrough-music-marketing (accessed August 15, 2011).

12 Jenna Wortham, "In Digital Era, Music Spotters Feed a Machine," *New York Times*, February 14, 2011.

13 Ibid.

14 The Huffington Post, "Glenn Beck's Last Fox News Show: Recap Of The Finale," huffingtonpost.com/2011/06/30/glenn-beck-fox-news-last-show_n _888155.html, (accessed August 13, 2011).

15 Brian Stelter, "Glenn Beck to charge fee for online show," *New York Times*, June 7, 2011.

16 Brian Stelter, "Is Hulu Boxed In?" *New York Times*, July 24, 2011.

17 Ibid.

18 The Creator's Project, "So what's this all about then?" thecreatorsproject.com/about (accessed August 14, 2011).

19 The Creator's Project, "Coachella 2011 April 15–17," thecreatorsproject.com/events/the-creators-project-coachella-2011 (accessed August 14, 2011).

20 VBS.TV, "What's all this VBS about, then?" vbs.tv/statics/about (accessed August 6, 2011).

21 Adapted from web coverage of the panel discussion, "Music in Games," bit.ly/Music-In-Games-Audio-SF (accessed August 13, 2011).

22 The American Society Of Composers, Authors And Publishers (ASCAP), "Licensing Songs for Video Games," ascap.com/music-career/articles-advice /ascapcorner/corner16.aspx (accessed August 13, 2011).

23 International Federation of the Phonographic Industry, (IFPI) 2010 Annual Report.

24 Hiroko Tabuchi, "With Sales Plummeting, Nintendo Pares Outlook And Cuts a Retail Price," *New York Times*, July 29, 2011.

25 Agata Kaczanowska, "Radio Broadcasting in the US," IBISWorld Industry Report 51311, July 2011, 7.

26 Ibid.

27 Evolver.fm, "Invite-Only Turntable.fm Takes 'Social Music' Beyond the Buzzword," Evolver.fm/2011/05/24/invite-only-turntable-fm-takes-social-music-beyond-the-buzzword/ (accessed August, 15, 2011).

28 Ibid.

29 Ibid.

30 Ibid.

31 John Jurgensen, "Beyond 'Thriller:' Reinventing The Music Video," *Wall Street Journal*, May 6, 2011.

32 Ibid.

33 Ibid.

34 www.reelseo.com/viewers-choosing-online-video-ads/

35 Elizabeth Olson, "She Hopes to Help a Dove Campaign Become a Hit," *New York Times*, August 25, 2011.

36 Jurgensen, "Reinventing The Music Video"

37 Ibid.

38 Ibid.

39 24–7 Ventures, Inc., "History of Apps Infographic," 247venturesinc.com/blog/2010/7/24/history-of-apps-infographic.html (accessed August 8, 2011).

40 Inc., "How to Make Money on iPhone Apps," inc.com/guides/making-money-iphone-apps.html (accessed August 30, 2011).

41 Andreas M. Kaplan and Michael Haenlein, "Users of the world, unite! The challenges and opportunities of social media," sciencedirect.com/science/article/pii/S0007681309001232 (accessed August 30, 2011).

42 Tania Yuki, "Blurring the Landscape: How TV is merging digital and traditional media," comScore webinar, comscore.com/Press_Events/Presentations_Whitepapers/2010/Blurring_the_Landscape_How_TV_is_Merging_Digital_and_Traditional_Media.com, June 17, 2010.

43 Agata Kaczanowska, Television Broadcasting in the US, IBISWorld Industry Report 51312, April 2011.

44 Kaczanowska, "Television Broadcasting."

45 Ibid.

46 Arbitron, Inc., "Radio Today—How Americans Listen to Radio," 2009 edition, arbitron.com/radio_stations/home.htm (accessed August 1, 2011).

47 Kaczanowska, "Radio Broadcasting."

48 Crunch Base, "Thumbplay," crunchbase.com/company/thumbplay (accessed August 6, 2011).

49 NielsenWire, "Americans Watching More TV Than Ever; Web and Mobile Video Up Too," blog.nielsen.com/nielsenwire/online_mobile/americans-watching-more-tv-than-ever/ (accessed July 10, 2012).

50 Kaczanowska, "The Sound of Success."

51 Kaczanowska, "The Sound of Success."

52 "The Fallout from the Telecommunications Act of 1996: Unintended Consequences and Lessons Learned," Common Cause Education Fund, May 19, 2005.

53 Federal Communications Commission, "What we do," fcc.gov/what-we-do (accessed August 9, 2011).

CHAPTER 12 CASE STUDY: FALCON MUSIC & ART—A JAZZ HAVEN ON THE HUDSON

1 Information in this case study is based on interviews with Tony Falco, Rosie Rion, and audience members in Marlboro, NY, May 4–5, 2010.

2 Todd Martens and Alex Pham, "Coachella is sweet music to promoters: The festival thrives as other parts of the music industry falter," *Los Angeles Times*, April 15, 2010: A.1.

3 Ibid.

4 Chris Richards, "Canceled shows, tours have industry in a sweat; Tickets go begging as acts from the Eagles to Rihanna bail out," *Washington Post*, Sunday Arts, 4 July 2010.

5 Ibid.

6 Ibid.

7 Ray Waddell, *Touring: booking binds*. Billboard, October 17, 2009.

8 livenation.com accessed July 7, 2010.

9 Ray Waddell, *Brave New World*. Billboard, March 27, 2010.

10 David Segal, "They're calling almost everyone's tune – Why the Music Industry is Quaking Over Ticketmaster's Merger," *New York Times Business*, April 25, 2010.

11 Waddell, October 17, 2009.

12 Ibid.

13 Ibid.

14 Biographical details provided in an email from Tony Falco, June 1, 2010.

15 Hudson River, "General Information About the Region," hudsonriver.com (accessed June 28, 2010).

16 MarlboroughNY.com, "General Information About the Region," marlboroughny.com/ (accessed June 28, 2010).

17 Hudson Valley Network, Inc., "Great Estates of the Hudson Valley," hvnet.com/houses/index.htm (accessed June 28, 2010).

18 Live at the Falcon, "About," liveatthefalcon.com/ (accessed April 13, 2010).

19 Hudson Valley Network, Inc. "Club Listings," hvmusic.com/listing/club_list.php (accessed June 28, 2010).

20 Dutchess Tourism, "Nightlife," dutchesstourism.com/nightlife.asp (accessed June 28, 2010).

21 Phone interview with Tony Falco, July 5, 2010.

CHAPTER 13 CASE STUDY: TICKETLEAP—SOCIAL MEDIA INTEGRATION IN THE CLOUD

1   Phone interview. Catherine Radbill and Keith Fitzgerald, 12/31/10.
2   Phone interview. Coster, Mayer, and Chris Stanchak, 10/18/10.
3   At the time, there was global concern about the possibility of computer failures when the date changed from December 31, 1999 to January 1, 2000, due to the global practice of abbreviating a four-digit year as two digits.
4   Phone interview. Radbill and James Thompson, 12/31/10.
5   "The Complete History of Social Networking—CBBS to Twitter" by Michael Simon. Posted 12/14/2009 to Mac/Life. maclife.com/ (accessed January 2, 2011).
6   Phone interview. Coster, Mayer, and Chris Stanchak, 10/18/10.
7   Ibid.
8   Phone interview. Radbill and Thompson, 12/31/10.
9   Phone interview. Coster, Mayer, and Chris Stanchak, 10/18/10.
10 Phone interview. Radbill and Thompson, 12/31/10.
11 Meeting. Allis, Avillez-Costa, Coster, Ennis, Mayer, and Radbill, 10/25/10.
12 Phone interview. Radbill and Fitzgerald 12/30/10.
13 TicketLeap Business Plan, dated Q1 2008.
14 *Wired Magazine* 10/23/07, wired.com/culture/lifestyle/multimedia/2007/11/pl_playlist?slide=3&slideView=3 (accessed January 5, 2011).
15 Email. Radbill and Stanchak.
16 TicketLeap Business Plan, dated Q1 2008.
17 Phone interview. Allis and Chris Stanchak, 11/22/10.
18 Meeting. Allis, Avillez-Costa, Coster, Ennis, Mayer, and Radbill, 10/25/10.
19 Phone interview. Radbill and Fitzgerald, 12/31/10.
20 "Ten Cloud Computing Predictions for 2009," written by Michael Sheehan, 12/2/08, head of public relations and marketing for GoGrid, a pure-play Infrastructure-as-a-Service (IaaS) provider specializing in Cloud Infrastructure solutions. blog.gogrid.com/2008/12/02/ten-cloud-computing-predictions-for-2009/ (accessed January 5, 2011).
21 Cloud Slam 2009 website, cloudslam09.com/node/65 (accessed January 5, 2011).
22 Phone interview. Radbill and Thompson, 12/31/10.

APPENDIX A VISIT TO 2012 WINTER NAMM

1   Randy Lewis, "Guitar Geek Festival 2012 this weekend in Anaheim," Pop & Hiss—The L.A. Times music blog, January 19, 2012, latimesblogs.latimes.com/music_blog/randy_lewis/ (accessed February 13, 2012).
2   NAMM Press Release, February 13, 2012.
3   Andrew Bansal, "NAMM 2012 Serves As Giant Melting Pot For Heavy Metal Greats," January 27, 2012, metalassault.com/gig_reviews/2012/01/27/namm2012-serves-as-giant-melting-pot-for-heavy-metal-greats/ (accessed February 13, 2012); John Corrigan, "John Mayer, Brian Wilson, Slash and others headed for NAMM," *Los Angeles Times*, January 13, 2012, latimes.com/business/money/la-fi-mo-namm-show-20120113,0,2159285.story (accessed February 13, 2012).

INDEX